BENEATH
THE STARRY
FLAG

BENEATH THE STARRY FLAG

New Jersey's Civil War Experience

ALAN A. SIEGEL

Rutgers University Press
NEW BRUNSWICK, NEW JERSEY

Library of Congress Cataloging-in-Publication Data

Siegel, Alan A., 1939–
Beneath the starry flag : New Jersey's Civil War experience / Alan A. Siegel.
p.   cm.
Includes bibliographical references and index.
ISBN 0-8135-2938-7 (cloth : alk. paper)—ISBN 0-8135-2943-3 (pbk. : alk. paper)
1. New Jersey—History—Civil War, 1861–1865.   2. New Jersey—
History—Civil War,
1861–1865—Sources. 3. United States—
History—Civil War, 1861–1865—Sources. I. Title.

E521 .S54 2001
973.7'449—dc21
00-045685

British Cataloging-in-Publication data for this book is available from the British Library.

Manufactured in the United States of America

Contents

Preface

Some years ago a well-known historian estimated that a new book about the American Civil War appeared on the average of once a week, a deluge that continues to this day. The latest edition of *Books in Print* includes over thirty-five hundred entries relating to the war. Amazon's web site lists five hundred titles, Barnes and Noble has more than nine hundred. Many bookstores carry at least fifty. Magazine articles are simply too numerous to count. The demand, apparently, is insatiable.

It's easy to understand why American readers have a love affair with the Civil War. It was the greatest military conflict ever fought on the North American continent, pitting millions of citizen-soldiers, brothers of the same blood, against each other on hundreds of battlefields flung across thousands of miles. The suffering on both sides, the valor of the soldiers, the deeds and misdeeds of the politicians and military commanders, the passions the war evoked, all are enough to make the Civil War memorable. But there is more than that: As Robert Penn Warren once wrote, "The Civil War is, for the American imagination, the great single event of our history." The war was the major turning point in our national story, and because it so pervasively changed America, the Civil War retains the power to fascinate.

New Jersey can be proud of its record in the Civil War. Eighty thousand men served in the Union army and navy, 6,400 of them would die, and countless others were imprisoned or wounded, many of them terribly. The valor of New Jersey's soldiers is remarkable: John Beech, a Trenton potter who served nearly four years, winning a Medal of Honor for bravery at Spotsylvania's Bloody Angle; Major General Robert McAllister of Oxford Furnace, always courageous in the face of the enemy; Peter Vredenburgh, a twenty-nine-year-old Eatontown lawyer who commanded Monmouth County's Fourteenth New Jersey Regiment, meeting death as he led a charge near Winchester, Virginia— "Forward men! Forward, and guide on me!" were his last words before a shell fragment struck him, killing him instantly; Captain Hugh Irish of the Thirteenth Regiment, less than a month out of civilian clothes, shot to death as he led his men into battle, crying, "Rally, boys! Rally!" and Colonel Hugh Janeway of Rahway, wounded twelve times, killed in action on April 5, 1865, the last New Jersey officer to die in combat. The thirty-three regiments of infantry, four of militia, three of cavalry and five artillery batteries supplied by the state saw action on every major Civil War battlefield. Almost three thousand black Jerseymen served with honor in the ranks of the United States Colored Troops. Another eight thousand men did duty as sailors and marines.

At home in New Jersey, thousands of patriotic men and women supported the Union cause, raising funds, encouraging men to enlist, sending clothing and medicines to the front. During the war, Jersey women served in the hospitals in and around Washington, and one, Cornelia Hancock, a young woman from Salem County, ministered to the Union wounded on battlefields from Gettysburg to Petersburg. Captain Henry Sawyer's wife rescued her husband virtually through sheer force of will from an almost certain death in a Confederate prison. There were others, of course, who despised Abraham Lincoln, viewed the war as an utter failure and did everything they could to undermine the Union effort. Somerset County's Daniel Cory, for example, said he would shoot the president if he could; the state's leading Copperhead newspapers denounced the draft and discouraged enlistments; and the State Legislature itself at one point called for a truce and negotiations to end the conflict.

In 1865 Walt Whitman, the Brooklyn journalist and poet who settled in Camden after the war, predicted that future generations "will never know the seething hell and black infernal background, the countless minor scenes and interiors of the secession war, and it is best that they should not. The real war," Whitman wrote, "will never get into the books." As it turned out, Whitman was wrong. The Americans who went to war in 1861 were an amazingly literate generation; no sooner had the conflict begun than there poured from their pens a vast record of what they saw and felt. New Jersey's newspapers of the day, some eighty dailies and weeklies, could not get enough of the news, whether written by correspondents in the field or copied from soldier's letters. After the war, individual memoirs and unit histories kept the presses busy. In later years the state's libraries collected unpublished soldiers' letters by the thousands. New Jersey's war record is preserved in countless books and pamphlets, innumerable manuscripts, and hundreds of reels of microfilm.

Preface

Not enough has been written about New Jersey and the Civil War, given both the state's amazing role and the vast available material. In recent years three valuable books have appeared, doing much to fill the need. Joseph G. Bilby and William C. Goble's *Remember You Are Jerseymen: A Military History of New Jersey's Troops in the Civil War,* published by Longstreet House in 1998, ably details the state's military role in the war. In 1995 Rutgers University Press published *Jersey Blue: Civil War Politics in New Jersey 1854–1865,* Professor William Gillette's insightful retelling of New Jersey's political role before, during and just after the war. The most recent addition to the literature is William J. Jackson's *New Jerseyans in the Civil War: For Union and Liberty,* a comprehensive history of the state during the war years published last year, also by Rutgers University Press.

Beneath the Starry Flag takes a different approach, offering the general reader a collection of richly detailed eyewitness accounts by New Jerseyans who lived through those four soul-stirring years. The motives and emotions and deeds of the people are told in their own words, drawn from a wide array of sources. Newspaper editors and reporters, men in the ranks, officers, politicians, and plain citizens, both patriots and Copperheads, speak to the reader again after 135 years. Except where absolutely necessary for clarity, the original texts have been left undisturbed.

The Civil War was the defining event in American history; it changed the nation, and New Jersey as well. *Beneath the Starry Flag* is about our state's fascinating role in that war told in the words of those who were there.

Acknowledgments

Grateful acknowledgment is made for permission to reprint excerpts from the following works: Herman J. Platt, ed., *Charles Perrin Smith, New Jersey Political Reminiscences, 1828–1882,* copyrighted 1965 by Rutgers University Press; James I. Robertson, Jr., ed., *The Civil War Letters of General Robert McAllister,* copyrighted 1965 by Rutgers University Press; Henrietta Stratton Jaquette, ed., *Letters of a Civil War Nurse, 1863–1865,* copyrighted by University of Nebraska Press, 1998; Ron E. Davis, ed., *The Civil War Diary and Letters of John Bacon Hoffman of Shiloh, New Jersey,* copyrighted 1979 by Dr. Ronald Davis; the letters of William S. Van Fleet, owned by Frances Kaminski, Archivist, from the collections of the Parsippany Historical & Preservation Society, Inc.; Charles Hopkins. "Hell and the Survivor," reprinted by permission of *American Heritage Magazine,* a division of Forbes, Inc., copyrighted by Forbes, Inc., 1982; and the Diary of George A. Bowen, from the collections of the Salem County Historical Society, Salem, New Jersey.

BENEATH THE STARRY FLAG

ONE

"A Carnival of Patriotism"

1861

Seven states had already left the Union by February 11, 1861, the day President-elect Lincoln boarded his train at the Springfield depot for a two-thousand-mile roundabout journey to Washington. "Everything looks like war," predicted a businessman in Morristown. "We hope against hope, and pray without faith that this madness may pass away," wrote another Jerseyan in mid-February. Yet the tide of history rolled inexorably on.[1]

Lincoln's ten-day journey through Illinois, Indiana, Ohio, Pennsylvania, and New York was a triumph of cheering crowds and tumultuous receptions. Lincoln said little of substance: "I come before you to see and be seen," he said at one brief stop. When Lincoln and his party arrived at Jersey City on February 21 to begin their seven-hour visit in the state, Jefferson Davis had been president of the newly minted Confederate States of America for three days.

The presidential entourage left New York City promptly at 8:15 a.m., reported the newspapers, taking the ferry for New Jersey:

At the Jersey City Ferry, in anticipation of his coming, crowds lined the passageways to the boat. . . . As the carriages were driven on board, Dodsworth's fine band struck up the National airs, congratulatory cannon boomed out a parting salute, and while the boat moved off the multitude sent up their parting cheers, and the shipping in the harbor displayed their national bunting.

Arrived at Jersey City, the party left the carriages and marched into the depot in procession. . . . The scene in the depot was magnificent, presenting as it did probably the largest indoor gathering witnessed by the President since his departure. The vast edifice was crowded in every part, the gallery which surrounds the interior being filled with a bright galaxy of the fair sex. The appearance of Mr. Lincoln was, of course, the signal for a general outburst of applause, prolonged until long after Mr. Lincoln had stepped upon the carpeted platform car prepared for him.

3

As he advanced and bowed in acknowledgment, cheer upon cheer broke forth, drowning completely the vain appeals for silence. . . .

The distinguished gentlemen on the platform were again introduced, but the crowd would not be appeased, and made a rush to get near Mr. Lincoln. The unfortunate reporters, who stood by the car, writing on the platform, were suddenly squeezed between the eager multitude and the object of their attention. It was like being in a hydraulic press, or going through a rolling-mill, or being run over by the cars, or pinched between the ferry-boat and the bridge, or suffering *hari kari*. Verily, our reporter's bowels ache when he mentally recalls that excruciating collapse.

In vain did the compressed unfortunate howl with pain—their agonizing cries were regarded as cheers for Lincoln. In vain did they implore the crowd to stand back. Mr. Lincoln heightened the excitement and increased the danger by reaching over the head of the people and shaking hands with a few, which only increased the desire of the many to get nearer. . . .

The Jersey Police were overwhelmed. Vainly did they brandish their clubs, and push the crowd back. . . . Mr. Lincoln . . . addressed the crowd again.

"Fellow-citizens. I appear before you, as I have on other occasions, simply to see you and allow you to see me, and so far as the upper tier is concerned (the ladies tier) they have the best of the bargain (laughter) but as regards the lower tier I intend to make no compromise (great laughter and applause)."

The crowd was still unappeased, and pressed closer to get a view of the idol of the hour, who hasn't had an idle hour since his election. At one time there seemed a probability of his being trampled under foot in the vehement rush.

At this time the vast audience was convulsed with laughter by a feat of Mickey Free, a well-known character in Jersey City. . . . Mickey had turned Wide-Awake, and had on a Wide-Awake cap, which he was evidently anxious the President should see, so he clambored up on the platform, and shaking his fringed garments, exhibiting his ivories, took Mr. Lincoln by the hand, and patted him on the back, amid uproarious laughter from all quarters.

The difficult feat now to be performed was to get Mr. Lincoln through the crowd to the cars. The police were no use, rather in the way than otherwise, but by dint of turning his suite into a body-guard, elbowing his way and moving slowly, Mr. Lincoln reached the car and disappeared within, the multitude peering in. . . . The train started from the depot at five minutes to nine o'clock, and moved away amid cheers from the crowd, "Hail Columbia" from Dodworth and a canon salute of 34 guns. . . . As we left the depot the track was lined for a long distance with thousands of beings anxious to catch a glimpse of the President. He bowed adieu from the rear car amid the cheering of the masses and the pealing of cannon.

We reached Newark at 9½ o'clock, and . . . drove through the city in carriages. . . . Mr. Lincoln, attended by his suite and the various gentlemen of the party, entered the [Newark] depot, which was filled with ladies and gentlemen, and was met by Mayor Bigelow, who, on behalf of the citizens, welcomed the President-elect to the thriving City of Newark. . . . After he had closed, Mr. Lincoln said:

"Mr. Mayor, I thank you for the reception at the City of Newark. With regard to the great work of which you speak, I will say that I bring to it a heart filled with love for my country and an honest desire to do what is right. I am sure, however, that I have not the ability to do anything unaided of God, and that without His support and that of this free, happy, prosperous and intelligent people no man can succeed in doing that the importance of which we all comprehend. . . ."

This was of course greeted with applause, and the party proceeded in procession to the carriages which were in readiness. Newark has a population of over seventy thousand, and I think it is entirely safe to say that at least two-thirds of them were out in the streets, thronging, swarming, jostling and hurraing in crowds of wonderful extent. An open barouche drawn by four splendid white horses, had been provided for Mr. Lincoln, who stood up therein bareheaded during the entire passage from depot to depot. The streets were filled, the houses were filled, the windows, the doors, the porches, the stoops, the plazzas, the roofs, the trees, the ash barrels, the everything you can think of were crowded to repletion with people who swarmed like bees, who seemed touched with electrick, and who must have had throats lined with brass.

Very many private carriages stood along the line, all of which were filled with bright-eyed ladies, who smiled and waved and huzzaed with as much enthusiasm, if not with as much noise, as the ruder specimens of humanity who surged by them on foot. We have never seen a more extensive and prettier display of "women, lovely women," than was made on the main street of Newark during the passage of the procession. Mr. Lincoln was struck by it, and thought if there are as many brave men as there are fair women in the city, Newark would be a difficult city to take.

Ladies waved their handkerchiefs, and men uncovered their heads. Small boys were all happy, and one, as he ran along by our carriage, wished he had his mother here. Thousands rushed wildly after the cortege, and one man falling down, there was soon a pile of men, about five feet high, accumulated. From one lamp post swung the effigy of a Secessionist, dressed in gray coat and pants, and bearing the inscription, "The fate of a Traitor." At the Public School, about one thousand small children were assembled in front of the building, and, as we passed, sang the well-known Hutchinson melody of "We are a Band of Brothers." Mr. Lincoln's carriage halted a moment; he bowed to them and we passed on.

When the depot . . . was reached, a terrible struggle occurred. An immense crowd followed close upon the Presidential heels. . . . The police with mighty efforts endeavored to stop the swelling tide, but as well might they have attempted to stop the waves of the ocean. Those far in the rear punched those in front and those in turn pushed on until we who occupied the rank by the cars were in danger of being smashed into parts, jelly or jam. . . . At last all were in [the cars], Mr. Lincoln made his farewell bow, the crowded cheered lustily, and on we sped. . . .

The president-elect's train slowed but did not stop as it passed through Elizabeth, Rahway, New Brunswick, and Princeton.

The very large proportion of ladies at all the places was especially noticeable, and as in numbers, so in enthusiasm did they outstrip the male population. . . . At Princeton, there was a large concourse, who cheered as we passed. . . . As we rushed on the people from every house on the road came out. At one place handkerchiefs failed the large hearts of the ladies, and sheets were substituted. Every farm house which could boast of a gun or large pistol, had them out, and gave us a salute.

[At Trenton] Mr. Lincoln was met by an additional Committee from the citizens, from the Council and the Legislature. Apparently every precaution had been taken to preserve good order, and to enable the Presidential party to pass quietly and unmolested through the city. We walked between walls of people with great ease, they meanwhile roaring, tumbling, and seething as one imagines the waves of the Red Sea did when Moses smote and divided them with his little old rod. So far, so good, but here it ends. The moment Mr. Lincoln took his seat in the carriage the mob became ungovernable. With a mighty rush they beat down the line of feeble constables, and without the least regard for decency, or the form of it, swamped the suite. . . . With the greatest difficulty, and only after repeated discomfitures, failures and struggles did

6

the entire party find seats in the conveyances. It seemed as if the crowd was the most obstreperous of any I had ever seen.

The party were then taken in carriages to the State House. The crowd of people to be seen [along the route] was perfectly alarming, yet the efficient police arrangements . . . enabled the party to reach the State Capitol in safety. . . .

After briefly addressing the State Senate, Lincoln walked over to the Assembly chamber, where he was introduced by the speaker of the house. The president-elect replied:

"It affords me pleasure to receive a welcome from the descendants of those who shed their blood in defence of the soil of their State—a State which has evidenced a determination to stand by the Union, and the people of which, I do not doubt, will now co-operate in any measures for the settlement of our present unfortunate difficulties.

"Already some of the stars of our bright confederacy are obscured by the dark clouds. I can only hope that the close of my administration may dispel those ominous messengers, and find all the Stars allied in a perfect Union.

"I have just enjoyed the honor of a reception by the other branch of your Legislature. To you, as to them, I tender my grateful thanks. It comes to me as the representative of the Chief Magistracy. I will reiterate to you my devotion to the Constitution, the Union and the perpetual liberties of the people. You have been pleased to allude to the difficulties which lie before me. These difficulties are my apology for entering into no elucidation of sentiments or my future policy. Moreover, it is but just that I should have the advantage of every fact and incident which may be developed prior to the day of my inauguration, in order that I may act with discretion and understanding. I hope that I shall be under no necessity of swerving or departing from the laws. I bear no malice toward any section. My prayer is to promote peace. I have no desire apart from peace and harmony. Such desires I hope may meet with peaceable results. I shall take all in good temper, and with what firmness I may.

"It may be necessary, however, to set the foot down firm. (Shouts of applause, prolonged for many minutes.) It may be necessary to take a stand. (Renewed shouts, and cries of "Good.") Gentlemen, if you think I am right, you will stand by me, won't you? ("Yes! Yes!") This is all I ask. If you weather the ship through the storm during four years, you may get at that time a better pilot."

After the speeches, a very discreditable rush was made at and upon the President and his suite. They were pulled, and hauled, and pushed, and mauled. It was an awful time. After an infinite amount of struggles, of fight and of persuasion, we were all seated and drove towards the hotel. There was gathered another terrific jam. They would on no account move from their positions and literal force alone enabled many of the party to secure an entrance to the hotel. . . . It is thought there were 20,000 people present.[2]

After a banquet at the Trenton House, Lincoln and his exhausted party took the train to Philadelphia.

The State Legislature's reception was surprisingly friendly, considering Lincoln's mediocre showing in the November election. The *Trenton State Gazette and Republican* viewed the president-elect's visit in a hopeful light:

The visit of the President elect to this city . . . gave great satisfaction to our citizens, and tended to dispel many prejudices which had existed in the minds of Democrats against him. We heard several prominent Democrats say on Thursday that, though they had come here with strong prejudices against Mr. Lincoln, they would return to their homes fully satisfied that he was "the right man for the right place." What he said, and the manner of his saying it, had made this change in their estimate of the man. No man could look upon Mr. Lincoln's face, and hear his voice, without becoming thoroughly satisfied that he was an honest man, and that he had no thought but what was in consonance with the good of his whole country. With such innate honesty of purpose, and with a will that knows no such word as "fail" in pursuing what he believes to be a right course, the whole country may rest satisfied that he will speedily bring the country out of its present difficulties, and again place it on the high road to prosperity.[3]

The cheers of the Jerseyans who lined the president-elect's route from Jersey City to Trenton failed to quiet the voices of those who had opposed him in the last election, and still doubted the wisdom of his policies. Typical of the Democratic press, the *Somerset Messenger* was far from impressed by the Illinois Republican:

At every stopping place he addressed the crowd that rushed to see him. None of his speeches evince either ability or statesmanship. On the contrary they are very common place and indifferent, and in some cases leaving the impress of "slang phrases," and evince generally ignorance of the events now taking place in our country. In one place he refers to our "bond of union" as a sort of "free love affair" held together by "passional attraction"—in another he congratulates the people that "nobody is hurt"[;] "nothing is suffering." The whole progress of the "President elect and his suite" is more like the moving of a crowned prince than the "is be ruler" of a Republican country—and is in fact a sort of "raree show" got up for the satisfaction of the gazers.[4]

If Lincoln's visit heartened the state's Unionists, it made little or no impression on those who believed that the state's proper place was with the South. As late as the first week of April 1861, former New Jersey Governor Rodman M. Price virtually urged secession. "I say emphatically," he wrote in a widely published letter, "[that New Jersey] should go with the South, from every wise, prudential and patriotic reason." Price believed that within months a new government would be formed by the union of New Jersey and other "conservative" Northern states with the South under the Confederate Constitution. Continued Price:

I believe the Southern Confederacy permanent. . . . If we find that to remain with the North, separated from those who have, heretofore, consumed our manufactured articles, and given employment to a large portion of our labor, deprived of that reciprocity of trade which we have hitherto enjoyed, our Commerce will cease, European competition will be invited to Southern markets, our people be compelled to seek employment elsewhere, our State becoming depopulated and impoverished, thereby affecting our agricultural interest. . . . These are the prospective results of remaining with the present Northern confederacy. Whereas, to join our destiny with the South will be to continue our trade and intercourse, our prosperity, progress, and happiness, uninterrupted, and perhaps in an augmented degree. Who is he that would advise New Jersey to pursue the path of desolation when one of prosperity is open before her, without any sacrifice of principle or honor, and without difficulty or danger; besides being the course and policy, in my judgment, most likely to reunite all the States under the glorious "Stars and Stripes"?

The action of our State will prove influential and, perhaps, potential, from our geographical position, upon the adjoining great States of Pennsylvania and New York; and I am confident that the people of those States, whose interests are identical with our own to a considerable degree, will, when they elect, choose also to cast their lot with the South.

And, after them, the Western and Northwestern States will be found in the same balance, which would be essentially a reconstruction of the Old Government. What is the difference whether we go to the South, or they come to us . . .?

It takes little discernment to see that one policy will enrich us, and the other impoverish us. Knowing our rights and interests we dare maintain them. The Delaware River only separates us from the State of Delaware for more than one hundred miles. A portion of our State extends south of Mason and Dixon's line, and south of Washington city. . . . Let us, then, save the country—let us do that which is likely to reunite the States, speedily and peacefully.[5]

The ex-governor's advice made good sense to many Jerseyans in the turbulent spring of 1861. With the South's economic and political ties with the North fraying, New Jersey's factory production slowed, leaving thousands unemployed. Those who disagreed with Governor Price were outraged by his gloomy forecast. "I am pained to hear that some of the politicians of New Jersey are advancing and urging the treasonable idea that our State will join the Southern Confederacy," wrote one Unionist.

Is New Jersey to follow the course laid out for her by politicians, to benefit her trade, when it is proverbial that politicians know but little about any trade . . . and care for it less if they can only fill their pockets from the Public Crib? Are New Jersey Freemen so lost to love of country, the Union, Constitution and the Laws, that she will throw herself into the arms of treason, hoping thereby to benefit her trade? I trust and believe that a large majority of her sons have that noble patriotism which will cause them to scorn such a treasonable proposition.[6]

The *Princeton Standard*, which had supported Lincoln in the November election, called Price's remarks "weak, treasonable [and] adventurous." One of the paper's correspondents, styling himself "A Mechanic," ridiculed the former governor's proposal:

As a Jerseyman, I want to know what authority Mr. Price has for saying that in six months we'll be under the Southern Confederacy. . . . I wish to know . . . the means by which it is supposed we will be thus speedily transferred, so that I may judge for myself whether to fly immediately to some land where liberty is still respected, or stay, hoping the plans of transfer to our Southern despotism may fail to be carried out. I have lived all my days in New Jersey, under a Government where life, liberty

10

and property are sacred, and now to be transferred to one where neither life, liberty nor property are respected, but are at the mercy of every drunken mob—where stealing, perjury and murder are not crimes; where lying and treason are not even venial sins in the eyes of [doctor's of divinity] of the secession stripe, and the people are to have no voice in the Government is entirely too much of a change for me.

Come now, Ex Governor, do explain, that we may judge for ourselves the chances of escape from this worse than Vandal government of the South.[7]

As one after another Southern state followed South Carolina's example, Republicans along with a growing number of Democrats rallied to the Union cause. In early February 1861, while delegates from seven states met to adopt a constitution for the newly formed Confederate States of America, Trenton Republicans filled every seat and standing place in Temperance Hall, cheering "several eminent speakers" with "great enthusiasm." Unanimously adopting resolutions that denounced "the pro-slavery party of the South," Trenton Republicans minced no words:

The open seizure of the National forts, arsenals and navy yards, the firing upon the National flag, and the robbery of the national mints and Sub-Treasuries by the Secessionists of the South, are acts of treason and should be punished as such; it is the bounden duty of the National Government forthwith to despatch a sufficient naval and military force to recover and protect all the national property, to enforce the laws in all parts of the Union, and summarily to arrest and punish all who violate them.[8]

Later the same week "An Honest Democrat" aired his views in the columns of the *Princeton Standard*:

We have approached a period in our history, when the great question should not be, will our party be weakened by taking measures in favor of the government, or be strengthened by opposition? but, will it be for the good of this nation, to meet the enemy and put down anything that may tend to a dissolution of these United States . . . ?

The men of the South . . . have taken measures to withdraw from this Union, which measures cannot be looked upon in any other light than acts of treason. . . .

In view of all this, what course shall the government pursue? Make compromises with them? they have been made and as often broken;

give them the reigns of government in their own hands? they have had this for a long period in a great measure, and even now they have the majority in both houses. Shall it let them go and set up for themselves? in doing so, they break the compact, which is the foundation of the reputation of this Republic with other nations.

The union of these States must be preserved; the stars and stripes, which have so proudly waved over us, must be unfurled to the breeze and continue to float over succeeding generations, not one star or stripe being erased, or clouded by the hand of vile men.[9]

On April 12 Confederate batteries opened their long-expected bombardment of Fort Sumter, smothering New Jersey's voices of disunion with a noisy outpouring of patriotism. Crowds gathered outside newspaper offices in every part of the state, awaiting the latest news from South Carolina. The anxiety in Newark was palpable as news of "the long dreaded calamity" clicked off the telegraph repeater.

We have never witnessed such intense excitement as was manifested in this city on Saturday evening and Sunday. Up to 5 o'clock the despatches announced nothing but misfortunes at Charleston, the conflagration in Fort Sumter, etc. At that hour the rumor spread that the Fort had capitulated, and was confirmed by some private despatches. Our regular despatch announcing the fact did not arrive till about 6½ o'clock, and the information spread with electric rapidity, causing a most painful sensation. Throughout the evening the streets and public places were thronged by agitated groups, and almost everybody discredited the intelligence. On Sunday it was corroborated by the papers, which were sold in the city by thousands. The various despatches were analyzed, and their announcements generally rejected as contradictory and improbable. Many actually believed that no conflict had taken place, and that the secessionists were telegraphing the various accounts only to alarm the North. The final confirmation this morning produced feelings of acutest grief, and at the same time the sternest determination to sustain and reestablish the honor of the country. These feelings are almost unanimous. Whatever may have been the former political divisions, there are but few sympathizers here with the rebels in this community, and a deep seated indignation is felt against them.[10]

The Confederate attack on Fort Sumter solidified political opinion in New Jersey behind the president, at least for a time. The *Somerset Messenger* spoke for many Democrats:

To admit that secession is right is to admit that this Union is a failure and Government by the "people" a farce. This we cannot admit. It is then the duty of every good citizen to oppose secession and support the Government and the Constitution; to stand by the Union and preserve the institutions of this Confederacy. We see no cause now for party wranglings. The house is on fire, let us put it out, and then there will be time enough left to seek out the incendiaries. The Democratic party has always stood by the Country—the motto of that party always has been "OUR COUNTRY—RIGHT OR WRONG!" Let that be the motto still. That is our motto. We are for the Union, now and forever! come from whatever quarter the foes may, and this we believe to be the position of every democrat in the land.[11]

Elizabeth's leading newspaper, the *New-Jersey Journal,* neutral in the 1860 election, had assured its readers only in December that disunion was impossible. Now it called for "a stern determination to stand behind the banner":

It is infinitely better to sustain great hardships rather than to have the flag . . . trampled beneath the feet of those who have ceased to cherish its multiplied glories. War, in its sternest reality, is far less to be dreaded than dishonor. . . .

   The volumes which contain the glorious achievements of revolutionary worthies, will not, thank God, be sullied by records of their sons' degeneracy. The friends of the Union are unwilling that the blood and treasure poured out to cement its bonds shall have been vainly devoted. The fires of patriotism, though for a season they may have emitted but feeble light and heat, burn with a fervor that attests the care with which they are watched and trimmed. The events of the last few days have called forth a spontaneous outburst of enthusiasm highly gratifying to every lover of his country.[12]

The *Newark Daily Advertiser,* the most respected journalistic voice in the state, struck a somber note when it called on Jerseyans "to abandon partisan prejudice and take their stand either for the government or against it." The Union, said the paper in an editorial titled, "The Tragedy Begins," would never be destroyed:

After a series of bold and insulting robberies of the forts and other property of the United States, Jefferson Davis has at length consummated his audacious treason by an attack upon Fort Sumpter. . . . Never before, we sincerely believe, has it been attempted to array a rebellion against a government which has done its citizens no wrong whatever. . . . Why is this attack? Was there ever in the records of the past so perfectly unjustifiable a commencement of fratricidal war—how, where, and when ended, God only knows. . . .

What has the government of the Union done to justify this murderous attack upon its citizens in Fort Sumpter; what has it not done or offered to do to turn aside civil war, which was begun by Jefferson Davis on Thursday? The impartial American people and all nations must perceive this invasion of the United States to be a most wanton act of cowardice as well as cruelty. . . .

And does the conceited Davis imagine for a moment, that this great drama, which has its opening in the port of Charleston is to have its consummation and end there also? Never, never. The gallant little garrison may be starved out, they may see the walls of Sumpter reduced to dust by the iron balls and shells of infernal machines, and be obliged to surrender to the beleaguring foe comprised of the better part of the population of Carolina; but this will be but the first scene of the first act of a drama, which bids fair to become immortal. The Union and Constitution, which were the work of Washington and Jefferson, of Adams and Hamilton, shall never be crushed like the ramparts of Sumpter.

Before the work of these apostles of liberty and constitutional government shall be reduced to ruin, thousands of the stalwart forms of the freemen of the North will be laid low. And then the republic of the North will not be overthrown. If the fathers shall perish, their sons will fly with alacrity to the field of fight, where liberty and law are the prizes, and the American Republic shall continue to flourish. . . .

We then renew our former oaths of allegiance to our noble country, we pledge our lives and efforts to preserve and make it a blessing to posterity and we will swear, that what our illustrious fathers left us shall be transmitted, if willing hands and unterrified hearts can do it, to our posterity.[13]

News of Sumter's fall and Lincoln's call for 75,000 volunteers three days later stirred the spirit of the Northern states. In New Jersey, "[e]very town and city from Sussex to Cape May rang with the sounds of a state deliriously at war." Elizabeth's reaction, reported in the *New-Jersey Journal*, was typical:

The past week has been one of excitement and alarm. . . . From all parts of our country comes up the sound of gathering armies, and through the streets of our cities is heard the tramp of soldiers and the hurried muster

of troops. Every hour sends from point to point the news of what is transpiring in different sections, and men, excited and eager, catch the
words and pass them on, till the pulse of the people beats faster and
faster, and throbs painfully with uncertain expectation. War is upon us.
It is no time to sit idly down and speculate in what manner it came, or
how it has so suddenly assumed such gigantic proportions—no time to
hurl recriminations at this man or that State, nor to throw blame on
any party or section. There is no room for parlay now. The times demand action. Enough for every patriot to know that the laws are set at
naught, our government defied, our flag dishonored, and that traitors
are attacking the very vitals of our national existence. Our citizens have,
in common with those of every other place, been thoroughly waked up
to these facts during the past week, and have endeavored to testify their
devotion to the Union by hoisting flags of every size and kind; from the
large banner floating gracefully from the tapering flagstaff, to the minia-
ture stars and stripes decorating the harness of the horses on our streets.
And on Friday the feeling was fanned into a perfect blaze of enthusiasm
by the passage through our ward of the Providence [Rhode Island] Ma-
rine Corps of Artillery, on its way to the seat of war. . . . Great was the excitement here among all our citizens, and many were the souveniers left
by the gallant soldiers behind, in the way of handkerchiefs and rings and
buttons cut from their uniforms, and given to our fair damsels who were
watching the transfer at the depot.[14]

"Bordentown for the Union!" proclaimed that town's newspaper:

The spirit of maintaining the Union as our fathers made it, is growing
stronger, and is becoming more ardent as the motives of the secessionists become more and more fully known. Every aggressive stroke made
by the secessionists only tend[s] to draw tighter the bonds which unite
the patriot's heart to his country; and the longer the traitors continue in
their rebellious course, and the oftener they insult or dishonor the flag
of our Union, the more terrible will be the punishment of the rebels
when the freemen of the North rise in their might to assert their rights
and redress their wrongs. The people of all the cities and of every large
town are driving from their midst all those who affiliate the course of the
secessionists.

On Monday last the Union men of all parties began their search for
traitors. . . . Down with the traitors! We say; make them loyal through
fear or drive them from our borders.

A grand Union meeting, composed of men of all political parties, was held in the City Hall last Monday evening. The greatest enthusiasm was manifested. The meeting was got up on the spur of the moment of only a few hours' notice, yet the large hall was filled to overflowing. A large flag—the stars and stripes—was floating in the breeze the greater part of the day, and was gazed upon by many, who regarded it as the only true emblem of their country's greatness and of their country's glory.

About 8 o'clock in the evening the tide of humanity began to flow in, and but a few minutes were occupied in filling the Hall to a perfect jam. . . . It was a meeting well calculated to do much good and to cement the bond of true Union feelings more stronger in the heart of every patriot. When the "old stars and stripes, which have floated proudly o'er land and sea for more than eighty years," were alluded to, the burst of applause was truly grand; and when the question, "Jerseymen, would you see the flag of your countrymen dishonored without rushing to its defence?" was asked, there came a mighty response from the audience in such an affirmative voice that all felt the good old flag was still safe, so far, at least, as it laid in their power to protect it. A few persons were present who had previously justified the South in her arrogance, but all their sympathy was lost in the feeling of patriotism awakened in their bosoms for their country and their country's honor. The meeting . . . adjourned with nine hearty cheers.

So much for Bordentown! We understand that there are about 25 of our young men enrolled for their country's sake, and are now awaiting an opportunity to enter its service in defence of the stars and stripes. There is loyalty in Bordentown. It is a hot place for traitors and for aiders and sympathizers with secessionists and traitors, and although a few weeks since we could hear an occasional sympathizer with the Jeff. Davis confederacy, but since the unprovoked attack upon Fort Sumter and Major Anderson, they have all disappeared, and but one sentiment prevails, and that is—"The Union, the Constitution and the enforcement of the laws."[15]

"The war fever rages high in old Sussex," reported the *New Jersey Herald*:

The streets and residences of the citizens of Newton are literally festooned with flags and banners. The red, white and blue is not only worn by the gentlemen, but even the ladies share largely in the excitement, all talking and advocating the Union. It is almost dangerous for anyone to even hint at anything like sympathy for the South in Newton. The unanimous voice of our people is in favor of maintaining the stars and stripes.

By this is meant no act of aggression against the Constitutional rights of the South, but "the Union of the States must and shall be maintained!"[16]

Princeton, too, was ablaze with patriotism.

At this time, the Stars and Stripes are seen in many parts of our town. They may be seen over the drill room of the Governor's Guards. They confront you as you enter Governor Olden's mansion. . . . The colors were also seen yesterday morning floating from the top of Nassau Hall—the same flag which was seen there in the Revolutionary war. . . . When the evening mail arrives at the Theological Seminary, the tap of the bell calls the students together to hear the news, and the Government receives their endorsement with an emphasis and ardor of patriotism which characterize all our young men. There is but one excitement here, and the unity has been as sudden as if effected by electricity. Indeed the whole State, like the whole North, is festooned with the Stars and Stripes. The lion of the North is aroused.[17]

The "duty of Jerseymen" was clear, wrote one Essex County resident:

The flag of our country trails in the dust. Rebellion has seized upon the government property, and trampled upon the stars and stripes. Major Anderson no longer upholds the honor of the country. The traitors' cannon have sounded war, and now threaten to plant their standard upon the walls of Washington. To-day we know no party, it is our country and its honor. The heritage of the revolution, the constitution of our fathers, with the beloved institutions of the land, are in danger. The success of the traitors of Sumpter will precipitate them into daring acts of aggression. Let the North be prepared to meet them as it becomes patriots, and beat back the tide of rebellion with the means they have invoked. Let every traitor in our midst, who dares breathe his sympathy for the villainous acts of the rebels, be remembered, so that when history shall record the terrible events now transpiring, and our country comes purified from this fiery ordeal, the finger of scorn shall mark him who would sell his country to a band of traitors. Thank God for the faith that few such will be found among Jerseymen. . . .

Shall not Jerseymen be the very first to march under the stars and stripes to defend its honor, to preserve its fame?

50,000 men from the North should be on the march to Washington within twenty-four hours to protect the government there, or the . . .

rebel flag [may] float over the walls of our Capitol. There is not a moment to be lost, and our Governor should at once take the necessary steps to move our troops. Our military will respond with alacrity! Every hour's delay adds to the danger. If we temporize for a few weeks we may have a divided North, and rivers of blood will be shed to atone for the delay.

Let the call go forth, and from every valley and hill top the hearty response will be given, and ten thousand Jerseymen will stand ready to do their country's bidding.[18]

One of New Jersey's leading Democrats and a delegate to the Peace Conference held in Washington in February, Commodore Robert F. Stockton spoke for many of his fellow party members in those heady days of April when he wrote to Governor Olden:

My dear Sir, You are aware that I have for months, without regard to personal reproach or convenience, done but little else than to use my best efforts to preserve the peace of the country. In spite, however, of my efforts, and your efforts, and the efforts of the whole people of New Jersey, War is upon us. . . .

I will therefore take the liberty to suggest, that after you have complied with the requisition of the National Government for troops, you consider the best means to preserve our own State from aggression. You remember that it is only the river Delaware which separates New Jersey from the Slave States. . . .

This is not time to palter about past differences of opinion, or to criticize the administration of public affairs. We are in the presence of an awful danger. We feel throes of political convulsion, which threatens to bring down to ruins the noblest fabric of Government ever constructed for the purposes of civilization and humanity.

Every citizen should feel that any sacrifice that he is called upon to make in such a crisis is as nothing. I am ready to do all I can to maintain our own rights and to preserve peace.

I will hoist the Star Spangled Banner at Morven, the former residence of one of the signers of the Declaration of Independence; that flag . . . which the immortal Washington, in the name of our Country, OUR WHOLE COUNTRY, planted on the ramparts of Liberty.[19]

Charles P. Smith, clerk of the Supreme Court and member of the Republican Party's State Executive Committee, was in Trenton during April 1861. "The bombardment [of Fort Sumter] continued several days," he wrote:

Thousands of people gathered in the streets mournfully discussing the imperfect items, and conjecturing as to the result. Suddenly flashed over the wires, "The Flag is down, and the Fort in flames!" Then burst forth the long pent patriotic enthusiasm! The cities suddenly became resplendent with flags! Men, women and children vied in displaying the National Colors, in badges, rosettes, and in every possible manner. Crowds paraded the streets, with drums and shouts, visiting the residents of supposed disloyalists, and demanding that they "show their colors!"

Then came rumors that Washington City was threatened; the burning of the National Armory at Harper's Ferry, and the cowardly destruction of the Navy Yard at Norfolk; its vast accumulation of munition, and a large portion of the ships of the Navy, by our own incompetent or treasonable officials!

How we thronged around the cars at the Trenton railway station, grasping the hands, and wishing "God's speed" to the First Massachusetts regiment of volunteers, hastening to the defence of Washington. Then the news that this, and certain unarmed Pennsylvania Regiments, had been assaulted by overwhelming numbers in the streets of Baltimore. Then the hurrying through of the New York Seventh Regiment, and, also, their welcome by our citizens.

Then the burning of the bridges and consequent severing of rail-road communication with the National Capitol, and, for a period, the virtual separation of the loyal North from the seat of Government. Then, after a painful suspense, the mortifying realization of the fact that while the rebels were fully prepared the North had every thing to provide.[20]

Within a week of Lincoln's call for troops one hundred companies of volunteers, ten thousand men, had offered their services, three times New Jersey's quota. "Every fireside shone with the lustre of patriotic feeling," remembered John Y. Foster, editor of the *Newark Daily Mercury*, "and even the schools shared in the absorbing excitement. It was a carnival of patriotism, from one end of the State to another."[21]

"The people of Ocean County are enthusiastically aroused, and fully determined to respond to the call of the President, in aiding to drive back the Rebels who have raised their guilty hands against the Constitution, the laws and the flag of our country," reported the *Ocean Emblem* of Toms River:

On Monday night the following notice was sent out, by special carriers, from this village, into every township in the county: FREEMEN, TO ARMS: The citizens of Ocean County, without distinction, are called to meet in County Convention, at the Court House, in the village of Tom's River, on Thursday, at 12 o'clock, noon, for the purpose of adopting measures to give fitting expression respecting the Traitor's Rebellion against the laws of our country. . . . The public houses of our village, and many of the private residences of our citizens, have the Stars and Stripes hung out. The stages are also decorated with that emblem of our National Glory.[22]

Typical of most New Jersey towns, Bridgeton in Cumberland County was awash in red, white, and blue.

For some time past our town has been enlivened by the stirring sound of the fife and drum, and the appearance of the "Cumberland Greys" frequently on parade. On Wednesday morning last they came out in their new uniform, presenting a most imposing appearance. The suits were manufactured by Messrs. Grosscup, Thompson and Burt, of this place, and reflect much credit on the manufacturers, who have not only executed the work well, but given the company what *they* will give the Southern rebels if they get an opportunity—fits.

On Wednesday afternoon the company met in Grosscup's Hall, which was crowded with spectators, who had assembled for the purpose of witnessing the presentation of a beautiful silk flag to the "Cumberland Greys." The Bridgeton Brass Band added materially to the interest of the occasion, by the performance of several national airs. The company marched through town to their armory, headed by the Band and their new flag, which was a most beautiful specimen of the Stars and Stripes, for which the ladies deserve much credit.[23]

In Bordentown a subscription was opened to purchase three large flags to fly in front of the town's hotels:

There was a gala time here on Saturday last, it being the occasion of the raising of a large pole and flag in front of the American House. . . .

The crowd began to assemble at 3 o'clock p.m., and continued to swell until near five o'clock at which time the pole was firmly fixed in its place and our worthy townsman, Capt. G. B. Raymond, proceeded to raise the Star Spangled Banner to the top of the flagstaff amid the cheers of the hundreds assembled.

One of the most singular and pleasing things of the occasion was, immediately after the raising of the liberty pole, there appeared high in the sky—higher than we ever saw a bird—two eagles. When first discovered they appeared to be almost directly above the pole, where they remained apparently motionless for about a minute, and then separated. . . . Their flight was slow and circuitous, and, as they occasionally dipped their wings or showed certain parts of their bodies so as the sun's rays would range with the eye, one imagined he was gazing on a polished plate of silver. The birds were watched eagerly until they were lost in the distance. Every one thought they were a good omen, and when the "Old Flag" went up, the welkin rang more fiercely for the good harbinger that so opportunely made its appearance. It was a happy occasion.[24]

The government's call for 75,000 militiamen to serve for three months roused the North. New Jersey's quota, four regiments of 780 men each, was quickly oversubscribed. Within weeks there were over a thousand men in camp at Trenton, led by thirty-eight-year-old Brigadier General Theodore Runyon, a Newark Democrat who had commanded Essex County's militia. Bordentown's contingent departed for Trenton on April 14, amid scenes that would be repeated time and again during the next four years:

Early on Wednesday morning our streets were alive with the sounds of martial music and the tramp of the citizens and recruits. The Cook Rifle Company were ordered to form in line at half-past six o'clock, preparatory to their departure for the rendezvous at Trenton. At six o'clock the brass field-piece was brought out in front of the American Hotel and salutes fired out of it, which soon drew together a large number of citizens and ladies, some of the latter being the mothers of the young soldiers, who had come to bid a final adieu and shed another tear for their offspring. Others, perhaps, their sisters who had come to exchange some memento of tenderness to him who had been reared in the same house, had shared the same joys or sorrows, and who now wished to bid a lingering and perhaps last farewell. Others still, the sweethearts of some as noble and fine-looking men as are to be found, came with words of cheer and encouragement to the manly hearts of the brave fellows who were about to leave their native town to defend the flag of their country, and to say to them, "God speed you in the good cause," and to renew vows of plighted faith and pledges of fidelity till they return from the war. There was still another class—the wives of the soldiers. They came, without doubt, sadder than all the rest; but amid their tears you could plainly see the smiling fortitude of women's patriotic heart beaming out in radiant rays of cheer as she looked upon him whom she had long since learned to lean for support, and, as she waved a silent adieu, her heart was doubtless cheered at the thought of the good cause in which he had enlisted and that the generous souls of Bordentown would not allow her or the little ones to suffer during his absence.

It was a sorrowful, yet joyous time. The noble fellows who had just gone through the ordeal of parting, were as happy as could be. They took their departure amid the shouts of hundreds of their fellow citizens and the waving of hundreds of handkerchiefs.[25]

The First Regiment left Newark on April 29, cheered by the biggest crowd the place had ever seen. "The city yesterday passed through one of the greatest excitements it has known for years," reported the *Daily Mercury*. "The whole population was on the qui vive."

At the early hour of six o'clock, thousands had congregated upon the streets and about Military Park, where the First Regiment had orders to form at five, and an hour later all the vicinity was crowded with an excited multitude, embracing men, women and children. All the movements were watched with the greatest interest, and when, at 7½ o'clock, the several companies left the parade-ground and proceeded to the armories, a vast crowd of enthusiastic admirers surged behind them. During the whole morning the multitude seemed to increase, and everywhere evidences of warlike preparations were visible, appealing with irresistible force to the patriotism of every loyal heart. The firemen of the city . . . gathered in full force, many with Union badges in their hats, and all with hearts burning with patriotic purpose—happy that they were permitted to add anything to the brilliancy of the occasion, and attest their sympathy with the noble thousand who go forth to the country's defence. . . .

At twelve o'clock, the Regimental line was re-formed, and . . . the farewell march was commenced, the whole Fire Department acting as an escort. At this time, 10,000 or 15,000 people were collected at the Park, and the wildest excitement prevailed.

All the men were uniformed, having also overcoats and blankets. Many, however, were without muskets; these will be supplied at Trenton. . . .

At last the . . . order was given to "fall in," and headed by Rubsam's Band, and escorted and flanked by the Fire Department, the Regiment marched out of the Park up Broad st., . . . to the High School—followed by the concourse of people, who completely blocked the streets . . . besides filling all the house-tops and windows overlooking the scene.

The school was trimmed with flags and presented a fine appearance.

The scholars were ranged around a platform erected in Linden street. The Regiment being drawn up, . . . [the] City Superintendent of Schools advanced and presented [a] flag. . . . The children then sang "Hail Columbia," and the regiment gave three cheers, and the band playing the "Star Spangled Banner."

At three o'clock, the line was again formed, and the Regiment marched towards the depot, the same innumerable multitude thronging the streets. Past walls of throbbing hearts, lining all the streets; past balconies crowded with fair faces, smiling kindly farewells; past windows white with fluttering handkerchiefs' flinging benedictions upon the brave; past long blocks hung all the way with starry banners, and animated with applauding thousands—past all these, with beating drums, and waving flags, and steady tread, and hopeful faces, the gallant First marched on, the skies overhead smiling upon them, the people at every step saluting them with royal majesty of presence. Every inch of sidewalk space, every elevation, doorways, piazzas, windows, roofs, were crowded with spectators as we have never seen them crowded before. Mingling in the crowd, and perched in the windows, were many—sisters, wives and mothers—in whose eyes the parting had left tears of sorrow.

In passing through Park street, the troops were reviewed by Mayor Bigelow, who appeared well pleased with their appearance, upon Broad street, the enthusiasm was universal, and at the Depot, scenes the most affecting were exhibited. At least 20,000 people were congregated upon the Avenue. There was of course some delay, but at last everything was ready, and the train swept out amid the huzzas of the multitude.

Thus our gallant soldiery, at last, are gone to the battle-field. May God go with them. May victory perch upon their standards. May rebellion be crushed, and the Union be maintained, and the Jersey Blues come home at last covered with glory.[26]

On May 3 General Runyon embarked his men, equipped with obsolete smoothbore muskets, from the dock at Bordentown for the slow trip down the Delaware to Annapolis, Maryland, and from there to Washington.

Last Friday evening the four regiments of New Jersey volunteers left the wharf at the foot of Main street, in sixteen propellers. . . . The soldiers were as happy a set of fellows as you would wish to see—marching down the street in a severe rain storm, singing and shouting for the "Flag of our Union" as if they were going on a pleasure excursion. . . .

It is true, they were not all fully equipped; nor had all the necessary

23

accoutrements for a conflict with the traitors, but the soldiers expected, having been assured by their officers, that they should have rifles, bayonets and all when they reached Washington. . . .

Give our Jersey boys an equal chance with those of other States, and we have no fear about them making their mark, and when they return after the victory they shall have a warm reception from their friends and fellow citizens. On to victory, gallant Jersey Blues! Strike for your country and your flag; for your rights and your liberty.[27]

Virginia's secession on April 17 and the ensuing riots in Baltimore cut Washington's communications with the North. Even the telegraph lines went dead. For six long days the nation's capital was isolated from the loyal states; then on April 27 the first of what would soon turn into a torrent of soldiers began to arrive at the depot, delivering the city from possible attack. On May 6 four regiments of Jerseyans were marching through Washington, the first fully organized brigade of any state to reach the capital. At home, meanwhile, Governor Olden easily borrowed $450,000 from private banks to support the state's war effort. A special emergency session of the State Legislature quickly voted a $2 million war chest. Enthusiasm for the war was matched only by confidence that it would be over quickly. "This rebellion," said a New Jersey congressman a few weeks after Fort Sumter, "could easily be put down by a few women with broomsticks!"[28]

"It seemed," wrote one soldier, "as if all the able-bodied men in the country were moving, with all their property on their backs, to agreeable, but dusty lodgings on the Potomac." Soldiers in gray and blue, Zouaves in picturesque uniforms, firemen in red shirts, regiments from New York, Pennsylvania, Connecticut, Vermont, New Jersey, and Michigan mingled in the streets of Washington. Although the business at hand was serious, and the soldiers knew it, a country fair atmosphere prevailed. A Burlington County soldier took pen in hand two days after New Jersey's regiments arrived in Federal City:

Yesterday was a proud day for the New Jersey Brigade. The whole four regiments were out in full parade on Pennsylvania Avenue. They presented a most formidable appearance, and were cheered at almost every point by the hundreds who had assembled to see them. They marched through the grounds at the White House, where the President stood, with hat in hand to receive them. He remarked that New Jersey, according to her population, had presented a fuller and more completely equipped body of men, than any other State. Every man felt proud that he was a Jerseyan, and especially a Jersey volunteer.

In the morning a band of music serenaded Major Anderson and General Runyon, at Willard's hotel. Major Anderson first appeared and made a short speech. General Runyon was wildly called for, and being inspired by the occasion, made a most eloquent speech. . . .

Yesterday the Commissary Department were busy in supplying the Jersey regiments with cookingstoves, kettles, wood, &c., &c. It is quite likely we shall be camped out in the open fields, in a few days. I ate my dinner today, cooked by two persons selected out of the company. It consisted of a piece of pork, four biscuits and a tin cup full of coffee. I relished it well. After dinner, our men all said, "Well, now we are beginning to live."[29]

On May 12 Major James S. Yard of the Third Militia Regiment caught a glimpse of the president:

During the afternoon . . . we were surprised by a visit from Mr. Lincoln, Secretaries Chase and Seward, and C. M. Clay, of Kentucky. The party was recognized by the soldiers, the news spread, and they crowded eagerly around; directly they burst into three cheers for President Lincoln. He bowed in acknowledgment of the compliment, and then in a free easy way waved his hand toward Mr. Seward, saying: "This is the Secretary of State—give him three cheers." It was done, and he then turned towards Mr. Chase, saying: "This is the paymaster, who gives you your pay—three cheers for him;" and again turning, pointed to Mr. Clay, saying: "And now three cheers for Old Kentuck." The boys responded heartily, and the President and his party seemed to enjoy it highly. After a few words of compliment, and interchange of bows, they walked off as unceremoniously as they came.[30]

A few days later Yard, a Freehold newspaper editor, saw Lincoln and his family close-up at a gala White House reception.

The great event of the past week was the President's Levee on Thursday evening. All the commissioned officers in the city were invited, and there was the greatest gathering of epauletts and scarlet sashes ever seen in this county. . . .

On reaching the White House, [we] were ushered into an ante-room, where our caps were deposited in pigeon holes, and a check issued for them; we then passed through a hall to the door of the "Blue Room," just inside of which stood the President. At his left stood a gentleman to whom we each in turn whispered our names, and were then formally introduced. After shaking hands we passed along to make room for others. To some the President would say a few words, but the mass were dismissed with a shake and a smile. I took a position near the wall and opposite to the President, where I remained a few minutes to watch the proceedings. He is exceedingly easy and familiar in his bearing, and makes everybody around him at ease. There appears to be no more stiffness among the guests than at a Freehold Sociable, and there was a total absence of that reserve that one expects to find in a man occupying the high position of President of the United States. As to his personal appearance, . . . he is not the ugly man represented—he is a plain, everyday man, and as good-looking as the common run of folks. Mrs. Lincoln was present, and after the introduction to the President, the guests were all presented to her. She is a plain, unpretending looking woman, of medium height, was very richly dressed in blue trimmed with white. A stiff bow was the etiquette here. She was surrounded by a bevy of ladies, and she chatted away perfectly at ease. A little son trotted around among the guests, and gave the whole the appearance of a family party.[31]

Twenty-four hours after the citizens of Virginia voted three to one in favor of secession, Federal troops advanced across the Potomac, occupying Alexandria and establishing a ring of forts to defend the capital. On May 24 elements of the New Jersey Brigade crossed onto enemy soil, making camp on Arlington Heights. "Washington and its suburbs presents the appearance of one immense camp," wrote the *Trenton State Gazette's* correspondent:

On every side camp tents spread out, while the stars and stripes float triumphantly from scores of staffs in and about the city. There are a few troops still quartered within the city, and the drilling of these from morn to dewy eve, with the occasional rushing of mounted cavalry, pell mell through the streets, gives the whole city a very military aspect. There are now over 30,000 troops here, and many of them are fairly "spoiling" for a fight. If Jeff Davis, with almost any number of troops, will present himself just now I think he would be cordially welcomed and *warmly* received.

The three New Jersey Regiments encamped on Meridian Hill, about two miles north of the city, are getting along quite comfortable at present, though they have suffered considerably heretofore, for want of proper food, clothing and shelter. Captain Yard is about having erected a large bake-oven on the camp ground so that pretty soon they will be independent of Washington bakeries and have good fresh bread instead of dry bread and still drier biscuit. . . . I visited the camp yesterday and to-day, and had a very pleasant and satisfactory interview with officers and men. It does them all good to see and talk with a Trentonian, especially since each one then has an opportunity to send a little private message of his own to his friends at home. . . .

Quite a little excitement was created among the Jersey boys yesterday by the arrest of Samuel Hanna, formerly postmaster at Camden. He was arrested as a spy by Col. Baker, and after a brief examination by Gen. Runyon, committed to the District jail. Some documents were found upon his person of a very suspicious character.[32]

Jersey's soldiers, used to the prosperous villages and farms of their home state, were taken aback by the poverty they found in Virginia. Wrote a Burlington County volunteer:

We have been hard at work, throwing up entrenchments for our defence, in case of an attack. . . . The country around us is wretchedly poor. Off in the distance, you can see the fine residence of General Lee, the commander of the Virginia forces . . . and a few others, but the general character of the houses is poor and dilapidated. . . . Everything looks poor—houses, cows, hogs, chickens. . . .

We found an old widow occupying a small house, opposite our camp. To our surprise, we found her in possession of several barrels of whiskey, and very little else. She had some tea and a few eggs. I paid a shilling for a cup of tea. As soon as the whiskey was discovered, the old lady had a grand rush, so great that a guard of men had to be placed at the door. When the officers saw that the whole camp was about to get drunk, Gen. Runyon dispatched a soldier to tell her to sell no more; she continued to do so nevertheless, when the General sent some men to knock in the heads of the barrels. The old lady declared she was ruined. The chickens and pigs have very extensive privileges in the houses about here. They can be found in every part. While a few of us were eating a scanty supply of breakfast from one of the farmer's tables, the hogs stood at the door and chickens were running under our feet and on the bench on which we were sitting at the table.[33]

Even as Union troops were preparing to cross the Potomac, Federal authorities began to realize that a force larger than 75,000 ninety-day militiamen would be needed to suppress the rebellion. On May 3, Lincoln called for 42,000 three-year volunteers; when Congress reconvened in July it went him one better, authorizing another million soldiers. New Jersey's first quota was four regiments, the First, Second, Third, and Fourth New Jersey Volunteers, comprising the First New Jersey Brigade.

The president's proclamation reached Elizabeth at 7 a.m. on May 4, and by 8 a.m. thirty-one-year-old David Hatfield, a private in the Mexican War, began to enroll a company. Two weeks later the 100-man company left Elizabeth:

On May 16th, 1861, while marching to the station to take the train for Trenton, the company was halted in front of No. 165 Broad street, when a sword and sash was presented to Captain Hatfield by the citizens of Elizabeth by Mr. C. C. Suydam. On presenting the sword Mr. Suydam said: "Captain David Hatfield, our fellow-citizens are desirous, upon this, the eve of your departure for service in your country's great and just cause, to present you with some substantial token of their appreciation and high esteem. In furtherance of this object they have caused to be prepared this sword, and this sash, and they request, through me, your acceptance of the same. We are confident, sir, that in bestowing this sword upon you we are intrusting it to no unwilling or doubtful hand, and that wherever glory and honor are to be achieved, there will the name of David Hatfield be enrolled. We have no fear for the safety of our glorious Stars and Stripes when committed to your care. . . . Accept then these, sir, as an earnest of the full confidence and esteem of your fellow-citizens of Elizabeth, both for yourself and your noble command."

Captain Hatfield seemed much affected on receiving this token of regard, and said in response, that he felt that he was going forth to battle in the cause of Divine Right, and that so long as he had a right hand to hold it he would wield it in defense of his country. He touchingly requested that when those present knelt at the family altar they would remember his command. When they gathered in the Sanctuary they would see vacant seats, and asked to be remembered there, as also in the Sabbath School. After expressing gratitude to his friends and neighbors he bade them farewell and the company then marched on.[34]

Major Hatfield would die on July 30, 1862, from wounds received in action at the Battle of Gaines' Mill, Virginia.

The First, Second, and Third New Jersey rendezvoused at Trenton's Camp Olden (the Fourth joined the brigade after the Battle of Bull Run), where it received its equipment and a month's worth of training. A correspondent for the *New-Brunswick Fredonian* visited the camp at the end of May:

On Tuesday we visited the soldiers at Trenton—at Camps Olden and Perrine and at the Arsenal. Camp Olden is situated near the "Sandtown Road," two and a half miles east of the Trenton Locomotive Works and Rolling Mills, and is reached by hacks and other conveyances which are constantly plying between the Camp and the Trenton House which charge the *moderate* sum of a quarter of a dollar. The Camp is in a large field adjoining a wood, and quite pleasantly situated. Along the road, without the grounds, were a number of shanties and wagons in which a thriving business was apparently being done in the way of selling cakes, pies and refreshments to the soldiers on furlough and their friends who visited them. The Camp grounds were surrounded by strong picket-guard and none allowed to enter except by the aid of a pass, to be procured of some friendly captain or regimental officer. . . .

We found the New Brunswick boys all in good health and spirits, and well pleased with their quarters and officers. They were quartered in Sibley tents, from twelve to fifteen in each tent—the bottom of which is well covered with straw. In some tents the men have ticks filled with straw to sleep on. . . . Outside the tents each company has a parade ground of about forty feet in width and perhaps a hundred and fifty yards long. While we were there a portion of "Company I" were engaged in leveling off and grading their parade, and appeared to be in great glee over their work—some hoeing, shoveling and raking the ground; while about twelve or fifteen were harnessed to a plow, turning up the sandy soil in fine style. . . . At one end of each row of company tents is a rude shed where the cooking is done—each company cooking its own food, cooks being appointed in regular turns. The soldiers all declared that the quality of their food was excellent, but some complained of not having enough. . . . Colonel Montgomery, of the First Regiment, who has seen twenty-five years' service in the regular army of the United States, was on the ground while we were there, and we heard him instruct the Orderlies of the different companies present in their duties, and he promised the men that they would be properly provided for, and that he would bring to a speedy account anyone who did not do his whole duty in this particular.

In the rear of the Camp is a hospital tent in which we learnt there were some half a dozen sick from the different companies. Not far distant was the guard house, in which were put the refractory soldiers who disobeyed orders. . . . As soon as the companies are sworn in and receive arms they are ordered to Camp Olden. The companies are now receiving old flintlock muskets, but expect to receive before leaving the State proper arms. The companies now on the ground drill three or four hours each day. The time they will be stationed there is not yet known, but probably several weeks. It is generally thought best to drill the three year's troops well before sending them off, if they are not really needed by the Government sooner, and therefore it will probably be sometime before the Jersey troops are called out of the State. . . .

After leaving the boys in Camp Olden, we went back to Trenton to see the Olden Guard . . . we met them coming back from the State House where they had been sworn in and examined. In their examination only one (a young man named Vacter) was rejected, and because he *stuttered!* He appeared to be much attached to the company, and the members of the Company to him, and he felt badly because he was rejected, and the last we saw of him later in the day, he was begging Captain Way to let him go with him in the capacity of cook, if he could not be received in any other way.[35]

A member of a Zouave company from Hudson County, assigned to the Second Militia Regiment, entertained readers of Jersey City's *American Standard* with a light-hearted account of his sojourn at Camp Olden:

You have no idea of the confusion that prevails in a camp of newly recruited soldiers. . . . Our Zouaves, after being nicely fitted out with new pantaloons and jackets, were summoned by Capt. Babcock for parade. After performing several evolutions, we at last got upon the "double quick," our peculiar drill; after going around the drilling ground a half dozen times we were surprised to find Capt. Baker's company trying the same movement. Both companies trotted around the grounds a half dozen times in pretty good order until the Zouaves, having become annoyed by following the other company, filled in a circle of less radius and soon were side by side with them. At this juncture, as we were about to pass Capt. Baker's company, his men broke into our ranks and threw us into confusion, and thereupon a grand foot race ensued between the fleetest members of each company which ended in the fainting of one man of the other company on the field from heat and fatigue. I saw him carried to his quarters where he was bled. Our boys I am pleased to say sustained no injury.

It would make you laugh if you should sit down to mess with us. Just imagine a long, low, narrow building, with three rows of tables set therein, extending the whole length of the building: then 500 men, or more, under Commissary Brown, marching in to partake of the comestibles, which consist of boiled salted beef and pork, bread and butter, and coffee contained in large tin pails. Our tables are rough pine boards laid upon frames—our table furniture is composed entirely of tin.

As soon as a company is seated, some one, usually the most hungry, calls out "fall to"—and immediately every member makes a dive with his pint tin cup in the coffee pails; then the cheapest brown sugar is used to sweeten this libation; milk is probably a condiment unknown to our messman, as we do not see, taste or handle it. It may be there are no cows in Trenton, and the solidified milk company has no agent here. Then we attack the huge chunks of meat, each man seizing (no rules of politeness are observable in our mess-room) a piece which he deems sufficient for himself; then bread and butter is eaten, according to pleasure.

For a meal or two this would do very well, but to feed us on the same dainties every meal, you yourself will admit, has a tendency to cloy if not nauseate one's appetite. In this manner we have been fed or rather forced to feed since Saturday last. To-day, at noon, however, some companies resolved to have a change of faire, and, accordingly, did it in their peculiar way, to wit: after being seated and having eaten a little they took the pails of coffee and poured them out of the window, then threw the meat and butter with it. For dessert they fell to shouting, tore up the table boards and threw them on the floor and retired, apparently well satisfied with the labor, to their respective tents.

This evening we had no supper; the messman, I suppose, was bent on revenge and therefore would not provide any more fodder. Rumor says that he has fled to some unknown locality, the report having reached his ears that some of the Jersey City boys meant to waylay him this evening and give him a sound thrashing for his treatment to us. I do not think they will do any such thing, for I have a better opinion of the boys, who, though they may be a little rude at times, are nevertheless good hearted and well disposed. . . .

Our friend came from Jersey City today, bringing lots of letters from our parents and, as I suspect, from some of our sweethearts; he also brought us the remainder of our equipments, so that we are completely accoutred; sabre-rifles, belts, cartridge and cap pouches having been furnished us from the arsenal this afternoon. We smiled all over when we were permitted to handle the dogs of war; in fact the feeling of the rifles was like that of shaking hands with an old friend, for we have had no weapons to handle since we left the shores of the Hudson.[36]

The New Jersey regiments left Trenton on May 28. "We have been constantly changing our position," a member of the Third Regiment wrote to his hometown newspaper, Gloucester County's *Woodbury Constitution,* "and I have been unable to write . . . but having found a piece of board this morning to write upon, with a knapsack for a seat, I will again resume my pen."

Camp Olden, June 28, 1861—This being the day set for shoving from this place to some place not known to any of us, our camp presented a very lively appearance this morning. Officers, soldiers, musicians and cooks were all busily engaged in packing baggage and arranging knapsacks. . . .

Gov. Olden and staff reviewed the troops, and each man ordered to pack in his haversack three days' provisions, with his knapsack, blanket, cartridge box, a canteen with two quarts of water, cap box, belt, side arms and musket, made a very heavy load for the men to carry, and caused them to look more like eastern dromedaries than soldiers.

The band struck up "Hail to the Chief" as the governor passed us, and, taking a last look at Camp Olden, we marched for Trenton, received ten charges of cartridges apiece, and stowed ourselves away in thirty-two cars, driven by two locomotives. We started off at 6 and reached Burlington at 7 o'clock, and an immense number of citizens were here assembled to witness our departure and bid a last good-bye to their own men who composed the Burlington Company in our regiment. Hundreds of the ladies passed from car to car, giving out with no sparing hand, water, lemonade, oranges, cakes and flowers. A short half hour was given for the leave taking. Hands were shaken, tears flowed freely, handkerchiefs were waved and kisses were given, as the iron horse, with a wild scream, again hurried us forward.

We were so delayed at the different stations, where hundreds bid us a hearty God-speed, that we did not reach Camden until 10 o'clock. We went on the boat and were again detained so that we did not land at [Philadelphia] until ten minutes past 11 o'clock.

And—well, I cannot describe the scene here. We marched through a perfect jam of citizens, more than 10,000 in number, to where we partook of a splendid collation gotten up for our benefit. On entering the eating saloon the first group we came near was a goodly number of Woodbury ladies, who were helping the soldiers take off their knapsacks, and serving out hot coffee and good wholesome provisions to all. Hundreds of our men received from their fair hands donations of all kinds for their comfort on the march. . . .

The bugle sounded and [our friends] bid us a long and, perhaps, a last farewell. Mothers, wives and children could be seen clinging to husbands and brothers, willing to part with them, yet loathe to see them go from them into the untried future; but the moment of parting came, and we tore ourselves away. It was now after 1 o'clock at night, and yet all the way to Broad and Pine streets, one continuous line of citizens cheered and encouraged us on. Thousands of ladies stood upon their doorsteps and in the streets to greet us on our way. We left Philadelphia at half past two and arrived at Wilmington at 4 o'clock.

Wilmington, Saturday morning, June 29—We are now enroute for Baltimore. Every bridge below this place is guarded by a strong force. . . . We went along slowly. Three miles below this place an awful groan echoed along the cars. On looking out we discovered the very dishonorable Jeff Davis suspended by the neck from a scaffold. An inscription on the hind part of his coattail told who it was.

We ran into Baltimore at 11 o'clock, left the cars, and immediately fixed bayonets and capped our guns. . . . After being inspected we marched a mile and a half to another depot, where we remained two hours. Here we were waited upon by many persons who were honest Union men. . . .

2 o'clock—Two huge locomotives, drawing forty six cars are now hurrying us onward. We stopped a few minutes at the Relay House. A large company is stationed here, and are fine looking men. We also stopped at Annapolis junction; another large body here. But at Bladensburg Station a terrific shout greeted us, and we shook hands with over 300 Jersey troops stationed there.

At the deep cut we passed two large camps. 5 o'clock—We are now at Washington, and 30,000 soldiers giving nine cheers for Jersey. At half past 7 we reached Abolition Hall, at the corner of Pennsylvania avenue and 4th street. We are to quarter here. It is an immense five story granite building, capable of accommodating 500 men. 400 of us sleep here tonight.

Sunday, June 30th—We felt much refreshed, after a good sleep, and at 8 o'clock this morning all are prepared to take a good look at the city. Through the kindness of one of our Washington friends we succeeded in making a grand tour through the capitol. From the dome we counted 11 large camps in sight in Virginia, Maryland and around Washington. There is now within three hours march of Washington 80,000 good soldiers and 30,000 more over in Western Virginia, all our men.

Arlington Heights stands forth conspicuous from here, while but three miles from us can be seen with a glass the pickets of the secessionists going their rounds. At Long Bridge are four regiments of our Jersey troops, at the aqueduct two, at Arlington Heights one. Four thousand men came in last night. . . . Our soldiers are much pleased with Washington. The Capitol is full all the time of men eager to see a place so much talked of.

Workmen are busy preparing the capitol rooms for the sitting of Congress. We sat this morning in Jeff Davis' seat in the Senate chamber. We pondered long on the treachery of this arch-traitor, and breathed a heartfelt malediction for his welfare. We also visited the [Washington] monument and gathered a few specimens of the different kinds of stones. It is not completed, but bids fair to be a magnificent work of art. At 4 o'clock we had a grand parade. In the evening we visited the White House and gardens, passed comment on the splendid statutes of the Goddess of Liberty, and that great wonder of art, the bronze equestrian statue of Jackson on his great war horse. . . .

Monday, July 1st—The first thing we heard this morning was that three of our pickets over in Maryland were shot last night by those most valorous Southerners, who stoop to such a mode of guerrilla warfare— Brave men indeed! 10 o'clock—Orders to pack up again and move. Everything in confusion. Streets filled with some 20,000 soldiers and citizens, officers, baggage wagons, mule trains, gun carriages, guards, regimental bands, artillery companies, women and children, with it seemed to us, an over considerable sprinkling of colored individuals of all shades of blackness. The green of the rifles, red of the artillery, blue of the infantry and yellow of cavalry, besides the innumerable variety of rich uniforms of many of the volunteer companies, who had dressed themselves at their own expense, created a beautiful scene that once looked upon was not soon forgotten. . . .

At 3 o'clock inspection, and at 4 took up the line of march southward from the capitol. Every man was on the qui vive to find out our destination. We passed the Washington Navy Yard and at half past 5 came to a halt on the bank of the Potomac, 2 miles below Washington, unslung our knapsacks and took our position, awaiting the baggage trains. Shortly after we arrived a terrific storm broke upon us. The wind howled fearfully and the rain fell in torrents. The men broke ranks and sought shelter wherever they could find it. Four hundred sought refuge in a lager beer brewery, 150 in a cow shed, some 200 in an open shanty, while the hen houses and small barns were full to overflowing. . . .

Tuesday morning, 6 o'clock—We are now pitching tents. The morning is beautiful, and the scenery on the Potomac is grand indeed. 8 o'clock—We are now seated on the ground eating breakfast, the first cooked victuals and the first coffee we have had since Friday morning. The men are very hungry and eat ravenously. We are now unpacking and find many of our things are lost. Our trunks are not here yet and two tents are missing. 12 o'clock, noon, A good dinner today, and our trunks and tents have just come. I have now got a place to write upon. . . .

The officers were very attentive, explaining everything to us, and giving us many little curiosities and relics. Three men are missing from our ranks. It is now 12 o'clock at night. The sentry's cry of all is well is ringing through the camp.[37]

Union Brigadier General Irvin McDowell now commanded the largest army ever assembled in North America, some 35,000 men camped in Washington and the surrounding hills. Clearly, the capital was no longer in any danger of a Confederate advance. But the presence of enemy forces less than a day's march away was intolerable, and pressure mounted for an attack. "Forward to Richmond!" was the cry, taken up by the press, the public, and the politicians: A quick thrust into Virginia and the rebellion would be over. Even Lincoln grew impatient, ordering McDowell to go on the offensive.

The Federal army started toward Confederate outposts at Fairfax Courthouse and Centreville on July 16 and 17. McDowell's plan was to clear the enemy from its advance positions, then attack the main Rebel army thought to be camped behind a stream called Bull Run, near Manassas Junction. By the time the main attack was finally launched on July 21, the Confederate defenders had already been reinforced by additional troops ferried by railroad from the Shenandoah Valley. The first great battle of the war developed into a bewildering fight: flags and uniforms so similar that friend and foe could not be distinguished; inexperienced officers who had never commanded more than a few hundred men; green Union troops equipped with antiquated arms whose ninety days' service was nearly over; and civilians who had ridden out from Washington, with picnic lunches, eager for a first-hand look at the South's humiliation.

It was a surprisingly vicious battle, given the untested soldiers on both sides, and McDowell's men came close, indeed, to success, but by late afternoon the Northern army was exhausted and discouraged. Stragglers began drifting toward the rear. Whole companies retreated, at first keeping up resistance, then, losing nerve, throwing away their guns and packs and fleeing. The retreat became a rout, then a general panic, as a confused jumble of demoralized soldiers, empty supply wagons, and frightened civilians scrambled toward the safety of Washington.

New Jersey's First Militia Regiment, and elements of the First and Second Volunteer Regiments, ordered to advance on Centreville on July 21, reached their destination hours after the Battle of Bull Run began. "Owing to some difficulty on the railroad," wrote a soldier with the First Militia Regiment, "it was six in the afternoon when we arrived."

From four A.M. Sunday, throughout the day, the roar of the cannon at Bull's Run could be distinctly heard, both at our location and on the road to Fairfax Station. I counted as many as thirteen cannon shots in one minute, and for four succeeding minutes seven each minute! This was extraordinary firing. The rumors reached us constantly that Bull's Run was taken, and even that Richmond was ours. We were all full of elatement, certain that the day was ours. We left our trains within a mile of Fairfax Station, to march thence to the Station. We had hardly left the cars before Dr. Craven, who had gone on before us, and had been all day of the battle-field, caring for the wounded, came to us, staggering us with the news that our own army, under Gen. McDowell, was retreating. We absolutely refused to believe it. . . . But when we reached Fairfax Station, we found all the excitement and the news confirmed.[38]

Lieutenant Colonel Isaac M. Tucker, in command of the Second New Jersey after the regiment's colonel went to the rear, supposedly to seek further orders, wrote two days after the battle of the confusion that met New Jersey's troops:

On Sunday morning our Regiment . . . received orders to proceed as soon as possible to Centreville and report ourselves to Gen. McDowell. . . . At three o'clock we got into line, and the First Regiment having started, we proceeded . . . marching on with our band playing "Dixie." Centreville is . . . about two miles this side of Bull's Run Bridge. The first news we had from the battle was cheering, and our men screamed with delight. When about two miles this side of Centreville, we met John R. Pierson, Esq., who had witnessed the battle nearly all day—who told us that our forces were retreating. Then the sad news came to us thick and fast. Soon we met baggage-wagons and carriages flying in confusion, strewing the road with implements, provisions and ammunition, &c. Then disorganized forces came straggling back. All communicated their detailed stories of the darkest day that ever dawned on this Union.

Having reached Centreville, I sent forward a messenger to Gen. McDowell or his aide, and reported our Regiment ready for service. It was then growing quite dark and we were surrounded by the wildest confusion I ever witnessed. Our whole regiment kept solid and close. After waiting about twenty minutes, I sent another messenger to find Gen. McDowell or his aide. After awhile they returned with information that neither could be found, and that the whole army was retreating, thoroughly demoralized and disorganized.[39]

"No retreat should have been ordered at Bull Run," Lieutenant Colonel Robert McAllister of the First New Jersey Volunteers wrote after the battle, "for the day was ours. The enemy were whipped. The men fought bravely enough, but we have too many cowardly officers." McAllister's regiment covered the Federal retreat, claiming the distinction of being the last to cross over to the safety of Union positions.

The roaring of artillery announced the opening of the battle of Bull Run. . . . We were soon on our way and moving rapidly toward the scene of conflict. We passed Germantown, the artillery sounding louder and louder. Some miles on this side of Centreville, we met a gentleman who said all was right, that the enemy were driven in toward Manassas Gap. On we went, feeling elated. After awhile the artillery ceased firing. We then knew that the battle was decided; but which way was the question. Soon the sad story was told by the confused masses of the retreating army. We determined to do what we could to stop the panic. We threw our columns across the road, appealed to their patriotism, to their honor, to the Flag, and urged them to return and help us fight the battle. But the panic was so great that our appeals were for the time unheeded. We then charged bayonets and stopped the stampede, letting only the wounded pass on.

   We turned into our ranks about five hundred of the stampeders, then marched through their retreating columns. We drew our swords and pistols on men and officers who would not willingly turn back. The whole scene beggars all description; and yet, strange to say, our officers and men were all cool. . . .

   Cheer after cheer went up for us as we advanced, and solemn promises were made on the part of the stampeders that they would fall in our rear if we advanced through them and formed line of battle. Others cried: "Go up yonder hill and you'll get it! You will be cut to pieces!" Still others encouraged us with hopes that we would save their retreat and bear the brunt of the battle.

   The stampede was now stopped and we were on the summit of a hill. Col. Montgomery had a conference with Genl. McDowell and urged the propriety of making a stand on the heights of Centreville—throwing up breastworks, holding the position, and not retreating to Washington. The General consented and ordered him to take his command to the other side of Centreville and form his lines for defense. We passed

Centreville and took up a position on the hill with our right resting on the road along which the enemy would have to come. But when we had accomplished this and were ready for battle, we found that our 2nd New Jersey Regiment had retreated. Two regiments under the command of Col. Blenker were the only troops left besides our own Regiment.

Col. Montgomery sent for McLean's regiment (the 2nd N.J.V.), and we waited in silence. Stillness reigned over that valley. Not a sound was heard save the groans of the wounded and dying in the hospitals not far distant. Our Surgeon Taylor was busily engaged amputating arms and legs. . . .

Having placed pickets out to give the alarm, the men laid down on their arms. Col. Montgomery and myself began to look around to see what was going on. We had a consultation with the colonel of a New York regiment—one of those under the command of Blenker, and we concluded to fight and stand by each other. We returned to our regiment. An hour passed away in silence. We then thought we heard something. On examination we found that our neighboring troops were moving off and that we alone would be in possession of the field. Now came the question: what are we to do?

We concluded to take another position around the lower hospital and across the road along which the Rebels would have to come. We re-formed in the new position but left the road clear. Yet we so arranged our forces as to sweep the road with a raking fire in case the cavalry came. I . . . waited in silence. Col. Montgomery and Maj. Hatfield left to call on Genl. McDowell, who was two miles off, to learn why Blenker's two regiments had left us alone, and to find out what was to be done.

McAllister soon learned that retreat was the order of the day.

As we marched [back] from Centreville, we had our rear column in a condition to defend. Cavalry was what we most feared. After marching several miles we reached the rear of the retreating column and thus protected them until we arrived at Fairfax, when we took a more advanced position for some miles. Afterward we formed protection for a battery and reached this place about 2 p.m. Monday, worn out and terrible hungry. We had not eaten anything for thirty hours save a dry piece of bread when we were in line of battle at Centreville. Almost all that time we were on duty, our horses had nothing to eat and no time to eat. Worn out by fatigue, many of our men sank down on the roadside and could not even be forced along.[40]

The Bull Run debacle ruined the military career of many a Federal officer, including the Second Regiment's Colonel George W. McLean, who resigned his commission before the year was out amid charges of incompetence. It also created one of New Jersey's first heroes, Lieutenant E. Burd Grubb. "During the battle of Bull Run, the Third Regiment . . . was ordered up the road as a reserve," reported the *Burlington County Advertiser*, "with orders to protect some ammunition at Burke's Station."

They went readily forward, longing to get into the fight, whose distant thundering reached their ears. Among these, it was necessary to detail some men to protect the ammunition; and to his great regret, spoiling his hopes of the battle, Lieut. Edward B. Grubb, of Company C, Third Regiment, with a Corporal and twenty-five men, was trusted with this duty.

The Lieutenant is a boy—not, I think, yet of age . . . of Burlington. . . . He disposed his men, set out his pickets, and leaving the Corporal in charge, "turned in" for a little rest. In less than fifteen minutes, came "the fleetest footed," the advance guard of the retreating army. The Corporal awoke his Lieutenant with the news, "The enemy are upon us!" In a moment he was out. Twenty of his men fell in with the troops that rushed by. He stood there, not knowing what it meant, and determined to stand his ground, come what would. The Corporal and five men stayed with him.

For more than an hour, the route rushed by, still they stood firm. A little while after came his regiment, under the Lieutenant-Colonel, who ordered him to fall in with their retreat, as the Army was routed and the enemy in full pursuit. "No," said Lt. Grubb, "Col. Taylor put me here, and nobody but Col. Taylor shall take me away." And for half an hour more he stayed, every moment looking for death. But the Colonel remembered him, and came to him; and not until he had destroyed every particle of the ammunition, did he leave his post, under the orders of his commanding officer.

By this gallant action, 30,000 ball cartridges were lost to the enemy, and much other valuable ammunition, which would have fallen into their hands, destroyed. But, best of all, it is an instance of that highest courage—strict obedience, with no thought of personal results—which deserves and has received notice and commendation.[41]

Grubb would later serve as colonel of the Twenty-third and Thirty-seventh New Jersey regiments, winning the brevet rank of brigadier general "for gallant and meritorious services during the war."

The dream of a short, swift war was abruptly shattered when news of the Federal rout at Bull Run reached New Jersey. "[E]nough is known," wrote the *Trenton State Gazette and Republican* as it sorted out conflicting accounts of the battle, "to warrant the statement that we have suffered in a degree which has cast gloom over the remnant of the army, and excited the deepest melancholy throughout Washington. The carnage has been tremendously heavy on both sides, and ours is represented as frightful."[42] The ignominious retreat of the Federal army emboldened New Jersey Copperheads, as the antiwar Democrats came to be known, to demand an immediate truce. Otherwise, predicted the *Newark Daily Journal*, the nation was in store for a long war that would surely end in Northern defeat:

No intelligent man now harbors the delusion that the South can be crushed or starved out, conquered or subjugated in months or years to come. . . . With our own time for preparation, with the choice of the battle-field, and the available military talent of the North at our command, we have offered the enemy battle in force, and in a fair and well contested fight, where our soldiers nobly vindicated the bravery of the country, we have been disasterously defeated, and our capital placed at the mercy of our enemies.

But does this defeat prove that the North may not again rise in her strength, and, gathering fresh armies to the field, meet and perhaps emerge successfully from the next campaign? By no means. We have still abundant resources, great credit, a determined will and the force of State organizations and overpowering numbers in our favor. We may raise a half million of soldiers and equip and appoint them as [an] army was never equipped and appointed. We may rectify the blunders of the past and retrieve its defeats by great victories. Success may perchance perch upon our banners for years; and yet, in the end, the North is destined to sure defeat.[43]

Conceding that it would be "useless to even attempt to disguise our mortification" at the outcome of Bull Run, the *State Gazette* denounced any notion of a truce. Bull Run, claimed the paper, meant nothing more than a six- to twelve-month delay before the Rebels were subdued:

Because defeated once, however, it is no reason for permanent despondency. Like, at the defeat of Fort Sumter the first impulse of the nation was to mourn and the second to avenge, so now, when the smoke of the battle shall have all cleared away; and the honored dead shall have been laid in their narrow tombs; and the first gush of anguish of those whose loved-ones have thus been hastily summoned away, shall have subsided, the whole North will again arouse itself to the great and glorious work of subduing this most unrighteous and causeless rebellion. Again upon the wings of the lightning will fly the order "To arms!" "To arms!" and from every town and hamlet—from every hill and valley, will come the response, "We are ready!"

We are no less confident of success now than before; and though the final triumph will doubtless be put off somewhat longer by the recent reverse, yet come it must and will, sooner or later.[44]

Before Bull Run, opponents of the war had been careful to keep their own counsel. Now, suddenly, there were reports of peace meetings where the Rebel flag was raised, and of armed units being formed to aid the South. Some of the boldest peace advocates grandly proclaimed that they would refuse to pay their federal taxes for the duration of the war. Although New Jersey's Copperheads were a minority, they were exceedingly vocal, and their activities produced a frenzied reaction. In the same editions that reported the Federal rout at Bull Run, the *Trenton State Gazette* printed a "General Prescription for the Treatment of Traitors."

By special request we re-publish the prescription given some days since for the treatment of traitors wherever found. It has been pronounced by several Political Doctors, in whose judgment we have great confidence, as one well adapted in all such cases, and one that ought to be universally adopted . . . in every town, village, neighborhood, or city where traitors are found. . . .

If it is once fairly determined that a community has in its midst a full-fledged traitor, an inquiry would very naturally arise—how he ought to be treated . . .?

Would you mob him? No. What would you do with him, then? LET HIM SEVERELY ALONE. By this course you would violate no law, and yet you would inflict upon the culprit a severer punishment than you could by a dozen mobbings of himself or his establishment. LET HIM SEVERELY ALONE—let no man speak to or notice him in any way. Avoid him as you would a walking pestilence. If he approaches you, turn your back upon him and walk away. If it be known that he is to be present at any public place, avoid that place, and advise all others to do so. *Mark* every man that does speak to him, and avoid him in the same way; for a man who will speak to, or notice a traitor in any way (except by exposing his treason in a public manner) is himself liable to suspicion. If he be the publisher of a paper, treat his paper as you do him—LET IT

SEVERELY ALONE. Neither buy it, read it, nor support it in any way. If your name is in it to an advertisement, or in any other way, get it out as speedily as possible, lest you, too, be suspected of sympathising in his traitorous sentiments. If you see that paper in any man's hand, or in any office, store, or work-shop, *mark* the man or place as you would a viper, or a viper's nest. Let it, and all who have anything to do with it, SEVERELY ALONE. If the traitor be a merchant, avoid his store—if a professional man, avoid his office—let each and all SEVERELY ALONE![45]

Copperhead editors such as Edward Fuller of the *Newark Daily Journal*, David Naar of the *Trenton True American*, and Charles Wilson of the *Plainfield Gazette* supported the antiwar faction by words alone, but others went further, reported the *Newark Daily Mercury* on August 14:

There is said to be a considerable nest of secessionists about Peapack, in Somerset county. A gentleman informs us that a secession company has been regularly formed, and that the postmaster of the place has been thrice notified to take down the American flag, the last notice being accompanied by a threat that if the demand was not complied with, he would be made to suffer. At other places in the same county, and also along the border of Union county, there are similar knots of traitors who are equally bold in their avowals.[46]

Other New Jerseyans were active on the South's behalf as well. According to a story in the *New-Brunswick Fredonian* on August 28, a Rahway merchant was one of them:

The examination of Mr. Phineas F. Frazee, of Rahway, charged with treason, was concluded . . . by holding the accused to bail in the sum of $1,000. . . . He is charged with recruiting for the Confederate Army, and furnishing passes to those he could trust, to carry them through the enemy's lines. The chief witness is a young man named Joseph Gabriel, who is now with the Second Regiment of Fire Zouaves in Washington, and who filed an affidavit in the U.S. Marshal's Office in New York last Friday before leaving with his Regiment. The arrest was made by the Deputy Marshal on Saturday afternoon, and created a great excitement in Rahway. He was taken to Newark. . . . Frazee is wealthy and has property in Rahway and at Columbia, S.C., and goes back and forth between the two places, being provided with both kinds of passes.[47]

Schraalenburg, now Dumont, had been the scene of a peace rally in late July. It featured in the news again in early September when Federal marshals disarmed some Confederate sympathizers found there:

Information having been received of the movements of a band of Secessionists at Schraalenburg, Bergen County, including their raising of a rebel flag on the barn of J. J. Zabriskie, Deputy U. S. Marshal French . . . proceeded to Schraalenburg yesterday with eleven men. They found no flag, but ascertained that a military company had organized, and were drilling regularly with U. S. muskets, of which they had forty, furnished by the State; and after receiving satisfactory proof that they had declared their purpose to support the secession leaders whenever an opportunity offered, the muskets were taken from them, and the new oath of allegiance administered to their leader, who took it with evident distaste, but without resistance.[48]

In mid-August the *Newark Daily Advertiser* published a letter that, it said, "had fallen into the hands of a Union man in Somerset county." Reprinted in most of the Unionist newspapers, the letter, supposedly written in New Brunswick by "J," caused a major fright.

Friend E. I received your letter on Tuesday. On Wednesday I went to Morristown—returned yesterday via Somerville. I was sorry you were not at home, as I wanted to see *you particularly.* Everything is encouraging all over the State. If we manage matters right there is nothing to prevent our sending the proper men to Trenton [in the elections] this fall.

"A" has full charge at Peapack and through Bedminster. There are a number of moderate Republicans and Douglas men there whom we can reach by use of the *right means.* He will see that the *right man* takes hold of it.

In regard to Neshanic neighborhood, I don't think "C" can attend to that properly. He will be apt to show his hand too plain; we have two or three devilish shrewd Union men to head off there. Can't you manage to go up soon! There need be but little money spent there, except among the "Yahoos" on the mountain; a barrel or two of whiskey properly distributed will keep them all right until election.

You say Bill Steele's coming back has upset some of your arrangements. You will agree with me now he was not the man for us. I knew last fall, it would not be safe to elect a Douglas man. You will have a chance to pay him yet I hope.

You had better drop that Peace Meeting arrangement. It will do no good, and may do a great deal of harm; let there be no publicity; you can't be too close mouthed. Try and have a *private* meeting soon and put matters in working shape. Some of us will be up next week. I will get a couple of hundred dollars, which I suppose will answer for the *present.* See how much more is necessary—only spend it judiciously. I will go to New York on Monday, and will try and see Dan. He is good in some ways, and will spend plenty of money—but I am afraid he talks too much. We must make the best of it, for we can't get along very well without him—though I hardly think it advisable to let him into *all* of our plans, for the present.[49]

Whether the letter was a clever forgery gotten up by some Union men, or a real communication between Copperhead conspirators, the newspapers that reprinted the correspondence took it seriously enough. The *Morristown Banner,* edited by a pro-Union Democrat, saw it as evidence "of an organized effort to usurp the organization of the Democratic party, and use it to carry out their own selfish plans."

These men want a legislature elected which will resolve that the war has gone far enough—which will refuse to vote any further supply of men or money for carrying it on, and which will declare that a recognition of the Southern Confederacy and a dissolution of the Union are preferable to a further continuance of the war. The next step in the programme is, as soon as things are ready, to place New Jersey under the dictatorship of Jeff. Davis. The people may discover when too late that this is *not fancy but fact.*[50]

Monmouth County was home to a good number of antiwar Democrats who took the Bull Run fiasco as proof that the war could not be won. Middletown Democrats arranged for a rally on August 28, inviting Thomas Dunn English, a rabid Copperhead editor from Fort Lee, as the principal speaker. Getting wind of the meeting, however, local Unionists assembled at the site chosen by the Democrats, holding their own rally. No sooner had the Union meeting gotten underway, reported the *Monmouth Democrat,* than "the Peace men arrived upon the ground in procession with a band of music, horsemen, carriages and the orator, Mr. English." When the Democrats prudently decided to hold their meeting elsewhere, a riot broke out:

Instantly there was a rush up the road to the carriage in which Joseph Hoff and Thomas Dunn English were about to leave the ground. The crowd hemmed horses and vehicle in on every side, and a hundred arms were stretched out to pull them out. In vain the men threatened to shoot, argued, and entreated; the clamor of a thousand tongues drowned their words, and in another minute the attempt to tilt over the carriage and spill them out was unsuccessful, only because of the solid wall of bodies at the other side. When the melee was at its worst, Mr. Benajah Deacon, United States Marshal for New Jersey, elbowed his way up to the carriage, and ordered English to dismount, so that he could save him from lynching. The mob desisting from their purpose of immediate punishment, English was got out, and rushed down the road to the speaker's platform by a tremendous crowd. The mob insisted that he should either speak for the Union, or they would take him in hand, and English, with a face blanched with fright, seemed so bewildered that he did not know what to do. The crush around him became terrible; men pulled and pushed, and shouted, hissed and groaned, and all attempts to move . . . became impossible. Just when it seemed as if English must fall into their hands, Marshal Deacon got the hotel door opened, and his prisoner was jerked inside and rushed up stairs to the garret, while the doors were forced to again and guards stationed at the staircase to prevent the ascent of the crowd.

The Marshal after examining Mr. English and finding there was "really nothing to warrant his arrest for treason" released him, and bade him depart. In attempting to do so he was again rushed upon by the crowd, but escaped.[51]

On August 30 Unionists convened "a large public meeting" in Shrewsbury in an effort to counter widespread "secessionist" talk. The gathering minced no words:

Whereas, Certain citizens of Monmouth county are known to have "Secession sympathies," and openly express them, thereby insulting all honest and patriotic men; we, the citizens of the village of Shrewsbury, do solemnly protest against all such men being allowed to utter any such sentiments, especially in times like these, and pledge ourselves to the utmost of our power to carry out the following resolutions:

Resolved, That a committee of five be appointed to wait on all opponents of our National Government.

Resolved, That no person or persons shall be allowed to dwell in this village, or vicinity expressing Secession sentiments, in whatever *manner or form.*[52]

Concerned about the rising tide of sedition in New Jersey, United States authorities decided to take action. In September a Federal grand jury condemned the *Newark Daily Journal, Plainfield Gazette,* and several other newspapers as treasonable. When a Burlington County politician named James W. Wall wrote a blistering letter to a member of Lincoln's cabinet, Benajah Deacon, the ever-vigilant United States marshal, arrested him on a charge of treason. Wall did not go quietly, reported the *Trenton Gazette:*

Having procured assistance, the Marshal about half-past two o'clock proceeded to Col. Wall's residence, and informed him that he was there for the purpose of arresting him. The Colonel, with a fierce oath, declared that he would not be arrested—that he had business of his own to attend to, and that he would be damned if he would suffer himself to be arrested. The Marshal was prepared for this, and calling in his assistants, directed them to take him. Upon this Wall started up the stairs, but was seized and brought down. He struggled and swore and struck one or two officers, but they did not release their hold. A man who was employed by him . . . came to the Colonel's assistance, but they were soon disposed of, and Mr. Wall, without any hat, his collar open, and cravat untied, was carried to Beldon's Hotel struggling and threatening the direst vengeance against the Marshal, the Secretary of War, and mankind in general. . . . When the 2 o'clock train from Philadelphia reached Burlington, the Colonel was put on board, and took his departure for Fort Lafayette, via Amboy. We understand he threatened to kill the Secretary of War on the first opportunity.[53]

Used as a military prison, New York's Fort Lafayette became home to another fiery Copperhead, Warren Township's Daniel Cory, in mid-September. A few days before his arrest the *Newark Daily Mercury* wrote about this "leader of Somerset rebeldom," saying:

A well-known citizen and politician of Somerset County . . . has for some time distinguished himself by his violent hostilities to the Government, even going to the extent of menacing the loyal men in his neighborhood. Recently this man declared publicly that he had organized a considerable body of men, all of like sentiment with himself, who were prepared to give all aid and comfort to the rebels and added that if circumstances should require, they would at any time unhesitatingly burn down about their ears the houses of all Union men who might oppose their measures. How far these statements of the traitor braggart are to be relied upon, we cannot say with certainty, but knowing something of the character of the neighborhood, we strongly incline to the belief that there is a good foundation for his boast.[54]

Arrested on September 16, Cory was released five weeks later upon taking an oath of allegiance to the United States "that he [would] neither enter nor correspond with the States in insurrection without permission from the Secretary of State, nor do any act hostile to the United States during the present insurrection." According to State Department records, Cory was officially charged "with disloyalty, with denouncing the Government and fomenting disloyalty."

It is shown by affidavits that he denounced President Lincoln as a tory and traitor who ought to be hung; he would like to put a bullet through him and said that the yellow-bellied Yankees who were going to fight the South ought to be shot and have their necks stretched.[55]

Bull Run had sobered the nation to the realities of war. "The fat is in the fire now," wrote Lincoln's private secretary, John Nicolay, "and we shall have to crow small until we can retrieve the disgrace somehow." Three days after the battle another requisition for five new regiments of three-year volunteers reached New Jersey, the state's share of one million men called up by the Federal government. The new units, the Fourth, Fifth, Sixth, Seventh, and Eighth Infantry and two batteries of artillery, were re-cruited during August and September and entrained for Washington by early October. Enlistment was brisk, although less frenetic than the heady days after Sumter fell. The Seventh Regiment's Company K, raised in Mor-ristown, left on October 2 following church services the evening previous.

The interest of this community in the company of Volunteers that has been gathering for a short time past, culminated on Tuesday evening in the First Presbyterian Church of this town, which was filled by the largest audience ever compressed within its walls. . . .

A large number of patriotic and earnest youth had gone from our midst since the commencement of the war and attached themselves to companies formed in our own or adjoining States, yet no complete com-pany organized and filled up by our own loyal citizens had gone to the seat of war. Capt. Brown, a highly respected gentleman of this Town, as-sisted by Henry C. Pitney, Esq., and others, determined to raise a com-pany of one hundred men, to be connected with the 7th Regiment, commanded by our gallant townsman, Colonel Revere. The effort was in a few days crowned with success. . . .

Long before the hour of services, the building was filled. . . . There were mothers with streaming eyes and swelling hearts, gazing, it might be for the last time, upon their noble boys; there were fathers with moistened cheeks, looking with manly pride upon the enthusiasm and patriotic bearing of the sons; wives, deeply moved, were present, commending their husbands to the preserving care and benignant smiles of a gracious Providence. Children looked upon the scene with variable feelings, knowing that on the morrow their fathers were to leave them; while not a few with peculiar emotions and the purist and strongest affections were scattered through the audience unable to restrain their feelings, check their thoughts or still their fears; and the hearts of all beat in harmony with the occasion, throbbing with mighty resolve and strong devotion to their country's flag, honor, and perpetuity.

The Company, as they marched in and took the assigned seats, were seen to be composed of material like the others that have gone to the war from the numerous towns and villages of the North. It had in it the hardy mechanic, the sturdy farmer, the young merchant, with not a few reared for other employment, drawn mainly from Morristown, Mendham, Boonton, and Madison. There was one without his coat, who hearing of the Company's departure, and fearing that he might be too late, left the place of his labor, and without bidding adieu to friends, started for the meeting. There is another who has near relatives in the South, sympathizing deeply with the rebels; a third has a brother in the Confederate army; a fourth was an only child; upon a fifth entered the hopes of a widowed mother; and each had a history peculiar to himself, and ties as strong to bind him to home and loved ones as the many who were present to bid him farewell. But love of country drowned every other consideration, and impelled them to rise above every obstacle that stood in their way, and go forth with the swelling hosts to maintain the honor of their country's flag, or die in its defense.

The services were opened with an appropriate prayer by Rev. Mr. Samuel L. Tuttle of Madison. . . . A beautiful sword, sash, belt, and pistol were presented to Captain Brown by Alfred Mills, Esq. in a neat and suitable address. . . . The Captain replied in a few pertinent and emphatic words, thanking the donors for their appreciative kindness, and in the name of his Company, thanking the gentlemen who had generously provided each member with an India rubber blanket. . . . The whole service was concluded by the choir and congregation singing the Army Hymn—"O Lord of Hosts, Almighty King, Behold the sacrifice we bring"—and then by the Benediction. . . .

Though a request was made by the pastor of the church that the audience would remember the solemnity of the occasion and the character of the house of worship, the pent feelings could not be repressed, but broke over all restraints. Never was the heart of the community more deeply stirred, and never was there a more united assembly for the furtherance of an object at any and all hazards. The enthusiasm thus aroused was in no way stilled by the slumbers of the night. Early next morning the town was alive, and as the volunteers marched to the cars, they were not only joined by new recruits, but were followed by hundreds to shake them by the hands, to speak a word of comfort, to bid the tearful farewell, and to give the parting benediction and the parting cheer.[56]

By the time New Jersey's newest regiments reached Washington, the Federal army in Virginia had a fresh commander, thirty-four-year-old George B. McClellan, and a new name, the Army of the Potomac. "Little Mac," as his soldiers called him, was a superb administrator and organizer who, in a few short months of intense effort, forged the raw, dispirited troops around Washington into an army the likes of which the world had never seen. Camps were organized in proper military fashion, food, munitions, and equipment distributed, the men drilled continuously, and incompetent officers weeded out. The soldiers admired him, Lincoln and his Cabinet deferred to him, the press lionized him. McClellan, exhibiting the vainglory that was to bring him to grief within a year, wrote to his wife, Ellen, in August: "The people call upon me to save the country—I must save it."

McClellan clearly knew how to organize an army, no one doubted that, but as autumn came and went with no action against the Confederates encamped within sight of Washington, some began to suspect his willingness to engage the enemy. The daily telegraphic bulletin, "All quiet along the Potomac," had reassured Northerners after the panic at Bull Run. Now it was a phrase of derision.

New Jersey's troops spent the remainder of 1861 in camps strung along the Potomac River, preparing for the active campaigning that never came. "All the boys are well and in good spirits," wrote Sergeant Louis Putoz of the Seventh Regiment. "As for food I am very happy to inform you that it is a great deal better than we used to get in the three month's service."[57] Captain James McKiernan of Company G, Seventh Regiment, writing in October, was equally upbeat:

We are encamped at a place called Camp Casey about three miles distant from the Washington depot. It is almost an impossibility to tell how long we shall remain here. Soldier life is not as hard as it has been represented. We get fresh meat four times a week, fresh bread every day, corned beef twice a week, and pork the remainder of the week. For a change, we have boiled rice sweetened with sugar, coffee three times a day, beans three or four times a week, and farina three times a week. You can see for yourself that there is no starvation in a soldier's life. The quality is of the first class. Every day that rolls around I like the soldier's life better. The boys are all contented, and appear to be satisfied with their lot. I think in the course of time the citizens of Paterson will have occasion to be proud of the Washington Rifles.[58]

At home in New Jersey, meanwhile, a massive effort was underway to support the troops in the field. Within days of Fort Sumter the first soldiers' relief association was formed in Newark, quickly followed by similar organizations in every part of the state, many of them led by women. Like their sisters throughout the North, the women of New Jersey played a critical role in the war, collecting clothing, bandages, medicine, and bedding for soldiers in the camps and hospitals near Washington.

Not all of New Jersey's contributions to the war effort were as practical as the supplies so eagerly forwarded by the relief associations. In late August the newspapers reported a novel idea:

The Messrs. Edge, the celebrated Pyrotechnists of Jersey City, are about to organize a Rocket Brigade to enlist in the service of the United States. For several years past the British, and other European governments have kept several standing regiments of this kind and they are said to be a most superior branch of the service. During the Crimean war several of the English Brigades armed with these terrible rockets, rendered efficient service in repelling cavalry. It is alleged that where an enemy is in ambush, or behind batteries, and surrounded by dense woods, as is the case with the rebels at Bull Run, these rockets will prove very destructive. They can be thrown with the greatest precision, and being of a combustible nature will set the woods on fire, before which the enemy cannot withstand, and affording a grand opportunity for our own cavalry and infantry to be brought into operation. Assurances have been received which lead the Messrs. Edge to believe that such a brigade will be accepted by the Government, and measures will be adopted at once to get the same into operation.[59]

Jersey City gained a different sort of notoriety in early October when a riot broke out between members of the Barney Rifles, quartered at the United States Arsenal, and some five hundred angry civilians.

At about nine o'clock in the evening one of the soldiers, either by accident or design, ran against a woman. This led to a fight between the soldier and a citizen who saw the occurrence, and the soldier was badly injured.

The soldier then went to the camp, giving information of his having been beaten, and a number of his comrades went to the Newkirk House near where the affray happened. Mr. Henry Newkirk was mistaken for the man that had beaten the soldier, and after an altercation an attack was made upon the house with stones and other missiles. The windows and blinds were demolished, and the inmates of the house narrowly escaped from serious injury. . . . The fire bell was sounded in a short time after the attack on the house, and between four and five hundred men assembled at the five corners.

At this time Col. Kozlay sent out a squad of men with muskets to bring in all the soldiers that were about the city. As the squad of men came near the Newkirk House they were attacked by the citizens, and some of the men were badly injured. Mayor Carpenter was present, and in trying to quell the disturbance was stabbed five or six times about the head and body, and is very seriously if not fatally injured. Coroner Donnelly interfered and saved the life of one of the soldiers who was armed with a hatchet. There were serious apprehensions of a riot yesterday, and it was said that in case of further difficulty, the fire-bells of Hudson City, Jersey City and Hoboken would be sounded, and that as many as 3,000 men could be brought together for an attack on the camp.

It was deemed advisable by the authorities to call out the Militia. . . . It was not anticipated that any trouble would occur last night, unless the soldiers should become unmanageable and make another attack upon the citizens. A number of special policemen were sworn in yesterday.

The citizens will insist upon having about forty of the soldiers delivered up to the authorities for trial, and in case of refusal, an attack will probably be made upon the camp tonight. The regiment were supplied with rifles this afternoon. During the stay of the regiment, Col. Kozlay will be strict with the men, and will grant but very few passes. Some of the soldiers, it is alleged, while out about the city, have insulted women to such an extent as to cause a bitter feeling against them. A large number of people visited the camp yesterday, and a great excitement prevailed both there and in the city.[60]

The sounds of battle were louder in Jersey City than along the Potomac. "All remains quiet at and around Washington," reported the *Paterson Daily Guardian* on October 8. "Balloon reconnoissances show that the

51

main body of the rebels is at Fairfax Courthouse. There are no signs of offensive movements, and it is thought that none are immediately contemplated by either side." For the men in camp, army life was becoming a dreary routine.

As the year wore down, Colonel George W. Taylor, commanding the Third Regiment, made plans "to rebuke the marauding parties of the rebel cavalry" that had been testing Federal lines near Fairfax Seminary, where the First Jersey Brigade was camped. In mid-December, Taylor led fifty picked men and a scout by the name of Newbury into enemy country.

Newbury had been anxious for a long time to try a plan of his, by which the rebel cavalry might be nonplussed, by means of a wire barricade. It was at his instance that at nightfall strong wires were stretched across a road frequented by the hostile troopers. This done, the force was divided, a part secreting themselves, so as to be in the rear of the enemy when they should reach the obstruction, and the other part lying near the barricade. About midnight, as was expected, the enemy came. The Orderly Sergeant in command first felt the check upon his horse and exclaimed, "Hallo here, there is something wrong." Others now were stopped, and confusion was soon apparent among them. They were about 40 in number. At this moment Lieut. Knight of the "Third" ordered his men to "fire," when a fearful volley of musketry was poured into the foe. The scene beggars description. . . . Shrieks, groans, imprecations and contrary orders were mingled with the few shots which the rebels fired. Eight men were seen to fall from their horses at the fire of our men. The orderly was shot in the forehead by a glancing shot, and yet showed fight, when a blow from a musket laid him senseless. Most of the troop galloped away.[61]

By December the well-drilled Army of the Potomac was in winter camp, leaving undisturbed the Rebel forces assembled across the river. "Visitors in crowds circulate through our camps," wrote one soldier.

A minister from New Jersey says he has been intensely interested, and would not have lost the chance of seeing the army for any considerations. Several ladies from Camden, after staying here several days, are ready to wish they could remain among our brave troops and minister to their wants, and feel that the sacrifice would be comparatively trifling. All are surprised at the comfort, contentment, good health and efficiency of our soldiers.[62]

No matter how contented the soldiers were, the people of the North were not. Morale was at its lowest ebb since Bull Run, and no one, not McClellan, not Lincoln, not Congress, knew what to do. "The Union is broken forever," wrote the London *Times* correspondent, "and the independence of the South virtually established." "There is no prospect of an immediate advance of the Army of the Potomac," said the *Paterson Daily Guardian*. "Reports . . . received at a late hour to-night, represent everything as quiet. The rebels won't, and we won't."[63]

TWO

"Rally, Boys! Rally!"

1862

Nothing seemed to go right for the Union during the winter of 1861–1862. Immense armies lay idle in the field, General-in-Chief McClellan had fallen sick, the war was costing $1.5 million a day, and yet no one, not the military brass or the politicians or the president himself, seemed to have a plan for ending the conflict. On January 10 a despondent Lincoln visited his quartermaster general, Montgomery Meigs. "General," he said, "what shall I do? The people are impatient; [Treasury Secretary] Chase has no money and he tells me he can raise no more; the General of the Army has typhoid fever. The bottom is out of the tub. What shall I do?" New Jersey's Unionists were equally gloomy. Lieutenant Colonel Robert McAllister of the First New Jersey , then camped near Alexandria, Virginia, wrote to his wife on Christmas Eve, 1861, complaining bitterly of people "at home sympathizing with Rebellion." Those who failed to support "our bleeding country" should be shipped to South America, added McAllister sarcastically, "where they will have a government that suits them."[1]

Toward the end of January military affairs took a decided and unexpected turn for the better. In the west Union troops under General Ulysses S. Grant advanced into northern Tennessee, capturing Forts Henry and Donelson and bagging 12,000 Rebel soldiers in the bargain. When the Confederate commander proposed an armistice, Grant demanded "unconditional and immediate surrender," brave words no Union general had ever before uttered. News of Grant's victory, and the capture on February 25 of Nashville, the first Confederate state capital to fall to Union arms, set Northern church bells ringing in celebration of victory. Grant was an instant hero, promoted to major general by a grateful president whose faith in his generals had been sorely tested ever since the opening battles of the war.

More good news came from North Carolina, where General Ambrose Burnside led a combined force of 100 ships and some 15,000 soldiers in an amphibious assault on the Outer Banks, easily capturing Roanoke Island,

Elizabeth City, and New Bern. The Union now controlled nearly all of North Carolina's coastline, making the task of the blockading fleet much easier. The Ninth New Jersey Infantry, recruited in the fall of 1861 from all parts of the state, was the only New Jersey unit assigned to Burnside's expedition. Composed almost entirely of experienced sharpshooters, including a company of German target shooters from Newark, the Ninth arrived at the Hatteras inlet on January 14 after a harrowing ten-day voyage through heavy seas and dense fog. Soon after their arrival at the inlet, wrote a soldier with the Ninth, a violent storm overtook the fleet, threatening the lives of the seasick volunteers.

Extra anchors were cast, but even this precaution did not avail to save several vessels of the fleet, which were drifted shore and became total wrecks. . . . The steamer "Pocahontas," laden with horses, on the passage down was driven ashore in the gale, its engines having become unmanageable, and but for the gallantry of Corp. Samuel J. Dilkes, of Company K, Ninth Regiment, the lives of all on board might have been lost. Dilkes bravely swimming ashore with a rope, fastened it securely by means of a stake driven firmly in the sand, and so enabled the crew to reach land in safety. The cook, an aged colored woman, being unable in this way to escape, Dilkes, with a heroism which filled all beholders with admiration, returned to the ship, now rapidly going to pieces, and binding the frightened woman to his person leaped into the sea, and by almost superhuman exertions succeeded in safely reaching the shore. . . .

On the following day, with the seas somewhat calmer, the regiment's colonel, lieutenant colonel, surgeon, adjutant, and quartermaster took the captain's gig to shore to report to General Burnside. On the return voyage tragedy overtook them:

Having concluded their interview with the general-in-chief, the party returned to their boat, which was rowed swiftly and safely towards the ship until the breakers just outside the inlet were reached, when suddenly a heavy sea, or water-spout, burst over the bow, sweeping to the stern, unshipping the oars. . . . Before the boat could be righted a second and stronger wave struck it from beneath, hurling it some distance in the air and precipitating all its occupants into the sea. The situation was fearful indeed, and the struggle with the seething waters desperate in the last degree. With great difficulty the boat was reached by several of the party and efforts made to right it; but this was soon found to be impossible. . . . Lt. Col Heckman and Adjt. Zabriskie, being expert swimmers, finding that Col. Allen and Surgeon Weller were in greater danger than the others, made several heroic attempts to save their lives, but all were unsuccessful, these officers, bravely struggling to the last, going down into the watery depths. By this time the capsized boat was drifting rapidly seaward; but the Lt. Col. and Adjt. finally succeeded in raising an oar, having fastened thereon a sailor's shirt, which signal being shortly afterwards discovered the alarm was given, and the steamer "Patuxent" at once hastened to give assistance. So overcome were the survivors by their exertions that upon reaching the decks of the steamer some of them sank into insensibility.[2]

After a bombardment by Federal warships silenced Confederate shore batteries, Burnside's troops boarded surf boats and came ashore on Roanoke Island on February 7. The First Brigade was the first to land, followed quickly by the Second Brigade, which included the Ninth New Jersey. "Company K was the first on shore," wrote Sergeant J. Madison Drake of Trenton:

We expected the enemy would repel and attempt to drive us back into the sea, but they did not come very near us, as our gunboats covered our landing. The rebel regiment was in line of battle, about half a mile from where we landed, (which was in a swamp) but the shells from our boats soon scattered them like chaff before the wind. They immediately fled, but not 'till they had wounded two of our soldiers. We waded through a swamp up to our knees in mud for about a mile, and then laid down on the wet sand and awaited the dawn of another day, which was the brightest and most glorious of the war. . . .

At daybreak on Saturday our pickets were fired on and driven in. In a few minutes three or four regiments of the 1st Brigade, with five small howitzers, made an advance. The enemy gave way before this force, and fell back through dense thickets into a battery, which contained three rifled cannons, and three thousand rebels. The 1st Brigade attacked the rebels in their stronghold with the greatest vigor, but the former had every advantage, superior numbers, and a splendidly constructed battery, while our men had to stand in the swamp which fronted their battery, up to our waists in mud and water. The engagement soon became general, and in a few minutes our brigade, which the gallant Ninth New Jersey headed, were in the midst of the conflict. Our regiment was in the midst of a galling fire over three hours, and we were within two hundred yards of the battery, Great Heavens! How they showered shell and grape at us; but thanks be to Providence (and their poor gunners) their missiles were thrown too high. . . .

We were compelled to hold our cartridge boxes up to our breasts, in order to keep them dry. . . . About noon our artillery got into position, and did its duty—then the Ninth N. J. stood up a little nearer. For over half an hour, at this period, our men poured a tremendous fire of leaden ball into their infantry, which turned the tide of the conflict. One of our Jersey Lieutenants from a tree saw that the enemy had broken and were fleeing; he sounded the joyful tidings, and in a moment more our company (who were in the advance) endeavored to make a charge on the villains from the swamp, where we had been fighting three hours.

At this moment our regiment was brought to a stand-still. We were being fired on from the rear! and that too, we soon discovered, by some of our own troops—Hawkins' Zouaves —who had but just arrived on the ground. We could not stand up under two such fires, so we "squatted a little," but the Zouaves who mistook us for rebels (whom they could not see at all) fired three rounds into our ranks. Of course this staggered us, but we endeavored again to cross the pond in order to flank the enemy, who had left their battery. In this we did not succeed, as a regiment, until the most of the Zouaves had crossed over the bridge and entered the vacant fort. A large number of us, however, succeeded in crossing the pond, and entering the fortifications with the Zouaves, who at once unfurled their flag to the breeze. Here we found the dead bodies of the rebels lying promiscuously around, while the wounded were groaning piteously. . . .

On getting into the bloody battery, we formed again and marched on after the fugitives. . . . We had a nice little "double quick" for two or three miles, when our regiment and a Massachusetts regiment marched into their hospital, on which we found flying a white flag. We left a guard here, and pressed forward through swamps and thickets, over hill and dale, 'till we ascended a mountain, where two companies of rebels were stationed. They endeavored to check us, but we killed six or seven of them, and put the rest to flight.

We marched on, and finally after a pretty long chase, we overhauled about a thousand of the rebels a short distance from their principal battery along the Sound. They had hoisted a white flag, so all we had to do was take charge of them and their arms.[3]

The Ninth New Jersey lost nine men killed and twenty-five wounded in the attack on Roanoke Island. Among the wounded was Corporal John Lorence of Company K. "Few cases of greater individual courage are recorded than that of Corporal Lorence, of Carpenter's Landing," wrote Company K's Lieutenant Jonathan Townley, Jr., who was himself wounded in the battle:

In the early part of the action at Roanoke, both of his legs were shot off just below the knees. As he was carried to the rear, his shattered limbs dangling in the bushes, he repeatedly said to the men passing on to the conflict, with all the energy he could command, "Go in, boys, go in; give it to them; I can't do any more." He was taken to the Surgeon's tent in the background, where his limbs were amputated and dressed. At length, the shout of victory rang through the forest. The Corporal inquired, "Who has won?" and upon being told that the rebels were running, raised himself on his stumps, swung his cap over his head, and, with an enthusiasm that thrilled every beholder, gave three cheers for the Union and the New Jersey Ninth! General Burnside being informed of the Corporal's brave conduct, visited him several times in the hospital, as did many other officers. Once when I was with him, as he lay suffering, he said that if his limbs would only heal, he would procure "a pair of wooden legs and fight on them." Of this I told General Burnside, who came in just at that moment, and who replied, "Corporal Lorence has done enough for his country; it is time now for the country to do something for him."[4]

Lorence recovered and was discharged from the army later that fall.

In mid-March Burnside's amphibious force landed on the North Carolina mainland at the Neuse River, routed the dispirited defenders, and captured New Bern. After an eight-mile march in "hot and sultry" weather, the Ninth New Jersey reached its first objective, an enemy battery near the Goldsborough and Morehead Railroad. "Here we halted and rested for a few minutes," wrote the ever-enthusiastic Sergeant Drake, who would later win the Medal of Honor for gallantry and bravery, "to give the stragglers a chance of joining their regiments":

After recovering our breath, we started again, the 1st Brigade advancing along on the turnpike road, while our Brigade . . . took the railroad. What a splendid time of it we had hobbling along the track on the ties. This was most tiresome. Nothing possibly could have fatigued us more, but we were eager to meet the traitorous horde so it was considered fine sport. A short time after dusk we filed off the railroad track, and after making night fires, we laid down on the wet grass. . . .

At seven o'clock on Friday morning we rolled up our wet blankets, and commenced the march again. . . . We had not gone over half a mile, perhaps, ere the sound of cannon and muskets was heard by us. . . . At half-past seven o'clock, our gallant regiment . . . filed off the track on the left and engaged three batteries on the extreme right of the enemy's fortifications. As we advanced through the woods and swamp, the enemy poured upon us grape, canister and shell, but with little effect. Nothing daunted, we continued to press on through mud and water, sometimes climbing over fallen pines, sometimes jumping over ditches; bullets fell around us on every hand as thick as hail, and yet we pressed forward eager to get in closer proximity to the cowardly thieves. When within two hundred yards of the batteries and rifle-pits we halted, and forming into regular line of battle, we deliberately poured into the rebels a well directed volley of our bullets, which for the time being silenced their artillery. We could now distinctly observe the rascals behind their breastworks, and we did not allow them to fire their cannon but twice afterwards. We stood on a commanding elevation, and for three hours and a half, continued to pick the rebels off, as they would show themselves. . . . [W]e stood our ground and picked them off one by one, until they slackened their fire at half past eleven o'clock, when we rushed out of the woods, through a heavy swamp up to our waists in water, and drove them out of the three batteries at the point of the bayonet. Our colors were planted first on all of the batteries, and seeing this, the rebels on the right flank threw their rifles away and precipitately fled. As the rebels rushed from behind their entrenchments, we poured into them a heavy fire, which cut down hundreds of their number.[5]

Union successes in Kentucky and Tennessee as well as North Carolina increased the pressure on McClellan to move his forces against the Confederates, arrayed only two days' march from Washington. By February 1862, McClellan had headed the Army of the Potomac for seven months. Money, men, and equipment were his in prodigious quantities, his army was acknowledged to be the largest and finest in modern history, but still the 100,000 bluebacks under his command kept to the tents.

Lincoln's impatience with Little Mac, as the soldiers fondly called him, prompted an extraordinary presidential order directing all Federal land and sea forces to move against the Confederates on Washington's Birthday. Although McClellan blithely ignored the order, the president resisted mounting pressure to replace him. Though impatient and dissatisfied with McClellan's sluggishness, Lincoln was not yet ready to make a change in command.

McClellan made his long-postponed move at the end of March, sending 55,000 men south to Fortress Monroe at the tip of the peninsula separating

Virginia's James and York Rivers. McClellan's plan was to move up the Peninsula against Richmond, some seventy miles northwest of his landing. Among the troops were the Fifth, Sixth, Seventh, and Eighth New Jersey Regiments, constituting the Second New Jersey Brigade, joined several weeks later by the First, Second, Third, and Fourth New Jersey Regiments, which made up the First New Jersey Brigade.

Little Mac's Peninsula campaign got off to an inauspicious start when 13,000 Rebel troops, dug in near the old Revolutionary War battlefield of Yorktown, held up the Union advance for nearly a month. After the Confederates evacuated their trenches at the beginning of May, a strong rear guard action near Williamsburg on May 5 held back the advancing Federal forces long enough for the Confederate army to retreat with its artillery and wagons intact. George A. Berdan, a private in the Seventh Regiment, survived the battle:

Since writing my last letter, we have had a great march and a bloody battle. . . . Leaving Yorktown far to our rear, we were kept marching until midnight. . . . We marched a distance of 14 miles in one afternoon and the sun's scorching heat poured down on us all the time. . . .

From the time we entered the outside forts at Yorktown, we were made aware of the dangerous grounds that we trod upon, by the death of about fifty men who were killed by the bursting of torpedoes, which the cursed rebels had placed all along the road. The torpedoes resembled cannon shells, and those placed in the ground were merely covered over with earth to screen them from sight. To them was attached a thin wire about two feet long. In walking along, our feet would get entangled in the wire, when off it would go. . . .

It was midnight when we laid down to rest. We had hardly gotten under our blankets when the rain poured down in torrents, wetting us completely through the skin—then it was impossible for us to sleep; so we had to grin and bear it until daylight, when we resumed our march. . . . The red mud was almost knee deep. . . . We proceeded along for two miles when we entered a heavy woods. Our Company and Company A were ordered out as skirmishers. . . . In groups of four we crawled along on our hands and knees through fallen trees for . . . 300 yards. Then we saw a body of men coming towards us. Immediately, three or four of our boys fired at them, when they took to their heels. Then the balance of our regiment came up to us, and we all formed in line of battle. In a few moments, another large body of men came toward us, carrying a white flag. They got within twenty yards of us, when one of them said "God damn you! Will you shoot your own men?" At that time we received orders from some of our head officers not to fire, as they thought they were our men. When the enemy said "don't shoot your own men" we saw them instantly move their hands to the triggers of their guns, when in a moment we dropped down behind trees and fired a volley at them. They retreated. We kept firing at them . . . for about half an hour. Our firing then ceased for nearly 20 minutes when the enemy advanced again. We again repulsed them. . . . Our brigade kept their position in the hottest part of the fight without being relieved for six hours. All this time we were laying on our bellies, fighting like good fellows. After we had fired about 20 rounds, our guns were so dirty that we had to punch the ball in by striking our rammers against the trees. All this time the rebel [bullets] were whistling and falling around us like hail. . . . We would each be screened by a stump or a tree, and woe be it to any man who exposed any part of his person, as he would be fired at by the enemy, who, like us, were always on their guard. Every once in a while I would raise my cap a little ways above the tree that concealed me, when bang would go a gun and I would let my cap fall; then instantly I would peep over and wait for a rebel to raise his head. . . . When I thought he was high enough, bang would go my gun, and down he would go. This is the way we fought for four hours when the rebels advanced too heavy upon us and we had to retreat. Our bands then commenced to play the National airs, when we formed a line and with terrific yells charged on them, when we made them retreat back again over the fallen trees, that seemed almost impossible for any human being to surmount. . . .

While fighting in the woods . . . shells were bursting all around us. . . . Our brigade is all cut to pieces, some companies only have twenty men left. . . . The enemy tried to deceive us in every way. They had flags with our colors on one side and three bars on the other. They also had . . . a black flag showing that we must not expect any mercy. We did not expect to be shown any, although we have shown mercy to their wounded. It was an awful sight to pass over the battlefield and see the wounded and dead lying around, both rebels and our own, also horses and broken cannons. . . .

In their retreat, the rebels crushed our wounded soldiers in the head, knocking their brains in, also running their bayonets through them. . . . We are now in possession of Yorktown and Williamsburg, Va. and today the Jersey boys have got a name that will not disgrace them as we have achieved a victory at such great odds. . . . After we were done fighting, our commanders took off their hats and gave three cheers for the Jersey boys. They said we were an honor to our state and that there was not another brigade in the army who would have held the position we held against such odds without relief for six hours.[6]

A week after the battle a letter from the Seventh New Jersey arrived in Paterson. Enclosed was a twenty-dollar Treasury note and two one-dollar bills, stained with blood:

Dear Sir: It is with feelings of the deepest sorrow and regret, that I have to inform you of the death of Daniel H. Ostrander. He was killed in engagement at Williamsburg, May 5, 1862. He was shot in the abdomen and was dead when his body was recovered. He was buried in a separate grave with that of his comrade James Watson, on the battlefield in as decent a manner as possible. A board with his name and stating where he came from and date of his death was placed at his head. In his pockets were found twenty two dollars which you will please forward to his mother and also the news of his death, as we do not know her address.[7]

The battle at Williamsburg slowed McClellan's advance but did not halt it. The Confederates now drew their forces around Richmond as the Federal army marched slowly up the Peninsula over roads made wretched by the continual rain. By the end of May the spires of the Rebel capital were in sight, but after a series of bloody June battles north and south of the muddy Chickahominy River, the Army of the Potomac retreated southward toward Harrison's Landing on the James River. The seven days of battle at Fair Oaks, Gaines' Mill, Savage's Station, and Malvern Hill cost both sides heavily in dead, wounded, and missing—30,000 on both sides by conservative count. Now led by General Robert E. Lee, Confederate forces were unable to best McClellan's superior numbers, winning only one of the battles, Gaines' Mill, but in a series of maneuvers Lee effectively lifted the siege of Richmond. After six weeks at Harrison's Landing, McClellan, defeated by his own timidity, withdrew from the Peninsula.

The battle at Gaines' Mill pitted 55,000 Rebels against the Federal V Corps's 35,000, commanded by General Fitz-John Porter. Fighting began around 2 p.m. on June 27, see-sawed through the hot afternoon, and reached its climax at 7 p.m. after Lee was finally able to get his divisions to act in concert. Launching an all-out attack that pierced the Union lines, Lee forced the bluecoats to retire across the Chickahominy during the night. The First New Jersey Brigade was ordered across the river early on June 27 to reinforce Porter's corps, fought stubbornly throughout the day, and when it retreated left behind nearly half its force killed, wounded, captured, or missing in action. "I will try and inform you that I am well and alive," wrote Abram H. Paxton, First Sergeant of Company I, Second Regiment, a few days after the fight. "I hardly know how to commence to inform you of what I have seen and experienced this last week."

Friday a week ago, June 27th we got orders to go and assist Gen. Porter across the Chickahominy. Well we had to go over three miles to get there, and I tell you when we did get there it was a beautiful sight to see all the troops in position to receive the rebels, and I tell you we had no more than seen the beautiful sight than the battle commenced. At first we were placed in reserve for our artillery, but some General . . . ordered us to the front in the edge of the woods, there was bales of hay for breastworks. . . . Well we had not fought over half an hour before the rebels had flanked us right and left and they was coming up on the left of our company front, marching by the flank as close as I ever saw troops.

All that had been shot in our company was two, as far as I can learn, that was our Captain and a young man by the name of Zabriskie. Our Company stood firm then yet. After I saw the rebels coming up in front with such strong force I looked back and I saw our troops running all over and the rebels coming in the rear of us. I started and I tell you the balls whistled around me like hail stones. How I escaped I cannot tell. Then it was when we lost so many of our Company. There is twenty-three killed, missing and wounded in that engagement. . . .

It was an awful sight to see the dead and wounded left behind and to see them all run for life. What made it worse for us we had no reserve to fall back on, they skedaddled before we got to them. I tell you it was a regular stampede.[8]

Colonel Isaac M. Tucker was one of the Second Regiment's first casualties. Early on, wrote Chaplain Robert Proudfit of New Brunswick, the men "were posted partly behind a low fence and partly behind some bales of hay," maintaining their ground in the face of superior numbers.

At last, however, one of our men, Sergeant Pierson of Co. H, perceiving that the federal regiment on our left had fallen back, called the attention of the Col. to this fact. The Colonel could not believe it at first, but at length, seeing the white coats of the rebels then gaining our flank, he ordered the colors to be moved to the rear, and the men to fall back and rally. While our regiment was executing this maneuvre, the flanking rebel regiment poured in a deadly cross-fire. Just after waving his sword and calling on his men to stand by their flag, Col. Tucker fell, pierced by a bullet in the side.

Several immediately sprang to his assistance and began to bear him from the field. The barbarous enemy, not regarding the suffering and disabled condition of the wounded man, or the errand of mercy in which his carriers were engaged, made the little party a target for their special fire. Lieut. J. H. Root of Newark was thus soon wounded in three places. A moment after, the Colonel, wounded by another ball, exclaimed, "The cowardly fellows, they fire on wounded men." Then, feeling that his wounds were mortal, he told his bearers to lay him down and save themselves. They bore him a little farther, and then placed him under some bushes, remaining with him till his death. He soon expired, but in that brief period the enemy were almost upon the party. Three of them took refuge in the bushes and were probably captured. The fourth, Sergeant Pierson, running the gauntlet of the heavy fire from one of our own batteries, as well as that of the rebels, narrowly, and providentially, escaped unharmed. Private Berdan of Co. I had a like narrow escape. Much exhausted with his efforts in assisting our severely wounded Major, he was unable to run. Scarcely hoping to escape, he walked slowly forward amid a storm of shells, aimed apparently at him. Yet he passed on and escaped untouched.[9]

During the next several days the First Brigade, exhausted and diminished, was lucky enough to be spared the worst of the fighting at White Oak Swamp and Malvern Hill. "Well, I got across the Chickahominy again safe," continued Paxton, "and I never was so tired in my life before."

I stopped a while and then I got with two or three of our boys and we went back to camp. So in the morning the boys kept coming in and then we got orders to pack up everything and get ready to move. . . . Well it turned out to be true. . . . They woke us up, and we started; how far we marched I hardly can tell, but we marched till Sunday afternoon. . . . Monday our rear guard came up to us, and we were all put in position to receive the rebels again. Dan, it is awful to hear the cannonading on both sides all day but our side throwed two shells to their one. About five o'clock all firing ceased on both sides for about half an hour, and then the infantry advanced on the rebels' side. . . .

When all the firing ceases on both sides, it seems to me it was so still that I could hear a pin drop, and then all at once the cheering commenced I did not know what to make of it, and then the rebels cheered. Their cheer I don't like to hear, it sounds deceitful to me. As soon as they cheered they commenced battle. It raged till it got so dark that we could not see each other. It seemed as if the rebels were determined to break through our lines; they fight desperately. They say all their canteens that they find are filled with whiskey and it is mixed with gun powder and salt petre. It makes a man perfectly wild.[10]

McClellan's heavy losses during the seven days' hard fighting that ended on July 1 stunned the people of the North. Hearing the news, Lincoln admitted he was "as nearly inconsolable as I could be and live." The New York stock market fell, the value of the Union greenback collapsed, and people everywhere, North as well as South, began to think the unthinkable—that Southern independence might become a reality.

Lincoln did not falter. "I expect to maintain this contest," he informed state governors, "until successful, or till I die, or am conquered . . . or Congress or the country forsakes me." On the very day the appalling casualty lists were beginning to appear in the North's newspapers, the president issued a call for 300,000 volunteers to serve for three years "so as to bring this unnecessary and injurious civil war to a speedy and satisfactory conclusion." In August, another 300,000 men were levied for nine months' service and, as if to make certain there was no misunderstanding the seriousness of the matter, Lincoln authorized the secretary of war to issue the North's first call for a draft, 300,000 militiamen to serve for nine months if the earlier quotas could not be filled. For the first time, bounty money, Federal as well as local, was dangled in front of prospective recruits.

Despite the horrendous bloodletting of the Peninsula campaign, the men of New Jersey stepped forward in answer to Lincoln's call. Gone were the stirring days of 1861 when almost every able-bodied man, or so it seemed, wanted to enlist; yet volunteer they did, until by the fall the state had sixteen new regiments in the field, the Eleventh through Fifteenth for three years, the Twenty-first through Thirty-first for nine months. Ira S. Dodd of Orange, who joined the Twenty-sixth, remembered the "imperious spirit of the hour" and the "shame" of holding back when others in the neighborhood were coming forward.[11] "Why I and the other fellows, came to enlist, is something I never could explain," wrote Paterson's Joseph E. Crowell, who signed up with the Thirteenth.

I think I am safe in saying that, at the moment, genuine patriotism hardly entered into the question. Of course there were some who enlisted from patriotic motives; but . . . I believe a majority of the boys were induced to go for other motives. Most probably it was the general excitement of the times. It was simply a furore to go to war. To many it was a change from the ordinary humdrum of life. To others it was looked upon as a picnic. And then in every boy's heart there is an inherent spirit of adventure.[12]

The Reverend James F. Brewster, pastor of Chester's First Presbyterian Church, left little doubt what the young men of his congregation must do:

To every unprejudiced mind the path of duty is clear. We must stand by our government and defend its honor. We must put down insurrection . . . even though it cost millions of treasure and long years of struggle; though it take the last dollar from our pockets and the last man from our soil. But we want the spirit of earnest, determined, conscientious men— the spirit that enters upon stern deeds only from a sense of duty, and is therefore all the more determined and brave—the spirit of unselfish devotion which Heaven will bless and on which God will smile. An army of Christian soldiers is invincible.[13]

War meetings were held in nearly every city, town, village, and hamlet in the state to encourage enlistment lest the dreaded draft take place. Committees were appointed to canvas each neighborhood. "The National life is in danger," read the notice of Warren County's war meeting. "The army of the Potomac reduced by disease and battle, standing in front of and keeping at bay overwhelming numbers of the enemy, cannot advance the National Flag, without large reinforcements. Patriotism, humanity, and true economy alike demand that these reinforcements should be speedily mustered into service."[14]

As preachers thundered from the pulpit and orators stirred the crowds, so too did the state's Unionist newspapers beat the drums of recruitment. Not surprisingly, the prospect of a draft hung like the sword of Damocles over the state. No time must be lost, said Newark's *Sentinel of Freedom*:

Both sides—patriot and rebel—are now engaged in a race. Each are striving to outdo the other in massing the greatest number of troops, preparatory to a life or death struggle. There must therefore be redoubled exertions; and if any slackness is shown by the people, the Government owes it to the country to stop at no effort which will assure, without loss of time, all the reinforcements to the old regiments and all the additional strength for the new, that may be required.

If volunteering falters, there should be no tender-footedness about drafting. It has been resorted to by the rebels with tremendous effect, and there should be no hesitation on our part from any sentimental notions as to the honor or dishonor involved. Private interests and feelings must be postponed to the public necessities, and these require an immediate and overwhelming accession to our military strength. . . . The sole thing to be considered is how to increase our army—how to beat the rebels in the struggle to secure an overwhelming force, and to this all minor considerations must give way. . . . It is our national existence we are contending for, and no measures should be neglected which will ensure it.[15]

The choice was simple, said another newspaper—"men may choose whether they will wear the honourable name of volunteer, or the compulsory title of conscript."

We do not know how many strong-limbed, athletic, able-bodied unmarried men between eighteen and forty-five there are in this community, but we are sure the number must be large enough to more than fill the quota of soldiers required from New Jersey. To every one of this class the direct appeal is made, and there is no escaping it. Why do you not enlist? It is not even yet clearly the duty of *every* man to go, but there are those whose duty it *is*, clearly enough. Every unmarried man who has no one but himself to support, and who has strength to shoulder a musket has but one path of duty now, and that leads *to the field.* Thousands of men are leaving wives, children, business,—everything at their country's call. Shall the young men who have nothing to leave ignobly hold back? Let every young man think of this. Honor and Manhood are not now in the workshop—behind the counter; they are *in the field.* Those who remain at home must one day face their old comrades returning with their honorable scars, and under their proud banners blazing with the names of fields which their gallantry has made illustrious. How will they feel who were recreant in the hour of peril, as they meet the scornful gaze of the brave men whose strong cry for help they failed to heed? How will they answer their just reproaches? Young man, that excuse must be indeed weighty which keeps you from the field to-day.[16]

Besides, said the newspapers, "the very enormity of the preparations makes it almost certain that . . . few of the new soldiers called into service will see any fighting at all. . . . The great contest has been practically fought and won," promised Newark's *Daily Mercury.* "Now it but remains to strike one overwhelming blow, and the war is over." Jersey City's *American Standard* agreed:

It seems quite probable now that the nine months men will be used principally for garrison duty. . . . Their labor will be light, their pay better than any other country ever offered; their term of service during the winter months, when labor of all kinds is hard to be had, and their coming back home will be about June next; so their service will avoid all the extreme hot weather, and give them the pleasantest and healthiest months in the year. The aggregate of the pay will be a better sum per day than most men get at home.[17]

Gradually, the ranks began to fill. "Our town is the central point of the military excitement that now prevails," wrote Freehold's newspaper on September 4:

On Saturday noble men from the several townships came pouring in to swell the lists of volunteer patriots who are willing to live or die for their country's honor. They came with a will. . . . They came in wagons and on foot; with fife and drum, and full brass band, pouring forth the strains of martial music; with banners waving in the breeze, they came, a host of freemen, to save their townships from the stigma of the draft, and help to preserve the existence of the Union. Matteawan, whose loyalty has been mistrusted, was among the earliest in, with more than her full number; bearing a banner with the words, "Matteawan—full quota." She came preceded by the Keyport Cornet Band.[18]

Not everyone was anxious to join the Union's ranks. "In strong contrast with the patriotic processions that have come into town," wrote the *Monmouth Democrat*, "have been the scenes about the Court House" where men who claimed exemption pleaded their cases.

Of course there were men who really should be exempted from military service . . . but these were outnumbered by those who were desirous to shirk their duty by the use of subterfuge and falsehood. Men of most robust appearance claimed to be dying of consumption. Naturalized citizens pretended to be aliens. . . . There were about 1,200 applications for exemption . . . so that we have a full regiment of exempts in the county.[19]

Millstone, in Somerset County, experienced a similar epidemic of sudden-onset illness, according to that town's newspaper:

On Wednesday morning last men and boys between the ages of 18 and 45 years were seen pouring into the quiet village of Millstone from all

parts of the County. There were men who were hearty and robust looking, who appeared as if they never had a sick day in their lives, and could
out-work horses almost, coming like a parcel of children to get a certificate of exemption from the draft. There were men who had all sorts of
diseases and complaints. Some had sprained wrists, weak knees, weak
backs, and some near-sighted. Some had no teeth. Some . . . were suddenly taken ill, and were so lame that they could but just hobble along
the streets. Others were troubled with severe colds, coughs and weak
lungs. Some were badly ruptured, but they never knew it until just now.[20]

**The scene at the Newark Custom House, where Essex County's would-be
exempts as well as willing recruits waited their turn to be examined, was a
study in contrast:**

Commissioner E. N. Miller took his seat in the U.S. Court room at the
Custom House this morning, where a crowd, provided with certificates
of various kinds, was already gathered. Mr. Miller prefaced the important business before him, by reading to those assembled, the opinion of
the Attorney General, as to who were exempt, and, designating the description of affidavits with which it would be necessary for applicants to
be provided. Many, finding their claims for exemption to fall short of the
requisitions of the case, summarily left the room. . . .

In and about the examining room of Dr. Coles a homogeneous mass
of "sick and disabled" were gathered, anxiously awaiting their turn to
undergo the tests which the Doctor rigidly applies. Many were crowding
their way to the room set apart for enrolling the names of would-be-
exempts, and it required the utmost exertions of two police officers to
preserve order and keep open a narrow gangway. Numerous jokes were
indulged in by the *garde des invalides* during the tedious waiting hours,
and we could not but commend them for one soldierly quality —that of
patient endurance under discouraging inflictions.

At the other end of the building quite a different scene was being enacted. There Dr. Dodd was examining men, who, having determined to enlist, were most anxious to prove themselves vigorous and sound. One poor
fellow, otherwise a good subject, was rejected because his front teeth were
nearly all gone—not enough being left to bite off a cartridge or amputate
one of Uncle Sam's hard crackers. He begged hard for the Doctor's approval, but the imperfection was a serious one and he could not be passed.[21]

**In Orange, Essex County's second largest city, there were some anxious
moments:**

Monday last [September 1] was an exciting day in Orange. It was the time appointed to marshal the brave volunteers of Orange and send them down to Camp Frelinghuysen. Early in the morning flags were flying, the old "revolutioner" belched forth its thunder, and strains of martial and band music, lent their inspiring strains to the scenes of excitement. Men, women and children thronged the streets, and many a sad farewell was taken, and a "God bless you" uttered, as the men were formed on the Green opposite the Park House about noon.

Upon inspecting the ranks, however, it was ascertained that there were some fifteen men short. . . . At length the company was formed into line by Captain Cairns, and marched up and down Main street, in the hope that the few required would "fall in;" but such was not the result. The afternoon was spent in endeavoring to procure the requisite number, without effect, headquarters being established at Willow Hall. All day crowds thronged the hall, and many serious and ludicrous scenes were enacted. At about six o'clock in the evening it was thought best to adjourn until 7 o'clock the next morning when after reading the roll, and it being that only 9 men were wanted, the company were dismissed, each man rising in his place and promising to be on hand at the time named the next morning, and determining to do all he could to fill up the ranks.

Tuesday morning dawned upon us clear and cool, after a refreshing shower during the previous night; but many misgivings were expressed as to our ability to procure the necessary number, which was now only 160 instead of 210. The belief was quite generally entertained that we should yet have to submit to the draft. . . . Thus matters stood until about 11 o'clock on Tuesday, when the desired number of men having been obtained, the large company were formed in line, and led by Rubsam's brass band of Newark, proceeded in fine order to Camp Frelinghuysen in Roseville. . . .

On the afternoon of Tuesday . . . we visited them [in camp]. They had been sworn into the service, and were receiving their bounty money. Mr. Charles A. Lighthipe, President of the Orange Bank, and Treasurer of the finance committee, went down to the camp with $18,000 in cash, and a similar amount in certificate of the town. The money was put up in neat packages of $100, in Orange Bank bills, and as the name of each volunteer was called, he came forward, signed a receipt and received his pay.[22]

Word of the dismal results of the Second Battle of Bull Run, on August 28 and 29, reached New Jersey too late to have any real effect on enlistment.

"Last week was another week of battles and terrific slaughter in Virginia," wrote the *Plainfield Union* on September 2. "Fighting has been going on there almost every day. . . . The loss on both sides is heavy." There were 16,000 casualties at Second Bull Run, the bluecoats had been beaten again, and now General Lee's army was apparently poised to strike at Washington, a mere twenty miles away. "If the darkest hour is just before daylight," said the *Princeton Standard* on September 5, "we have some reason to anticipate soon the glorious dawn of a bright day." News of the death of Major General Philip Kearny in action at Chantilly, Virginia, on September 1 reached New Jersey four days later, adding to the widespread feeling that the war had taken a new, more sanguinary turn. Kearny, who in peacetime lived at Belle Grove, his estate across the Passaic River from Newark, was a fearless commander greatly admired by the Jerseymen who fought under him. "The death of Gen. Kearny will everywhere be regarded as a national calamity, but here, in New Jersey, among his own people, it is felt by each citizen as a personal sorrow and loss," wrote the *Trenton State Gazette*. "His reputation and glory is a portion of our inheritance, and to avenge his death one of the most sacred of our duties."[23]

New Jersey's newest regiments left home in September with flags flying and bands playing, full of hope and some trepidation. Before they left, there was still time to blow off some last-minute steam. The Fourteenth Regiment was scheduled to leave Freehold by train, destined, thought some wishful thinkers, for Utah. Four days before its departure, reported the *Monmouth Democrat*, a battle royal broke out:

We had something of a "free fight" in town on Saturday night. On that day the advance bounty had been paid to the 14th Regiment, and a great number of them came into town on furlough. They patronized our drinking saloons to a liberal extent, and as early as 8 o'clock were so crazed with grog as to be ready for a fight with or without occasion. The greatest crowd was gathered at the hotel of Stillwell & McNulty, where the authorized officers were engaged in taking the legal oath of the volunteers. Here a fight commenced, in which several parties . . . were severely hurt. This difficulty was hardly quieted before another commenced. There followed a similar fight on the other side of the street . . . and two or three citizens were severely handled.[24]

"Some 600 to 800 of the New-Jersey nine month volunteers, encamped at Camp Frelinghuysen in Newark, took French leave on Saturday morning," recounted the *New York Times* on September 22:

There were some 2,300 soldiers in the camp, and . . . they had been promised a furlough to enable them to visit their homes before marching to the seat of war. The furlough was promised for Wednesday last; when the time came, they were requested to wait until they got their uniforms. The uniforms were furnished on Friday, when, to their surprise, they were informed that they were under marching orders, and could not have a furlough at all. This caused much ill-feeling in camp, but the soldiers, although they were determined to have their promised furlough, yet decided to proceed in a quiet and orderly manner. They therefore held a mass meeting, and appointed a Committee to wait upon the commanding officer and inform him that they should leave camp yesterday morning, with or without a furlough, and that they would all return again at any reasonable time that he would fix. Morning came, and, as the Colonel in command had decided that he had no power to grant furloughs while they were under marching orders, about a third of the men . . . skedaddled. Through the exertions of Capt. Walter H. Dodd, and Capt. Morris, of Newark, the remainder were persuaded to remain until arrangements could be made for their departure in a more soldier-like manner. Col. Van Vorst was finally prevailed upon to grant the men furloughs until 9 o'clock Monday morning. . . . Furloughs were accordingly given to the remainder, and they departed quietly.[25]

Most of the new regiments were still forming when the Thirteenth, led by Colonel Ezra A. Carman, took the train from Newark's Chestnut Street depot on August 31. Raised in Essex, Hudson, and Passaic counties, the Thirteenth was to win its laurels with the Army of the Potomac at Chancellorsville and Gettysburg and under Sherman before Atlanta and Savannah. But it was still an outfit of amateur soldiers, with only a few scant days of training under its belt, when it was thrown into its first engagement, the bloody battle near Antietam Creek in Maryland, northwest of Washington.

The Union repulse at Second Bull Run had sent the Federal army reeling in confusion back toward the national capital. A confident Army of Northern Virginia under General Lee's command was now free to move north through Maryland into Pennsylvania. It was a time of high Confederate hope: A successful invasion of the North might bring with it British recognition and perhaps Southern independence after all. But it was not to be. Withdrawn from the peninsula, the Army of the Potomac linked up with the disorganized remnants of the Federal army that had fought at Bull Run. Whipped quickly into shape by General McClellan, a Union army of 95,000 men marched out from Washington in early September to find Lee. It was an emergency of the first magnitude that demanded every available unit. The Thirteenth's training could wait. Assigned to the XII Corps, Carmen's men trooped across the mountains of western Maryland, arriving near Sharpsburg on September 16.

Warned that a Federal army was approaching, Lee determined to fight, concentrating his forces at Sharpsburg, a little hamlet seventeen miles from Harper's Ferry, just west of Antietam Creek. McClellan's battle plan was simplicity itself: Three full army corps would attack the Confederate line while a fourth would provide a diversion south of Lee's main forces. With dawn's first light, Major General Joseph Hooker's I Corps attacked the Rebel center through a bullet-swept cornfield near the Dunker Church. The Thirteenth was ordered to march toward the sound of the gunfire, recalled Joseph E. Crowell, an eighteen-year-old typesetter with the *Paterson Guardian.*

It was an hour or so before the first signs of daylight, and we had just thrown ourselves on the ground for a short rest after a tedious and fatiguing night's march. Then the shooting began a little distance in front of us. . . .

Although but two weeks away from home . . . we had become quite used to the sound of musketry, but never before did the shooting seem to have the same significance that it did now. We knew that we were in for it. We waited for daylight as the condemned murderer waits for the sun to rise on his last day, for there was not one of us that did not regard it as his last day. . . .

The long-delayed daylight finally arrived. The first gray streaks of dawn disclosed to our eyes a vast army, lying in battle array, all ready for the fight, it seemed. The first thing done was to serve us all with a ration of fresh beef. . . . We lighted fires. There was no use for secrecy now, for each army knew the proximity of the other. We stuck our fresh beef on the ends of sticks, held them in the flames of the camp fires and toasted them, as best we could. But before the meat was scarcely smoked we were ordered to change our position.

The Thirteenth was formed in "close column," which is a usual way to prepare for a battle. We had never been drilled in any such movement, and to get us in the right position it was almost necessary for the officers to lead each man by the shoulders and put him where he ought to be. And to tell the truth, most of the officers knew about as little of these movements as the men.

When we were in the right shape we were told that we might again light the fires and cook our meat for breakfast. But that breakfast was never cooked. We had scarcely got the fires started than the firing in the front began again more vigorously than we had ever heard it before. We were ordered to "fall in." Some of the men ate their beef raw. I was not used to that yet, and thrust my ration into my haversack. . . .

Then the firing of the rifles in the front became more continuous. That was followed by the artillery. First there was a single shot, as if it were a signal. Then there was an answering roar from a far-off hill. The Union artillery responded, and the rebels answered back. The shooting of big guns extended all along the line, and the scarce risen sun was greeted with a continuous salvo that sounded like ten thousand anvil choruses. The "boom-whiz-crash-boom" . . . was repeated and repeated a hundred, a thousand, yes, thousands of times, till the skies crashed like a thousand severe summer thunder-storms. It was simply awful! The noise was ear-splitting, and the effect on the nerves was terrible. . . .

We were temporarily halted along a piece of woods. . . . Then every man was startled by the most unearthly yelling. None had ever before heard such demoniacal shrieks. They sounded as if they came from a lost soul in the nethermost depths of purgatory. We were all startled. It made our blood run cold. . . . So we went over the edge of the woods from whence the unearthly shrieks were coming. . . . There lay a wounded soldier. He was a member of the One Hundred and Seventh New York, one of the regiments of our brigade, and whose face was instantly recognized. He had been struck by the fragments of a bursted shell, and both of his legs were torn off near the knees. The feet and ankles were gone entirely, but there protruded from the lacerated flesh the ends of the bones of the legs in a most horrible manner, making a sight that was simply sickening. Nearly every man of Company K went over to take a look at the wounded man and immediately turned away with a pallid face. There were plenty of wounded men now passing through to the rear, but their injuries were comparatively insignificant. This was the first time that any of us had seen a man mortally wounded and in the act of dying. . . . An order to "fall in" ended this painful scene. The wounded man must have died a few minutes later, for he was going fast when we left him. . . . We were ordered to take a slightly changed position, to support Hexamer's battery, which was banging away for dear life. As fast as the men could load the cannon they were sending shot and shell toward a rebel battery on an opposite hill, and the latter were sending back their shells, which were striking around us in the most reckless manner. The execution done by the enemy just then, to our intense relief, did not amount to much, for most of the shells went over us, and exploded somewhere further in the rear. . . .

Suddenly we were ordered to lie down flat, with space between each file sufficient for some one to pass through. This strange order was soon understood, for a moment later, the Sixty-ninth New York . . . came running through us in the double quick. They had been ordered to charge one of the rebel batteries. They went down the hill on the run with their guns on their shoulders, or hanging in their arms, and when they began to ascend the other side of the valley, they brought their muskets to a "charge bayonet!" A gallant charge they made, but they were repulsed. They were ordered back to their former position. Although a number of them had been killed, although there were some still in the ranks with blood streaming from their wounds, they came back through the Thirteenth with as much regularity as if they had been in a drill, and with a discipline that excited our admiration.

A ferocious seesaw fight in the cornfields and nearby woods ended in stalemate about 7 a.m. The Thirteenth was then ordered to march to the Hagerstown Turnpike. As the men began to climb the split-rail fence that ran along the road, they were raked by deadly fire from Rebel troops concealed to the west. It was, wrote Crowell, the regiment's "baptism of fire."

We were ordered forward! Over eight hundred strong, in battle front, we proceeded. The officers ordered us to "dress to the right," but it was a straggling line. The "z-z-z-ip" of the bullets could be heard whistling past us. And a moment later the first man of Company K fell. It was Fred King. He was mortally wounded. . . . The feeling at seeing one of our own men fall out this way was indescribable. . . . But no matter who fell we must obey orders. And the pitiless, relentless order was "Forward!" The cannon balls and shells struck around us, tearing up the earth, and sometimes ricochetting or bouncing along the ground a great distance, like a flat stone skims across the water of a pond. Wounded men lay everywhere. Some were writhing and kicking. Others lay still. Some of the human forms were already quiet in death. The number of dead horses was enormous. They seemed to lie everywhere. But it was still "Forward!"

We climbed over a rail fence. It was a road . . . that yet runs from Hagerstown to Sharpsburg. We did not take the road, however, for the order was still "Forward!" We climbed over the fence on the other side of the road. We marched some fifteen or twenty feet into what was then a meadow. We could not see any of the enemy, although their bullets were whistling past our heads. The rebels seemed to be in a woods on the other side of the meadow. Suddenly, something occurred that seemed almost supernatural. A vast number of the enemy appeared to

rise straight out of the solid earth, and they poured into us a deadly volley of leaden hail. . . .

It was behind [a ledge of rock] . . . that the rebels had concealed
themselves, and quietly waited till we had got within shooting distance
and then suddenly stood up and fired into us. . . . They fired into us a
murderous volley. Surprised, demoralized, we wavered and fell back
and made for the first fence, on the nearest side of the road . . . !

Most of the officers . . . were marvelously cool and collected in that
terrible scene. They succeeded in stopping the stampede. They re-
formed us on the road before we had climbed the second fence, and we
were again turned against the enemy. A cessation, for a few moments,
not entirely, but partially, of the firing, enabled us to collect our shattered senses as we gazed over the meadow we had just left. Then we saw
the murderous effect of the volley that had been fired into our ranks by
the enemy concealed behind those natural breastworks. There in the
meadow lay nine dead and sixty wounded men of the Thirteenth Regiment—the work of a single volley!

There was but one man there who seemed not to be wounded. It was
Heber Wells, one of the bravest men in battle that ever lived. . . . Why
had he remained behind in the storm of bullets that were whistling past
him, when everybody else had fled? He had remained beside the body
of his dead captain. Captain Irish had been killed! When the captain saw
the company wavering, he raised his sword aloft and cried out. . . .

"Rally, boys! Rally!"

And just as he said this he fell, pierced by a bullet. Sergeant Wells
saw him fall and returned to his side. Wells imagined at first that the
captain had been shot in the head, but could not find the wound.

"Captain," said he, "are you hurt?"

"Heber, I'm killed!"

Captain Irish pressed his hand on his right breast, glanced gratefully
at his faithful friend Heber, gasped painfully and was dead . . . ! When
the members of Company K realized what had happened they were paralyzed with horror. . . .

Heber Wells tore open the captain's coat and shirt, and found a small
wound near the right nipple of his breast. There was not a particle of
blood oozing from it. But it had reached a vital spot. Wells put his ear to
the captain's breast, and heard the last fluttering of his stilling heart.
Then Wells searched the pockets, taking from them the captain's watch,
the papers and memorandums, and unfastened his sword. He tried to
get the pocket knife and other things on the other side, but could not, on
account of the way the body was twisted around. There was imminent

danger of the Union troops being repulsed and the body falling into the hands of the rebels, and Heber did not want any of the contents of the captain's pockets to fall into the hands of the enemy.

Then Wells made up his mind to rescue the body. The bullets were still whistling about his ears in a dangerous fashion, but he seemed to care naught for that. Picking up the things he had removed from the captain's pockets, and his sword, he took them over to the road and called for volunteers to rescue the captain's body. There were plenty of responses of this noble, yet sad duty, dangerous though it was. Of the volunteers, Wells selected Jacob Engle, Lewellen T. Probert and Jacob Berdan, and the four carried the captain's body over the fence and laid it in the road.

Captain Irish's final words, widely reported in New Jersey's newspapers a few days after his death, made him posthumously famous.

The captain being dead, the command of the company fell on First Lieutenant Scott. But he was hors de combat too. The lieutenant was not killed, but sick, very sick. When Sergeant Wells went to look for him, he found the lieutenant lying alongside the fence, doubled up with cramps and vomiting like a dog. Sergeant Wells ordered a couple of men to take the lieutenant to the rear, and assumed command of the company himself. . . .

Not much account of the time of day is kept during a battle, but everybody seems to agree that it was about 9 o'clock in the morning when Captain Irish was killed. The battle . . . was not over yet, nor was the part the Thirteenth New Jersey played in it. From its position on the pike the regiment was ordered back into the woods, pretty nearly the same it had occupied before proceeding down to its baptism. We had scarcely got there before the enemy made his appearance in full force on the other side of the turnpike. Then our artillery opened upon them in good shape. This attack of the Confederates had evidently been intended to capture that battery on the hill, which was giving them a good deal of trouble. But they didn't get that battery, not by a long shot. The enemy was given a hot dose of shot and shell and shrapnel and canister, and the enemy was promptly sent back to his shelter at the edge of the woods.

The Thirteenth Regiment, already demoralized by the volley down in the meadow, where Captain Irish had been killed and so many wounded, had not got over it, and this second attack very much scattered them. It took some time for the officers to get them together in good shape again, but they finally succeeded in doing so. Just then an order came for the regiment to report to General Green, over by the Dunker church, where the enemy was massing in force and pressing the Union troops dangerously.

The Thirteenth marched about a mile to its left, and up the hill back of the Dunker church, a small brick structure about the size of a country schoolhouse, right into the thick of the afternoon's battle, wrote Crowell.

Up back of this church the Thirteenth Regiment, led by General George Greene himself, came near being captured. The enemy advanced toward us with their guns held as if they were either out of ammunition or else wanted to surrender, and quietly marched down to the right as if going peaceably to the rear. Adjutant Charles A. Hopkins with another officer went out with a white handkerchief on a sword as a sort of truce to see what was meant by these mysterious movements. Hopkins had got out into the open field where he was exposed to every danger, when it became evident to everybody that the crafty enemy was trying to work the dodge of getting in our rear, and thus putting us between two fires, which would have annihilated the Thirteenth in a few moments. The scheme was discovered by the Union troops, and the fact that it was seen through was discovered by the Confederates almost simultaneously, and the firing began at once on both sides in a very lively sort of a manner. Those who were there say that the horror of the fight that was commenced was almost offset by the sight of Adjutant Hopkins and his companions skedaddling over that field to get out of the way of the bullets that came from both directions at once. As if by a miracle, however, neither of them was struck.[26]

Flanked by the enemy, and mostly out of ammunition, the men of the Thirteenth retreated to a safer position, to be replaced by fresh troops. Although they would see no more active fighting at Antietam, the bloodiest single day's engagement in American military history, the Thirteenth had performed magnificently. "I have no words but praise for their conduct," wrote the commander of their brigade. "They fought like veterans. . . . They were led by those who inspired them with courage, and they followed with a determination to conquer or die."

The battle at Antietam ended at about 5:30 p.m., with nearly 23,000 dead, wounded, and missing, one out of every four men in action that day. The battlefield itself was a gruesome scene of horror, a "ghastly spectacle," wrote one war correspondent, with dead and wounded sprawled every-

where. The pitiful cries of the wounded echoed through the night air as
both armies slept on their arms. Private Crowell never forgot that night.
Unable to sleep, the men talked "about the horrors of the day." Then a
sound interrupted their conversation.

"For the love of God, don't. . . ." This came over from the direction of
the barn. . . . It was not like a cry. It was a shriek. It was a loud-cracked
voice, that seemed to come from the very depths of some human soul. I
never heard such a tone of voice in my life again.

Crowell and several companions went to investigate. "I wished that I never
had."

The old barn was being utilized as a field hospital. . . . The floor was covered with wounded men, lying closely side by side. On the bare floor, in
a row, as thick as they could lie, were the maimed human beings that
had just been operated upon. Some were conscious, but the most of
them were moaning and groaning. These moans and groans arose in the
night air like a chorus. . . .

I passed between the rows of wounded men, many of whom would
never be removed from their hard couches, except as corpses. I stopped
to look more fully at one poor fellow whose face seemed familiar. This
poor wretch . . . had just suffered an amputation of the left arm at the
shoulder joint. He looked at me appealingly, as if he wished to say something. I knelt at his side and held down my ear. He made an effort to
speak, but not a sound came from his lips. On the contrary he simply
turned his head and there ran from his mouth a stream of what looked
like dark-green paint. His legs stiffened out, a convulsion passed over
him, an ashen hue suffused his face. He was dead!

Horror-stricken I rushed through the barn and out of the rear
side. . . . We had better have gone the other way, for here were horrors a
thousand times worse. The surgeons were at their ghoulish work on this
side of the barn.

Upon a board, laid upon two barrels was stretched a human form.
Perhaps it was the same poor fellow whose yell of anguish had aroused
and startled us. But he was silent now. A young medical cadet was holding a chloroform-saturated handkerchief to his nose. The doctors were
about to amputate the shattered mass of flesh that was once a leg. The
surgeons were in their shirt sleeves. The aprons that some of them wore
were as red with blood as if they had been butchers. Assistants held candles to light the operation. I saw the doctor give one cut into the fleshy

part of the man's thigh—and fled! But I ran straight into another amputating table—a board over two barrels. Here they were taking off an arm! Turning I ran against another! In every direction that I might go, I would run against one of the horrid things.

Blinded with fright and terror, I tried to escape. I don't know what became of my companion. Seeing an apparently open way, I deliriously rushed in that direction, but meeting some obstruction I stumbled and fell. What had I fallen into? In grasping to steady myself, I caught hold of something wet and slimy! It was quite dark, but I could see! I could see all too plainly. Would to heaven I could not see!

I had fallen headlong into a heap of horrors—a pile of human legs and arms that had just been amputated. I shall not attempt to say how many there were. Were I to say there were a dozen wagon-loads of arms and legs, hands and feet, in that ghastly pile, I might not be believed![27]

Lewis Irish left Paterson on September 22 to search for his brother's body, relieved to find that "[h]e is carefully buried in such a manner that there will be no difficulty in removing his remains."

On my way to Frederick City I began to see the sad effects of this war. The city is one vast hospital; the finest dwellings, hotels and shanties are filled with the wounded. Not finding any among the wounded that I knew, I started in a hired conveyance for the battlefield. . . . All along the route was crowded with ambulances, wagons and wounded soldiers on foot, dragging their weary limbs along. It was like riding through one great burying ground. Dead horses lay thickly around, and the mounds pointed out the last resting places of many a poor soldier. The ground was thickly strewn with pieces of clothing, haversacks, caps, broken wagons, guns, pistols, and the trees, fences and orchards, and everything in the vicinity, bears the work of the terrible conflict.[28]

Antietam was a turning point in the war, shattering Southern dreams of foreign recognition and giving President Lincoln the victory he needed to issue the Emancipation Proclamation. As Lee's battered army retreated south to Virginia, the president announced that as of January 1, 1863, the slaves of persons in rebellion against the government were to be forever free. "Viewed as a political measure this proclamation is as absurd as it is fanatical," mocked Newark's *Daily Journal* on September 23. "The slaves cannot be emancipated until we conquer their masters who are in arms, and obtain control of their territory, a fact which is yet apparently very far from accomplishment. The President might as well issue a proclamation to the Mormons to cast off their superfluous wives before the first of next January, or to every man in the country to quit drinking whiskey on or before that day." Emancipation was decidedly not popular in New Jersey even among Union men, many of whom swallowed hard and accepted it only as a means of punishing the South.

New Jersey's fall election was vigorously contested. "All who prefer freedom to slavery, true Democracy to slavish aristocracy, the Union to disunion, honor to dishonor" will vote Republican, claimed the *New Brunswick Fredonian* on October 23. Democrats saw the matter differently, appealing—in the words of a Somerville newspaper—to "those who love the Union more than the negro." A tide of anti-Republican sentiment swept the state on Election Day, awarding the Democrats the governor's chair as well as both houses of the legislature. "The victory . . . is a rebuke to the fanatics who have attempted to divert the war from its holy purpose, and make it a political war for the abolition of slavery," heralded the *Monmouth Democrat* on November 6, an opinion seconded by the *Trenton Weekly True American*:

We regard the clean sweep just made by the Democracy in this State as only confirming the opinion we have frequently expressed, that abolitionism can gain no foothold in New Jersey. . . . Besides, as an eminently conservative people, the people of New Jersey look with suspicion upon the wild experiments which abolitionism contemplates. All such schemes incur their hostility. Such radical measures as changing the social conditions of four millions of laborers with a stroke of the pen or a legislative enactment, and giving rise to problems which no foresight can solve, find no favor with men whose reason yet preserves its mastery over passion and fanaticism.[29]

Many Republicans were disheartened by the election results, others philosophical. Governor-elect Parker was, after all, a strong Union man, they reasoned, and had the soldiers in the field been allowed to vote, the result might have been different. Similar Democrat victories in New York, Illinois, Indiana, Ohio, and Pennsylvania were interpreted by many as evidence of the North's frustration that after pouring out so much "blood and treasure" the rebellion was no closer to being put down than it was when it began.

McClellan's strategic victory at Antietam proved to be a hollow one. For the next forty days the Army of the Potomac lay immobile, while Lee regrouped his forces. No amount of prodding from Washington could move the inert mass; when yet another telegram arrived from McClellan complaining of broken-down horses, the president could stand it no more. "I have just read your despatch about sore tongued and fatigued horses," replied Lincoln. "Will you pardon me for asking what the horses of your army have done since the battle of Antietam that fatigue anything?" Still McClellan did not move.

On November 7 the president acted, replacing McClellan with Major General Ambrose E. Burnside, the hero of North Carolina. Although doubting his ability to command an army of 130,000, Burnside acted with dispatch, marching his men with unexpected speed to Falmouth, across the Rappahannock from Fredericksburg. His plan was straightforward, and might have succeeded if effected before Lee could react. Crossing the Rappahannock on pontoons, the Federals would seize Fredericksburg, make it their base, then drive toward Richmond. In its opening stages Burnside's plan went well, the Union army (including eleven regiments from New Jersey) occupying the heights opposite Fredericksburg by mid-November. By the time the needed pontoons arrived, however, Lee and most of his 75,000 men were solidly dug in along the hills south of the river. Unable to think of an alternative plan, Burnside decided to move ahead with his river crossing, leading to what proved to be, wrote Sergeant Joseph Mosley of the Twenty-fifth New Jersey, "a blundering attack" on "impregnable works."

Friday morning, Dec. 12th, hostilities commenced with daylight, and desultory firing . . . was kept up during the whole day at short intervals, along the line, which stretched some ten or twelve miles along the course of the Rappahannock, every shot being replied to by the rebels. . . . During the afternoon the firing began to get warmer, and Union soldiers were at their work laying two pontoon bridges . . . above and below the city.

The rebels did their utmost to drive them out, and failing to do it with shot, sent down their sharp-shooters, who displayed their skill in picking off a large number of our men, firing from the windows and doors of the city, completely riddling the boats as they were placed in the river. Their fire was so severe that it was necessary to call on volunteers to finish the work.

Once the pontoon bridges were completed, the Federal troops crossed the river, occupied the city, and threw out picket lines.

At nine o'clock in the morning, Dec. 13th, the ball commenced in good earnest, up and down the river, our forces engaging the rebels hand to hand, driving them at every charge back upon their strongly entrenched works, not being able to draw them out for a fair stand up fight, and of course we were working against terrible odds. At every chance they would open a cross fire of grape and canister upon our boys, cutting them down like grass, wherever they exposed themselves. The rattle of musketry and the roar of cannon was terrific, shaking the earth for miles. The fight continued without advantage to our side, and with terrible loss to our army, all day, and only ceased for about one hour just before sundown. There was one universal pelting from right to left, and the scene, as I witnessed it from an elevated position near the centre, beggars description. It was a terrible sight to see these brave men rush up to the cannon's mouth and offer themselves as sacrifices on the blood-stained battle-field of Fredericksburg. As they charged on a battery, the rebels would charge on them from their numerous earthworks sending death and destruction in their ranks, and at every charge they fell like grass before the scythe. I cannot call this, as some do, a grand and sublime scene; it is rather a disgusting, soul-harrowing and sickening sight, one that I hope it will never be necessary for any one to attempt a description of, for if there is anything grand in seeing men fall into the jaws of certain death, then I pray God deliver me from the sight; but this was not the worst that took place before the close of this day's work.

Shortly before 5 p.m. the Twenty-fifth was ordered to charge the Confederate line, entrenched behind a stone wall at the base of Marye's Heights behind Fredericksburg. Mosley's brother, Richard, was among those killed.

At dusk . . . the call to fall into line was sounded throughout the city. . . . After getting into line, the different regiments were filed by a four rank movement through the principle and centre streets of the city, until they covered the extent of ground that was required, when the command by the left flank, double quick march, now given, and the boys with terrific speed, rushed pell-mell through houses, over fences, up ally-ways, into ditches, and by every conceivable avenue that presented itself, becoming a completely disorganized and unmanageable mass, before reaching the enemy whom they expected to meet at every step; but who were far enough off to give them a reception that was not expected. It was well for them that that miserably managed charge had been conducted in the dark, for they were led as it were, right into a net prepared for them by the enemy, who had them at their mercy, and had they seen fit, could have annihilated every one of them or taken the whole body prisoners. Of course, nobody is to blame; but somebody must certainly have been drunk, and for my part of the affair, I shall hold the commander in charge responsible for the death of a dear brother. The slaughter of Saturday and of Saturday night was perfectly awful, and will result in a curse to the country, for there never was a more bewildered and disorganized body of men in God's world. . . . I do not believe any man with a thimble full of brains would have ordered such a piece of work. . . .

[W]hen the attack was made the Zouaves were to lead our 25th into the fight, which they did to perfection, for when the first fire came from the rebels the brave Zoo-Zoos had slid off sideways, and the brunt of the battle was left for our boys to stand, which they did, not a man going back on the glory of old Jersey.[30]

Secure behind their defenses, the Rebels mowed down the Yankees with bloody efficiency. By the time the fighting died down, the Twenty-fifth had lost six men killed, sixty-one wounded, and eighteen missing. The Fourth, Twenty-third, Twenty-fourth, and Twenty-eighth New Jersey regiments suffered equally heavy losses. New Jersey's other regiments at Fredericksburg missed most of the fighting, although there were casualties among them as well. Ordered out on picket duty, the Fifteenth lost its first man killed in action when Michael Mulvey was shot through the head. A fine marksman, Mulvey had been cautioned by an officer not to expose himself to enemy fire.

With a patriotic answer, he sprang forward to a pile of railroad ties. A rebel sharpshooter was posted on the opposite bank of a stream, behind a tree, and would load and fire when he could get a fair shot. Mulvey soon discovered him, and watched for his opportunity. The rebel put his head and rifle out from the tree; Mulvey did the same above the pile of ties. There was a double explosion. Mulvey fell back, pierced through the brain with a minié ball. The rebel marksman tumbled over, his body in full view, also pierced to the brain through his eye, from the unerring aim of poor Mulvey. At sundown the regiment held the ground in that part of the field and his comrades buried him, wrapped in his blanket (the soldier's shroud) in the field nearby, where the grass looked greener and the soil less disturbed. There was no monument to mark his grave— not even a board could be had.[31]

When darkness finally overtook the field at Fredericksburg, the Union army had suffered one of its worst defeats of the war. Nearly 13,000 casualties littered the ground, most of them in front of the Rebel positions at the base of Marye's Heights. "It can hardly be in human nature for men to show more valor," wrote a newspaper reporter, "or generals to manifest less judgment."

Sergeant-Major Amos J. Cummings of the Twenty-sixth Regiment combed the battlefield for the body of Private John Dries.

The rebel wounded and our own frequently lay side by side breathing their last. The hospital headquarters were situated in a large white frame house on the Northern bank of the river in which a small army of surgeons were busily engaged, night and day, in dismembering our poor, wounded braves, the shrieks and groans of whom were frequently heart rending. . . . As fast they expired they were buried in their blankets—three or four in a grave—on the river bank, their friends (if they had any) generally placing a piece of a cracker box at the head of the grave, detailing thereon their names, companies and regiments. . . . At the entrance of one of the tents, we observed a small pyramid of legs, arms, hands and feet—the result of hospital operations. But sickening as were the scenes in the hospital, they had not the influences upon one's nerves as the scenes on the field. Some of the dead were mashed into one complete jelly, their remains stringing over a distance of five yards, while others lay on their backs, hands clenched and toes turned in, a picture of stern determination and resolve which death alone could conquer. These were generally shot through the heart. Those shot in the head presented a horrible appearance, the blood and oozing brains hiding their features.[32]

When reports of the slaughter at Fredericksburg reached New Jersey, the people were aghast. Even Newark's pro-administration paper, the *Newark Daily Mercury,* called Fredericksburg a disaster, reporting "immense losses, whole brigades shattered and broken, and regiments almost obliterated, with thousands of dead and wounded lying in ghastly heaps upon the ground."[33] The Copperhead *Newark Daily Journal* called for peace through compromise. "The defeat of Burnside, if it does not stop the war, will at least convince the people of the disgraceful imbecility and utter want of capacity of the Administration," wrote the paper's editor, Edward Fuller, on December 17:

Their damning record is complete; and henceforth none but a fool or a knave will attempt to whitewash these abolition incapables, or defend their course. We have never believed that the grand enterprise of the fanatics to subjugate or conquer the South could meet with any success commensurate with its expense, loss of life and national position; but we had a right to suppose, with the immense resources of the country, the splendid nucleus for the establishment of a great army and navy, and the comparative weakness and lack of resources of war existing in the South, that at least the North could hold her own in the struggle. . . .

But the Administration has failed, signally failed to appreciate the position, and their blunders have caused the failure of one of the largest armies ever raised in modern history. Our military blunders can never be retrieved, but our political position might be preserved if the Administration would allow the people to take the matter into their own hands. . . . The people must now speak and demand that they be allowed to settle the difficulties. An armistice should be at once declared, for the war is an unquestioned failure on the part of the North.[34]

Burnside took the blame for the massacre at Fredericksburg but much of the nation laid the fault solely at the doorstep of the White House. "If there is a worse place than Hell," said the president, "I am in it."

THREE

"We Will Give Them Hell Yet"

1863

When the official New Year's Day reception at the White House was over, the president went upstairs to his office, where a small group of officials was waiting. "If my name ever goes into history, it will be for this act," he said as he signed the Emancipation Proclamation, freeing "all persons held as slaves within any state . . . in rebellion against the United States. . . . " "I never in my life felt more certain that I was doing right than I do in signing this paper," added Lincoln, his signature firm even after five hours of shaking hands with the public.

Emancipation had as much to do with the military situation as it did with Lincoln's belief that slavery was "at the root of the rebellion." The North's problem, it grew increasingly evident, was how to deploy its clear preponderance of strength in a sustained manner sufficient to collapse Confederate defenses, scatter its armies, and bring down the government in Richmond. Destroying the South's economy by encouraging its bondsmen to flee would now be part of the plan. Finding generals who could lead the Union's immense armies to victory was another, but it was vastly more perplexing. In the west Generals Grant and Rosecrans labored with some success. In the east, the main theater of the war, one difficulty followed another as the year 1863 began.

January 1863 was the nadir of Northern hope. The bloodshed of Fredericksburg fueled a swelling tide of frustration, anger, and recrimination that threatened to engulf the president, his administration, and the nation itself. Burnside, doubting his ability to command an army, tendered his resignation, and when Lincoln rejected his offer, he began drawing plans for yet another assault across the Rappahannock, this time eight miles north of Fredericksburg. On January 20 the men were assembled to hear Burnside's grandiloquent order of the day: "The commanding general announces to the Army of the Potomac that they are about to meet the enemy once more. The auspicious moment seems to have arrived to strike a great and mortal blow to the rebellion, and to gain that decisive victory which is due to the nation." Burnside's message "was listened to with marked silence," wrote a soldier in the Twenty-ninth New Jersey. "A peculiar indifference pervaded the whole army, owing in a measure to a lack of confidence in the management."[1]

For weeks the weather had been clear, and the roads were dry and firm. Despite some grumbling within the ranks, the march toward Banks' Ford began well enough, but around midafternoon the sky grew cloudy and a bitter winter wind began whistling through the trees. Just before dark a fine drizzle turned quickly into a driving downpour. "We bivouacked in the woods," wrote Sergeant-Major Amos Cummings of the Twenty-sixth, "and hardly were our fires lighted before the rain fell in torrents."[2] The Thirteenth New Jersey went into camp near Dumphries, alongside a little stream, recalled Private Crowell:

In the night the threatened storm broke loose. And such a storm! The "pup" tents were of no more use than so many sieves. They were called "shelter tents," but they were anything else than a shelter on that occasion. We spent the night standing up or walking around, on the principle that a man erect affords less surface to be exposed to the rain than a man lying down. Besides the water was apparently two or three inches deep on the ground, so that we might as well have undertaken to go to bed in a bath tub.

There was not a man who was not drenched to the skin. If we had been thrown into the river we could not have been more thoroughly soaked. The wood was so saturated that it was impossible to build a fire in the morning, and we consequently had to go without our much-needed hot coffee. The wet clothes, saturated knapsacks and other things almost doubled the load we had to carry. But all this made no difference. The relentless march was ordered to proceed.

Despite weather conditions that might have caused a less-determined commander to reverse course, Burnside ordered the advance to continue. Writes Crowell:

We had not gone far before we were compelled to throw away our woolen blankets and other things, which were so saturated with water as to be useless, and the weight was more than we could carry, And here it was in the dead of winter at that! The loss of the blankets unquestionably meant suffering for us when night came, but we could not help that. . . .

The mud had become deeper than ever, and the tramp of so many thousand feet made it sticky and mushy. We floundered around, seemingly aimlessly, for awhile and finally came to the banks of another creek, which we were expected to cross to get to where we were going, wherever that might be. Here another obstacle was encountered. The rain had swollen the creek several times its usual height, so that it could not be forded. Fortunately some big trees were growing in the neighborhood and these were felled and dragged to the creek and thrown across. . . .

It took five or six hours to get the infantry across on the rough bridge that had been completed, but then it was found that it was impossible to get the artillery and baggage wagons over. So there was another delay. The bridge had to be made more perfect for the wheeled vehicles. A row of logs was laid across the timbers of the bridge and the tops hewed off, till it formed a sort of corduroy road. The artillery was then brought across on this structure, but here another trouble was experienced. The wheels of the heavy cannons only mixed up the mud on the other side of the creek, till it became impossible to pull the artillery through, no matter how many horses and mules there might be harnessed up. It is no exaggeration to state that the mud was above the hubs of both the cannon wheels and those of the wagons and ambulances. But a small portion had got across when everything came to a dead halt. Not a wheel could be moved.[3]

The rain continued without let-up for thirty-six hours, turning the roads into creeks and the creeks into raging torrents. Artillery, supply wagons, ammunition trains, ambulances, pontoons, horses and mules, all were bogged down in knee-deep mud. "Our position was like that of liliputians in a great mud pie," said one soldier. After hundreds of horses and mules died from exhaustion, the army's engineers called on the men themselves for help. "We marched a mile or so back and forth across a field of almost bottomless mud, to be ready at a moment's notice to assist in getting the pontoons or artillery further in from the river," wrote Lieutenant Lewis Van Blarcum of the Fifteenth Regiment:

Co. A was detailed to pull a load of pontoon lumber about a mile and half to a brick church, where the pontoons and appendages were being concentrated. The boys caught hold of the rope attached to the wagon, and, with deafening yells, extricated it from the mud and took it to its destination, and have thereby earned the complimentary title of being "Uncle Sam's mules." It appears that the "Rebs" were aware of our dilemma, as a large board was to be seen on the opposite shore, marked in large letters of chalk, "BURNSIDE STUCK IN THE MUD!" which has now become a by-word in the army.[4]

Burnside finally realized that the situation was hopeless, and on January 23 gave the order to return to camp near Falmouth. "The march [back] soon degenerated into a grand straggle," recalled an officer, "for the men were literally worn out by the three days of terrible work which they had been through."

The Twenty-sixth kept together very well until we reached Falmouth. There rations were served out; among them, as an extra favor, a whiskey ration, which did more harm than good. After leaving Falmouth, the regiment dwindled rapidly away, one after another falling out of the ranks, until a mere handful was left. The whole army straggled; here you could see a group of men from two or three different regiments coolly making coffee around a fire, while others were plodding leisurely along, some in groups, some singly. Now and then there would be a wagon stuck so that ten mules could not pull it out, or perhaps a knot of wagons, ambulances and artillery so entangled that it seemed as if they could never be separated. Many a poor fellow lay down by the roadside utterly exhausted and helpless.[5]

The Mud March was one of the Army of the Potomac's darkest hours. The loss of horses and mules, weapons and equipment was enormous; worse, the army was thoroughly demoralized and its commander humiliated. On January 25 Major General Joseph Hooker replaced Burnside.

Discontent within the Army of the Potomac was rampant, with desertions running nearly two hundred a day by the end of January. "From what I can observe . . . , I am convinced that each day increases the dissatisfaction, and renders the morale of the army anything but satisfactory" complained Jacob R. Schenck, quartermaster sergeant, Twenty-ninth New Jersey, in a letter to the *Hunterdon Democrat*, a Copperhead newspaper.

Fighting will never accomplish what is sought after. I verily believe that the "Southron" is as firmly convinced of the justice and holiness of the cause he is defending, as were the patriotic warriors of the revolution, and they will maintain their rights by force of arms, *if no other means are proposed,* until every last mother's son of them bites the dust in the struggle. . . . Northern newspapers may write and prate about Union feeling in the South, to their heart's content, it is a myth—a fancy— pregnant in the brains of those who love to make assertions without the evidence to bear them up. I wish to God there was more of Union spirit both North and South; then there might be a lingering hope that this "carnival of blood" would cease, and that suffering humanity might return to contentment, where now all is misery and woe.[6]

The Twenty-second New Jersey, most of whom hailed from Bergen County, was one of the most discontented outfits in the Army of the Potomac. A majority of its men had little sympathy for the Union cause and even less interest in risking their necks in battle. In mid-January when the regiment was transferred from guard duty behind the lines to the I Corps, known as a fighting command, mutiny broke out.

The regiment left Camp Mercer, Acquia Creek, on Monday morning. . . . It was after a great deal of trouble and ordering that the regiment finally got started. . . . As soon as the orders were pretty well known by the line officers, a meeting was called by them. . . . A series of resolutions was drawn up by them which were presented to the Lt. Col. the following morning. One of the resolutions stated that the regiment was not properly disciplined to be sent into the field. Another asked for a three months' drill, and then four months back pay. . . . On Sunday morning the regiment was hub-hub and confusion, the men having got wind of the meeting the night before. Accordingly, what the officers of the regiment had started the men thought they could carry out to perfection. A petition was . . . circulated through the companies, and numerously signed by the boys. . . . The men asked for a three months' drill and also that they would not leave the ground until they received their pay. They had it so arranged that when they were ordered to fall in with their knapsacks, not to do it, but to fall out without them on. The order from their Captains [to fall in] was at first very reluctantly obeyed. . . .

After they were all properly drawn up [in front of the Colonel's quarters], the Col. mounted his steed, and said, "Men, this may be last time I ever address you as a regiment. . . . The men that started this affair are nothing but cowards and skulkers, and are the first to shrink from duty. . . . I will give you half an hour to fall in, and if my orders are not obeyed, every officer in this regiment will resign immediately, and you will be nothing but a disorganized mob."

Thirty minutes later when the drum roll sounded all but twenty-three privates and one sergeant from Company A fell into rank, knapsacks on. "All honor to those in the Regiment who promptly shoulder the musket when ordered so to do," editorialized Paterson's *Daily Guardian*, "and eternal shame to all men enlisted only for nine months, who after securing $200 bounty and serving without a fight through two thirds of their term, demand ... all the remaining period of their enlistment to drill. We never before heard of soldiers who were repugnant to getting into a fight." Two days later the malcontents returned to the regiment under guard.[7]

The Emancipation Proclamation divided New Jersey's soldiers as much as it did the public back home. "I got my box a day before yesterday and it made me feel good," Private Jacob Young, a farmer from Somerset County who had enlisted in the Thirty-first New Jersey, wrote to his father four days after the decree was issued.

I will name the things I found—One pair of boots, one pair of gloves, one pair of stockings, some butter, some paper and stamps, yarn and thread and a darn needle, six papers of tobacco and four plugs of tobacco, and two sticks of liquorice, but there was no chicken and only two apples. I guess my box had been opened before I got it, but there wasn't so much taken out. I am glad that they did take that chicken out for if they hadn't it would have spoiled the butter.

I guess there is going to be another big battle for the way things is a-moving. . . . When I was at home I was a Lincoln man, but I am set against him now for yesterday and day before yesterday there was a lot of niggers came through our camp and they said they was a-going to Washington. I thought they was a-going to take New Year's dinner with old Abe.[8]

"There is a storm brewing not only in the North but in the whole army that will yet make the abolitionists rue the day they were born," wrote Sergeant William R. Knapp of the Ninth Regiment in early February, echoing the views of many stateside Democrats.

Women of New Jersey, was it to fight for the freeing of negroes that you sent your sons to the field bidding them "God speed;" did you not send them into battle for the glorious old flag, the Constitution and the enforcement of the laws? Or did you send them to rob the South of those rights, which should be respected, when the Constitution contains nothing that favors their extinction. We know you did not: but alas noble Jersey, how thy loyalty has been abused. So long as we knew that we were fighting for a restoration of the Union as it was, we felt confident of success, but . . . we have never been as successful since the emancipation proclamation as before it was issued, and there is scarcely a man in the ranks of our army who approves of it. Many have deserted their regiments since then, and are still leaving whenever an opportunity arises.[9]

A soldier from Bergen County's Twenty-second Regiment was even more outspoken.

There is much dissatisfaction existing in the army on account of the President's proclamation. Desertions are numerous and frequent. . . . As the slaves become free only as our army advances, then who can deny we are fighting for the confounded nigger? I tell you what! These abolitionists and republicans at home must be mighty careful how they talk to soldiers when they return, or there will be some tall knock downs. It makes us mad when we think of it, that they remain at home and reap all the benefits of the war, while we who differ from them in opinion are up to our knees in mud, enduring all the privations and hardships of war and fighting for their favorite who—the nigger! The proclamation has done more to demoralize the army of the North than any good, practically or morally, that can possibly result from it. The nine months men are looking anxiously to the time when they can return home. I'm one of them.[10]

The Union army's reaction to emancipation was not altogether negative, as many had feared it would be. A soldier from Paterson proudly declared that he was "fighting for freedom. Every day makes me gather more hatred toward the South when I see the poor black people coming over here at the risk of their lives to gain their freedom, with their backs all lacerated with scars. It will make any man with sense to cry out against the South." Others saw that the destruction of slavery would be the ruination of the Confederacy. "We have heard men say that this is a war for the purpose of destroying the institution of slavery," wrote a member of the Twelfth Regiment. "So it is; that peculiar institution is the foundation of the rebellion, and in order to defeat the enemies of our government in open revolt, it is compulsory to destroy their power."[11]

Soldier morale had plunged to a new low by the time "Fighting Joe" Hooker assumed command of the Army of the Potomac. Of the 180,000 men officially on the rolls, nearly 85,000 were absent without leave. Scurvy and diarrhea plagued the troops; and the camps near Aquia Creek were little more than pigsties, with unbelievable filth and impenetrable mud everywhere. It was, said one soldier, a winter of despair.

Hooker tore into the army like a whirlwind. Fresh vegetables and soft bread baked in camp supplemented the monotony of hardtack, salt pork, and coffee. Peremptory orders went out to regimental commanders to establish company kitchens, clean up the camps, and enforce elementary sanitation. The men in the ranks were directed to cut their hair short, bathe regularly and put on clean underwear "at least once a week." A liberal furlough policy cut the tide of desertion while distribution of back pay did wonders for morale. Hooker's reforms had a near-miraculous effect on the army. "Cheerfulness, good order and military discipline," wrote one soldier, "at once took the place of grumbling, depression and want of confidence."[12]

Toward the end of February an unusually heavy snowfall blanketed northern Virginia. As soon as the skies cleared, men from four Vermont regiments that were brigaded with the Twenty-sixth Volunteers pounced on the unsuspecting Jersey soldiers.

The Vermonters twice made an attack on the encampment of the Twenty-Sixth, sending a perfect shower of snow balls at the head of every luckless Jerseyman who made his appearance without his tent. The first attack was a complete surprise to us, but we essayed a sally from the camp, and drove the attacking party back to their reserves. Being heavily re-enforced they charged on us again, and after a desperate resistance we were driven back into camp, fighting resolutely from the shelter of our tents until darkness put an end to the contest. Our casualties were quite heavy, but those of the enemy it is thought exceeded ours. A few days afterward the attack was renewed, but we took a strong position on a hill in the rear of the camp, and repulsed every assault of the foe. . . . The enemy raised a flag of truce, an armistice of a few hours was concluded, and then ensued that novel spectacle of war, men, who but a few minutes previous were engaged in one of the most sanguinary battles of modern times, harmonizing and fraternizing with clasped hands.

On February 25 the contest was renewed by the victorious Twenty-sixth, with disappointing results, wrote Sergeant-Major Cummings:

Col. Morrison sent a challenge to Col. Beaver of the Third Vermont, to engage in the open field at 3 o'clock P. M. The challenge was accepted, on the condition that the Fourth Vermont should be included with the Third. This was agreed to by the Colonel. Before the appointed time some of our men were detailed on fatigue duty, and at the time of the engagement we were only able to muster some three hundred men.

Nothing daunted by the superiority of numbers, Col. Morrison ordered Lieut. McCleese of Company C to fortify a small hill on our right, make as much ammunition as possible, and pile the snow balls in pyramids. This arduous duty was hastily performed. It was a strong position, a swollen brook at its base answering the purpose of a moat—too strong, in fact, for the Vermonters and they declined to attack us. . . . Commissioners were appointed, and after a parley, the Twenty-sixth was marched across the brook, and formed in line of battle on the field fronting the Vermonters. The hills were covered with spectators, and the eagerness to witness the novel contest knew no bounds. Companies A and B were thrown out as skirmishers. Company E occupied the right, C was given the centre and F rested on the left. The Colonel dashed over the field in all directions, encouraging the men to stand fast, amid the blue wreathe curling from a "brier wood" nonchalantly held in his left hand, and the Adjutant danced about on a spirited charger, apparently impatiently awaiting the hour of contest, the light of battle dilating within his eyes, and a quid of "navy plug" reposing beneath his cheek. . . . The line being formed and everything in readiness for the contest, a red flag was raised as a signal, and in a breath of time a strong body of the enemy drove in our skirmishers, and fiercely attacked our centre. At the same moment another strong force advanced against our right, but only as a feint; for they suddenly wheeled to the right, and joined their comrades in a furious charge on our centre. Major Morris ordered up Company E from our right, but too late to be of any advantage, and they were completely cut off from the main body of our army. Although flanked and pressed in front by overwhelming numbers, our centre heroically contested the advance of the enemy. Animated by the presence of the Colonel, they fought like veterans, and the white snow balls eddied through the air like popping corn from a frying pan. But the enemy were madly surging upon us in superior force and it was hardly within the power of human endurance to stand such a perfect *feu d'infer* any longer. Gradually the centre fell back inch by inch, the line then wavered to and fro, and finally the men broke in confusion and rolled down the hill followed by the victorious Vermonters. . . .

The boys never rallied. Lieutenant Woods made an attempt to rally them and form them in hollow square on the fortified hill to the right, but he was mistaken by the boys for a Vermonter, and unceremoniously pelted from their midst. But the Colonel was not totally deserted by his men. The Vermonters seized his horse by the bridle, and made a desperate attempt to take him prisoner. The fight at this point was terrific— beyond description. The men fought hand to hand. Colonel Seaver, the Achilles of the day, dashed through the combatants, seized Colonel

Morrison by the shoulder and called upon him to surrender; but his demand was choked by the incessant patter of snow balls on his
"physog. . . ." Amid the wild excitement consequent upon the shouting,
the rearing and plunging of horses, the Col. was drawn from his saddle
and taken by the enemy. Most of his "staff" followed him as prisoners. A
desperate attempt was made to rescue him, but it proved of no avail.
Major Morris fared no better. Adjutant White, however, made a bold attempt to retrieve the fortunes of the day. Dashing into the dense ranks
of the foe, he seized the bridle of Colonel Stoughton's Bucephalus and
gallantly attempted the impossibility of capturing the Colonel. . . . This
was at last observed by a shrewd Yankee, who dexterously slipped between the two horses, detached the supporting knee, and the Adjutant
fell from his lofty position like a tornado-stricken oak. This fall disheartened the Twenty-sixth, and only detached parties of a dozen scattered
over the field persisted in an obstinate resistance. The "Sergeant" received a solid shot in the back of the head, and was borne to the rear a
captive, and then, "The bugles sang truce."

Thus ended the great battle . . . unequaled in desperateness, and the
theme of many a future poet's cogitations. Our loss was very heavy, and
we were severely defeated. The spectators, acting on the well known
principle of kicking a man when he is down, pitched into us most un-
mercifully when our centre was broken, and prevented us from reform-
ing in line of battle. The slaughter of the enemy was fearful, and the
prowess of the Newark ball-players and fire men was displayed on their
battered visages. . . . The following is a fair recapitulation of the casualties on both sides: Bloody noses, 53, bunged peepers, 81, extraordinary
phrenological developments, 29, shot in the neck after the engagement,
unknown.[13]

By early March, Hooker had succeeded in reviving the spirits of the Army
of the Potomac. It took the enlisted men little time to see that at last they
had a commander who, as one said, "knew what to do and was going to do
it." Said another: "General Hooker enjoys the confidence of the troops under his command, and they have more . . . enthusiasm under him than under any other General."[14] The steadily improving April weather brought
with it increasing signs that something was afoot. Yankee observation balloons were airborne, and cavalry units ranged up and down the Rappahannock reconnoitering Rebel positions. "During the last few days," wrote the
chaplain of the Twenty-sixth Regiment in mid-April, "former quiet has
given place to change and commotion. . . . The plan of the campaign no one
seems able to divine. Gen. Hooker keeps his counsels well."[15]

Hooker's plan for the first great offensive of 1863 was a good one. Instead of striking directly at the heavily fortified heights at the rear of Fredericksburg, as Burnside had done with such disastrous results in December, Hooker proposed a classic pincer movement: Half of his army would march north along the Rappahannock River to Kelly's Ford, well above Fredericksburg, cross the river there, plunge south through a boggy forest known locally as The Wilderness, emerging at the enemy's rear, a few miles east of Chancellorsville; meanwhile, to divert Lee's attention, the other half of the Union army would cross the Rappahannock below Fredericksburg. If all went well, the Confederates would be caught between the two halves of the Union army. "My plans are perfect," Hooker told anyone who would listen, "and when I start to carry them out, may God have mercy on General Lee, for I will have none!"

On April 27 the Army of the Potomac broke camp. Ten New Jersey regiments joined the blue columns that hiked north to the fords above Fredericksburg. Crossing the Rappahannock and Rapidan Rivers unopposed, they pushed through The Wilderness, reaching Chancellorsville early on April 30. The Union's Sixth Corps, assigned the job of crossing the river below Fredericksburg, stepped off on April 28, made its way across on pontoons, and began entrenching the next day. Among its forty-seven regiments were eleven from New Jersey.

Genuinely surprised at first by Hooker's flanking movement, General Lee waited two days before deciding that the Yankee bridgehead below Fredericksburg was a feint. Once he realized that the main Union threat came from the north, Lee divided his forces, sending the bulk of his army toward The Wilderness with instructions to repulse the enemy. On May 2 and 3, the Confederates did just that, mounting a series of fearsome attacks all along the Union lines that came near to routing the entire army. Only by superhuman effort was a defensive perimeter established; on May 3 Union soldiers broke off the fight and retreated toward the safety of the river.

The Eleventh New Jersey, commanded by Colonel McAllister, distinguished itself at Chancellorsville, fighting almost nonstop for three days. On the evening of May 2 the regiment was formed in line of battle near the Chancellor House, General Hooker's headquarters, wrote First Sergeant John H. Smith:

Darkness came—the moon rose, and then, yelling like incarnate fiends, the rebel horde tried to break our first line. But a wall of flame flashed along our front, the rattle of musketry deepened into a roar, steady and unbroken; distant rebel batteries in our immediate rear opened their brazen mouths. The air grew hot and oppressive, the very vault of heaven seemed about to crack, and a sound as of roaring waters appeared to fill the atmosphere, varied with the whiz of bullets, the crack of artillery, the bursting of shell, the crash of timber, and the yells and cheers that arose again and again to be devoured in the louder roar of arms. . . .

"Soon after sunrise the fight opened in our front," continued Smith.

Ours being the second line of battle, we were not so exposed in the commencement; but the line in front at last gave way on our left. Our regiment immediately executed a left half wheel, in order to check the enemy with the fire of our full front, but hardly had this maneuver been accomplished ere it was ascertained that the regiment supporting us on the right had given way, and the enemy were flanking us in that direction. Our line was immediately swung around . . . and we again faced the foe in a new direction. The fighting here was terrible! Solid shot tore the ground about us and the storm of lead was terrific. Trees eight and ten inches through were cut off and hurled through the air as though but twigs, and the pattering of bullets as they struck the trees was not unlike the clatter of hailstones upon a roof. But to remain with our right and left unprotected was certain destruction, yet we fell back slowly, leaving our wounded in the woods, and when once in the opening we rallied and charged back in the bushes. Again and again did we rally and charge, but we were outnumbered, and rallying finally about the colors we brought them off across the plank road through a murderous fire of solid shot and shell. Regiments had become mixed and confused, but taking up a position in the open field, our regiment joined in a final charge upon the rifle pits on the left. But the tatterdemallion rebel horde were pouring *en masse* over the knolls and the charge was of no avail. Retreating to the Chancellor building, and supporting a battery, we were again subject to a murderous fire of artillery. The Chancellor building, used as a hospital and filled with wounded, was shelled and burned with its wretched inmates, and the wounded left in the woods perished in great numbers from the leaves taking fire.[16]

To the south, meantime, unaware of the debacle at Chancellorsville, the Sixth Corps prepared to storm Mayre's Heights, a heavily fortified position that was the key to Rebel defenses. The Twenty-first and Twenty-sixth New Jersey regiments, together with troops from New York, Maine, and Vermont, were assigned to assault Lee's Hill, just south of the Heights. "I was in the fight," wrote Sergeant-Major Cummings of the Twenty-sixth. "I waved my sword, fired a musket, yelled, cursed, and swore as much as anybody, I saw enough to satisfy the most bloodthirsty."

The distance between the road in which we lay and the bottom of the hills on which the rebel batteries were situated was probably three-fourths of a mile, and these flats were seamed with three ditches beside the railroad cut, which was quite deep. Another deep ditch was situated at the foot of the rebel ridge, in which were concealed the enemy's riflemen. To the 2d Vermont, 26th New Jersey, and a regiment from the Light Brigade, was assigned the arduous task of storming the enemy's position. . . . To say that I was pleased to hear that the Twenty-sixth was among the honored ones selected for the fearful work in front would be a lie. I actually turned pale, and could hardly repress a shiver at the bare thought. I never could believe it possible that we could storm those heights, fortified as they were, when the veterans of many a hard-fought field had twice been repulsed from them while in their crude state. A splendid brick house lay on the side of the hill directly in our front, and behind it a battery of bright brass pieces was belching shell and solid shot toward us continually. We were ordered to charge a battery situated on the hill a little to the right of a natural indentation on the hillside running parallel to the side of the house.

At ten o'clock . . . the signal for the charge was given. Our batteries were already piling the positions of the enemy with shell. "Forward, Twenty-sixth!" shouted the Colonel, and over the high bank we went at a double quick. My heart was in my mouth in an instant at the very idea of a nine months regiment on such a desperate charge, and yet I had been told that new troops were better than old ones in bayonet charges. Hardly had we debouched upon the plain before the enemy's guns had opened upon us, and the shot and shell were already screeching above our ranks. With a yell, however, the boys pressed forward in fine style, clearing the first ditch, and still preserving a good line. Already the shrieks and heart-rending groans of the wounded were heard, but the cheers overbalanced the groans. The shells howled above us with a most fearful energy, and we could hardly hear the commands of our Colonel, but could see him in front, almost standing in his saddle and bravely waving us onward with his sword. The railroad was passed, but within its protecting banks numerous "dead beats" sought a shelter from the iron hail mercilessly bursting above us. In vain Major Morris called them cowards, and applied his sword to their backs. Fear had in a measure paralyzed them, and they lay upon their bellies like overturned statues. . . .

Once more the word was "Forward!" and once more the regiment raised a feeble shout, and again broke forward at a double quick. Another ditch was crossed. Half the plain was behind us. The men were out of breath, and becoming exhausted. The rebels had obtained our range, and were doing fearful execution in our ranks. The men began to scatter and drop upon the turf. The wounded shrieked pitifully, and dead men rolled upon the ground like logs of wood. The moment was an exciting one. "Forward, boys!" shouted the Colonel, and the command was repeated by the Major. The "dead beats" were pricked forward, and again the regiment pressed to the front, first by the right and then by the left flanks, confusing the range of the enemy's guns as much as possible. The incessant roar of artillery and the pitiless explosion of shells rendered it impossible for the orders to be clearly heard, and the men scattered like a mess of chickens; but still each one pressed individually toward the heights. "Your brother is shot!" shouted one of the boys to me, and at the same moment a shell exploded so near that I absolutely thought my head was off, I had no time to think. . . . A shell exploded beneath the Lieutenant Colonel's horse, nearly lifting him from his saddle, but his only reply was "Forward, men—act like Jerseymen!" and toward the heights the reeling human wave again surged.

Three-quarters of the distance was passed. The regiment was much scattered, despite the gallant efforts of its field officers. Shells were exploding every second above them; the rebel riflemen had opened upon us from the ditch at the foot of the hill, and a tempest of grape and cannister was rained upon us from above. It was too much. The column of brave Jerseymen reeled like a ship in a storm, and the officer of the picket line implored our Colonel to fall back 'ere it was too late, as the attempt to storm the batteries must prove futile. Faster and faster fell the iron tempest, and symptoms of a break became discernable. But no; the 2d Vermont had reached the ditch on our right, and were gallantly cheering us onward. Our spirits revived, and with one last yell of determined energy the men pressed forward, drove the sharpshooters from the ditch, and mounted the hill, carrying everything before them. The rebels were flying in dismay, and throwing away everything. Any quantity of knapsacks, blankets and equipments were strewn through the woods. The heights of Fredericksburg were ours![17]

The Twenty-sixth suffered five killed, forty-eight wounded, and seventy-one missing in the attack on Lee's Hill and the fighting later at Salem Church. But it was all for nothing. On May 5 the Sixth Corps retreated across the Rappahannock, pulling up its pontoon bridges behind it. By the morning of May 6 the Army of the Potomac was once again on the north side of the river, minus 17,000 casualties.

New Jersey's reaction to Hooker's defeat was milder than might have been expected. Though appalled at the heavy losses, the state was not plunged into that same despondency that had followed earlier defeats. Some saw in the curious response an indifference spawned by two years of fruitless warfare. Others, perhaps nearer the mark, suggested a new resolve among the people that this war would be fought to an end, no matter the cost in blood and treasure. Predictably, the Copperhead press called for an end to the killing. "The Army of the Potomac has suffered another dreadful reverse," wrote the *Bergen Democrat* on May 15. The public, it said, should "repair to our closets, and on bended knees, entreat ALMIGHTY GOD to stop the dreadful carnage, and the inhuman merciless butchery which is desolating the land and disgracing civilization." In Somerville, the pro-Democrat *Messenger* reported the huge toll of dead and wounded: "Once more the gallant Army of the Potomac, controlled by an imbecile department and led by an incompetent general, has been marched to fruitless slaughter."[18] The *Orange Journal,* generally pro-Lincoln, conceded that "the incapacity or want of success in the conduct of the war by the administration at Washington have well nigh discouraged the country." Calling upon the public to throw off its feelings of "despondency and indifference," the paper urged "immediate and efficient action" to raise still more troops "to supply the places of the fallen."

However we may deplore the immense loss of life that has already taken place and which must necessarily continue whilst the war lasts, that painful consideration even should induce no one to slacken his efforts in support of the government. Whatever may have caused the war, though a fit subject for consideration at any time, should not influence our action in the performance of our duty to our country. There is no other way now than to fight until the rebels shall cease to resist the legal authorities and submit to the constitution.[19]

New Jersey's Twenty-seventh Regiment, recruited in Morris and Sussex Counties, was held in reserve during the battle of Fredericksburg, then ordered south to Fortress Monroe, Virginia, in mid-February. In March new orders came assigning the regiment to General Burnside's command, then chasing after Rebels in Kentucky and East Tennessee. On May 5 the Twenty-seventh was attempting to cross the Cumberland River when tragedy struck:

In the morning bright and early we started for the Cumberland River, a distance of thirteen miles. We reached its banks at 3 o'clock p.m. The means of ferrying us over was flat boats—or, rather, coal barges—thirty feet long. To prevent the boats being washed down by the current two ropes were stretched across like a letter V, the two uniting in one on the opposite shore. The means of propelling us consisted of six men placed in the bow of the boat, who would grab the rope, pull, let go and grab again. The upper boat was used by the infantry, while the artillery and transportation train were carried over by the lower boat. All the companies with the exception of parts of companies C, B, and L had passed over without accident. Fifty or sixty men were carried over at each trip. Captain [John T.] Alexander was in command of Company L. The boat that contained these companies had reached within forty feet of the opposite bank when the men at the bow lost hold of the rope and could not regain it. The boat started down stream, driven by a rapid current. The men became panic stricken and rushed to the opposite end of the boat, which caused it to sink, and in less time than it has taken me to write this account the whole boat-load was swept by the lower rope into the rapid Cumberland. Those who could swim were seized by the death grasp of those who could not swim. It was an awful sight. May God spare me from being again a spectator of such a scene. The men had on their cartridge boxes, filled with sixty rounds, and were fully armed, and equipped with tents, overcoats, blankets etc., which hindered many from saving themselves. I saw Captain Alexander and Orderly Sergeant [Albert D.] Wiggins go down. . . . After the accident we remained on the bank for a day for the purpose of recovering the bodies that might float to our side of the river, as the rebels held the other side.[20]

Thirty-three soldiers drowned, including nineteen men in Company L, all of them from Morris County's Rockaway Township.

Death from enemy or friendly fire, wounds, sickness, accidents, and desertions thinned the ranks of Jersey's regiments. If caught, deserters were routinely court-martialed, fined, flogged, imprisoned, or sentenced to make up time lost. Only a few were executed, usually to set an example. On June 19, a private in the Thirteenth Regiment paid the ultimate penalty for his cowardice.

Two members of the Forty-sixth Pennsylvania . . . and Christopher Krubart, of Co. B, Thirteenth Regiment, had been found guilty of desertion and were sentenced to be shot. . . . The day was a perfect one. The sky was cloudless; the sun shone resplendent. . . . When the information first reached the troops, a hushed stillness pervaded the whole of the First Division, and as the drums of the different Regiments beat the first "Assembly" call, the men marched to their positions with sobered looks. The order announcing the findings and sentence of the court martial was read, and a detail, to comprise the firing party, was ordered from the Division, the Regiments to which the condemned men belonged being exempt. Promptly at twelve o'clock each Brigade of the Division proceeded to the place of execution and formed a "hollow square." The marching of the troops, their formation into line, the subdued voices in which the officers repeated the various commands, the deep thud of the rifles as they came simultaneously to the ground at the command "Order Arms," and the rigid aspect of the men as they took the position of "Parade Rest," formed a grand, impressive, solemn and never to be forgotten sight. The wagons containing the coffins soon rumbled upon the scene, followed by an ambulance, closely guarded, containing the doomed men. Arriving at the spot where the three graves had been dug, a coffin was placed at the head of each, and the condemned men seated upon them. Their eyes were blindfolded, their hands tied behind their backs and their feet fastened in front. The firing party comprised thirty-six men in all, eight being detailed to each of the condemned men, with twelve men as a reserve. The guns had been loaded at Division headquarters under the personal supervision of the Provost-Marshal of the Division, three rifles being left unloaded. When the firing party received their rifles not one of them knew, therefore, whether his gun contained a blank cartridge or a ball. They marched with slow and measured step to the place of execution, the details comprising the firing party taking their assigned position a short distance in front of the unfortunate men, the reserve being placed in position to the rear of the centre detail. The death sentence was then read, and Chaplain Beck, of the Thirteenth Regiment, offered a short prayer. The officer in command of the firing party gave the order, "Ready," every piece came to the proper position, and then omitting the word "aim" commanded "FIRE!" A sharp report followed, and three lifeless bodies fell backward upon their coffins. The troops were then marched past the graves and the men shudderingly looked upon the ghastly sight. Krubart's body was pierced by seven balls in the vicinity of the heart. No burial service was read. The bodies were placed in the coffins prepared for them, and at once consigned to mother earth.[21]

The First New Jersey Cavalry was one of the Union Army's best mounted regiments, fighting in almost a hundred engagements with great dash and bravery. Under the command of an English soldier of fortune, Sir Percy Wyndham, the regiment was ordered to take part in a reconnaisance in force sent by General Hooker to scout out the whereabouts of the Rebel army. On June 9, 10,000 Federal cavalry, joined by artillery and infantry, crossed the Rappahannock some twenty-five miles above Fredericksburg and almost immediately surprised 8,000 Confederate cavalry camped at Brandy Station under the command of General J.E.B. Stuart. The ensuing twelve-hour engagement, the greatest cavalry battle ever fought on American soil, nearly resulted in Stuart's capture. When it was over the Rebels just barely held the field, but the Union cavalry, usually hopelessly outclassed by Confederate horse soldiers, had shown that it could hold its own with the best of them. "It was the prettiest cavalry fight that you ever saw," said Adjutant Marcus L. W. Kitchen afterward. "At four o'clock on the morning of the 9th we . . . got across the Ford [of the Rappahannock] without interruption or discovery." Captain P. Jones Yorke of Company I "was in the advance, and as we moved he managed so well that he bagged every picket on the road. Thus we had got almost upon the rebel camp before we were discovered."[22]

As [the rebel cavalry] hastily formed to receive us, the First New Jersey Cavalry dashed out of the woods, charging down among them. Without even an attempt to charge, the rebel line broke in confusion; and driving them back, pell-mell, the regiment pressed upon their rear. With a hundred and fifty prisoners, taken by a body of only two hundred and fifty-nine enlisted men, the regiment then rallied and re-formed for the greater work before them.

Nearly half a mile apart, on two eminences of a continuous line of hill, stood a couple of country houses. . . . At the one facing the right of the line General Stuart had established his headquarters, and each of them was protected by a battery of horse artillery. Leaving the First Pennsylvania Regiment to support his battery, Wyndham formed the First Jersey for a charge. Lieutenant-Colonel [Virgil] Broderick was at its head, and in column of battalions it advanced, with a steady trot, its line more accurate than ever in parade. As it passed over the difficult ground in the vicinity of the railroad, there was danger of its front being compressed by the narrowness of the defile. Without a pause, [Lt. John] Hobensack led the left squadron of the first line down the steep bank of the cutting and up the other side—a steep descent and rise of nine feet each way, taken by the whole body without a waver or hesitation. While the right squadrons of the other battalions followed Broderick against Stuart's headquarters, the left wings, under [Captain John

H.] Lucas and [Lieutenant Moses] Maulsbury, accompanied Hobensack and dashed at the hill on which stood the other battery. So rapid
was the advance of both columns that the batteries of the enemy endeavored in vain to get range upon them; while our own guns . . .
played with terrible effect upon the stationary rebel line. With a ringing cheer Broderick rode up the gentle ascent that led to Stuart's headquarters, the men gripping hard their sabres, and the horses taking
ravines and ditches in their stride. As the rebels poured in a random
and ineffectual volley, the troopers of the First Jersey were among
them, riding over one gun, breaking to pieces the brigade in front of
them, and forcing the enemy in confusion down the opposite slope of
the hill. Stuart's headquarters were in our hands, and his favorite regiments in flight before us. . . . By the same orderly who carried off Stuart's official papers, Wyndham ordered up a section of his battery and
the regiment of Pennsylvanians. Leaving the artillery to the support of
the First Maryland, the noble Pennsylvanians came to the attack. It
was time that they did so; for a fresh brigade of rebels was charging the
hundred men of Broderick. Gallantly did the Lieutenant-Colonel meet
the charge. As the enemy advanced, down against them rode our men:
Broderick and his adjutant in front, [Captains] Hart, Wynkoop, Cox,
Jemison, Harper, Sawyer, Brooks and Hughes, all in their places, leading their respective men. With a crash, in went the little band of Jerseymen into the leading rebel regiment, the impetus of the attack
scattering the faltering enemy in confusion right and left. Through the
proud Twelfth Virginia they then rode, with no check to their headlong
onset; and with dripping sabres and panting steeds emerged into the
field beyond. No longer in line of battle, fighting hand to hand with
small parties of the enemy, and with many a wounded horse sinking to
the earth, they met a third regiment of the rebels, no longer faltering
before an unbroken enemy, but rushing eagerly upon the scattered
groups of combatants. Even in this emergency the confidence of the
men was not shaken in their leaders. Against that swarm of opposers
each individual officer opposed himself, with such men as collected
round him; and slowly fighting, breaking the enemy with themselves
into bands of independent combatants, the Jersey fell back up the
bloody hillside.[23]

Two of the Rebel horsemen rode straight at Adjutant Kitchen, who had
been left alone for a moment. "The crowd with whom Broderick was engaged was a little distance from me," remembered Kitchen, "and I had just
wheeled to ride up to his help when two fellows put at me."

The first one fired at me and missed; before he could again cock his revolver I succeeded in closing with him. My sabre took him just in the neck, and must have cut the jugular. The blood gushed out in a black looking stream; he gave a horrible yell and fell over the side of his horse, which galloped away. Then I gathered up my reins, spurred my horse, and went at the other one. I was riding the old black horse that used to belong to the signal sergeant, and it was in fine condition. As I drove in the spurs it gave a leap high in the air. That plunge saved my life. The rebel had a steady aim at me; but the ball went through the black horse's brain. His feet never touched ground again. With a terrible convulsive contraction of all his muscles, the black turned over in the air, and fell on his head and side stone dead, pitching me twenty feet. I lighted on my pistol, the butt forcing itself far into my side. My sabre sprang out of my hand, and I lay, with arms and legs abroad, stretched out like a dead man. Everybody had something else to do than to attend to me, and there I lay where I had fallen.

It seemed to me to have been an age before I began painfully to come to myself; but it could not have been many minutes. Every nerve was shaking; there was a terrible pain in my head, and a numbness through my side which was even worse. Fighting was still going on around me, and my first impulse was to get hold of my sword. I crawled to it, and sank down as I grasped it once more. That was only for a moment; for a rebel soldier, seeing me move, rode at me. The presence of danger roused me, and I managed to get to my horse, behind which I sank, resting my pistol on the saddle, and so contriving to get an aim. As soon as the man saw that, he turned off without attacking me. I was now able to stand and walk; and holding my pistol in one hand and my sabre in the other, I made my way across the fields to where our battery was posted, scaring some with my pistol and shooting others. Nobody managed to hit me through the whole fight. When I got up to the battery I found [Bugler James] Wood there. He sang out to me to wait and he would get me a horse. One of the men, who had just taken one, was going past, so Wood stopped him and got it for me.

Just at that moment [a rebel] battalion and some other troops came charging at the battery. . . . There was one rebel, on a splendid horse, who sabred three gunners while I was chasing him. He wheeled in and out, would dart away, and then come sweeping back and cut down another man in a manner that seemed almost supernatural. We at last succeeded in driving him away, but we could not catch or shoot him, and he got off without a scratch.[24]

In the middle of the fight, Broderick's horse fell dead beneath him.

Instantly his young orderly bugler, James Wood, sprang to the earth and remounted him. While the bugler himself sought for another horse, a rebel trooper rode at him with an order to surrender. As Wood was taken to the rear, he came upon a carbine lying upon the ground. Seizing it and leveling it at his captor, he forced the man to change places with him; and thus, with an empty weapon, repossessed himself of arms and horse, together with a prisoner. . . .

In the meantime, the left wing of the regiment had directed its efforts upon the other battery of the rebels. Keeping to the trot, their unbroken ranks moved steadily against the hill, on whose top stood the cannoneers and a few horsemen observing their approach. As they came nearer, all these men disappeared except one, who maintained his position; and as they came within two hundred yards of the summit, this man lifted his hat, beckoning with it to those in his rear. In one moment the whole hillside was black with rebel cavalry, charging down as foragers, pistol and carbine in hand. Hobensack glanced along his squadron. Not a man was out of place, and every horse was taking the gallop without a blunder or over-rush of speed. At the sight of this united band of enemies, the confused rebel crowd hesitated and shook. With an ill-directed, futile volley, they began to break away, and the next moment, a shrieking mass of fugitives, they were flying before the sabres of our men. The rebel battery of four guns was left with but two men near it, and with their eyes fixed upon it our officers pressed upon the fugitives. When within a hundred yards of the guns, and when looking over the hill, Lucas could see yet another brigade coming in the distance to reenforce the broken enemy, an ejaculation from Hobensack caused him to turn his eyes to his own rear. There was the main body of the force that had broken the right wing, coming in line of battle full upon their rear.

"Boys, there's a good many of them, but we must cut through," bellowed an officer. "Charge!"

Enthusiasm and desperation supplied the place of numbers, and cutting their way out, the little band opened a path toward the section of our battery. Three times was the guidon of Company E taken by the enemy. Twice it was retaken by our men; and the third time, when all seemed desperate, a little troop of the First Pennsylvania cut through the enemy and brought off the flag in safety. Once the rebels who hung upon the rear attempted to charge our retiring men; but the wheel of the rear division sufficed to check their assault, and the left wing of the Jersey reached Clark's two guns, annoyed only by the revolvers of the rebels. . . .

Broderick was dying in the enemy's hands; Shelmire lay dead across the body of a rebel; Sawyer and Hyde Crocker were prisoners; Lieutenant Brooks was disabled by a sabre stroke on his right arm; Wyndham himself had just received a bullet in his leg. Men and horses had been fighting for over three hours, and were now utterly exhausted. . . . The enemy were indeed terribly demoralized, and the charge of a dozen of our men again and again routed a hundred of the rebels; but now there were not a dozen horses that could charge—not a man who could shout above a whisper. The guns were across a ditch, which rendered their removal very difficult; and it was their fire which kept the rebels from crossing the hills to charge against us. So, with a desperate hope that [reinforcements] might come up after all, our worn-out troopers stood by the gallant cannoneers of the Sixth New York Independent Battery— New Yorkers by commission, but Jerseymen of Rahway in their origin.

Presently the apprehended moment came, and the last reserves of the rebels, fresh and strong, poured down on three sides upon the exhausted little knot of Jersey troopers. While the cavalry fought hand to hand across the guns, the artillerymen continued steadily serving their pieces and delivering their fire at the enemy upon the hill. Time after time, as a rebel trooper would strike at a cannoneer, he would dodge beneath a horse or a gun-carriage, and coming up on the other side, discharge his revolver at his assailant, and spring once more to his work. At length, from mere exhaustion, Hart, Hobensack and Beekman, with their comrades were forced back a little way from the guns; and while they were forming the men afresh, the rebels rode again upon the cannoneers.

As one of the gunners was ramming home a charge, a rebel officer cut him down, with three successive sabre strokes. Then, springing from his horse, he wheeled the piece toward our troopers, not fifty yards away. Hobensack turned to Hart, stretched out his hand, and said: "We must shut our eyes and take it. Good-bye!" and clasping each other's hands, they waited for their death. The roar of the piece thundered out, and the smoke wrapped them in its folds; but the charge flew harmlessly over their heads. The piece had been elevated against the hill, and the rebels had not thought of changing its angle. They were so savage at the harmlessness of the discharge, that they actually advanced halfway towards our men; but beyond that they dared not come; and the Jersey regiment marched calmly off the field without an effort being made to pursue them.[25]

Although the First Cavalry suffered fifty-two casualties at Brandy Station, its morale was never higher. "When the memory of the fight comes over me," wrote Kitchen, "I get almost as enthusiastic and excited as when it was going on. I am so proud of the regiment, officers and men."[26]

Brandy Station was merely a prelude to the historic battle at Gettysburg, the crucial turning point in the war. Since early June the Confederate army had been moving northward according to an audacious plan worked out at a conference in Richmond weeks before. Worried that Grant was on the verge of capturing Vicksburg, thus reopening the Mississippi and detaching Texas, Arkansas and Louisiana from the Confederacy, President Davis had proposed sending elements of Lee's army westward, where they could hook up with the beleaguered defenders and relieve the siege. Unwilling to weaken his army, Lee proposed instead a second invasion of the North. His army would march through the Shenandoah Valley, cross into Maryland, then plunder southern Pennsylvania. With his forces positioned to threaten Baltimore, Philadelphia, and even Washington, Lee felt confident that Federal troops would be recalled from the west, easing the pressure on Vicksburg. It was admittedly a gamble, but if the Confederates were able to deal a decisive blow to the Yankee army on its own soil, perhaps the North would sue for peace; at the least, France and Britain might finally recognize the Confederate States.

News that the Rebel army was approaching the Susquehanna River, less than sixty miles from New Jersey, set off a general panic. Besieged by demands that he take action, on June 17 Governor Parker called for volunteers:

JERSEYMEN! The State of Pennsylvania is invaded! A hostile army is now occupying and despoiling the towns of our sister State. She appeals to New Jersey . . . to aid in driving back the invading army. Let us respond to this call upon our patriotic State with unprecedented zeal. I therefore call upon the citizens of this State to meet and organize into companies, and report to the Adjutant General of the State as soon as possible, to be organized into Regiments as the Militia of New Jersey, and press forward to the assistance of Pennsylvania in this emergency.[27]

Nearly seven hundred men responded to the governor's call, and hastily entrained for Harrisburg. At home even the Copperheads saw the danger. The *Newark Daily Journal* supported the governor's call for volunteers;

the *Freehold Democrat* called Lee's invasion the worst crisis of the war.[28] "The best place to defend New Jersey today is on the banks of the Susquehanna," said the *Newark Daily Mercury*:

While there is apparently no danger apprehended of an invasion of our own State, yet Pennsylvania, it must be remembered, slept in fancied security two weeks ago. If Hooker should suffer a disastrous defeat, and the rebel army cross the Susquehanna, there is nothing in the world to prevent them from visiting Northern New Jersey, striking the Delaware at its upper waters, and entering this State at Easton or its neighborhood, the river being fordable at many points. Should they do so, their cavalry could easily ride from one end of the State to the other, and nothing could stop them. That this can be done experience shows plainly.[29]

On June 28 the Army of the Potomac got its fifth commander in less than a year when Lincoln, convinced that Hooker was not the man to turn back the Rebel invasion, named Major General George G. Meade in his place. When Meade took over the army, the main Federal force was near Frederick, Maryland, some thirty-five miles south of Gettysburg. Lee's army was divided, with part near Chambersburg, Pennsylvania, a corps at York, threatening to cross the Susquehanna, and the remainder at Carlisle, preparing to attack Harrisburg, the state capital. When word reached Lee that the Federal army was north of the Potomac, he decided to concentrate his scattered forces near the hamlet of Cashtown. Early on the morning of July 1 a division of Confederates broke camp at Cashtown and set out for Gettysburg, eight miles west, hoping to capture a much-needed supply of shoes. Instead, the graybacks ran into elements of a Federal cavalry division patrolling just west of the village. What began as a chance encounter soon became a furious three-day battle, a dreadful blood bath that left a staggering 50,000 casualties in its wake.

The fifteen New Jersey units that fought at Gettysburg, still on the march when the battle began, missed the first day's fighting. On July 2 Battery B of the First New Jersey Light Artillery, armed with six ten-pound Parrott guns, deployed near the base of Little Round Top, then moved forward to Sherfy's peach orchard. When a massive Confederate attack on the Union lines came late that afternoon, nearly eighty Federal guns awaited the signal to fire. "Hold this position while you have a shot in your limbers or a man to work your guns," the Federal commanding general instructed Captain A. Judson Clark just before the Rebels attacked, and hold it Battery B did, firing 1,342 rounds, more than any other Union battery fired in any single day throughout the entire war. Twenty-two-year-old Private Michael Hanifen was one of the survivors:

About 3:15 the enemy opened again with a terrific artillery fire from front and right flank, and at half past three the enemy commenced moving down from our front and right in three columns. A cloud of skirmishers covered their front. We opened fire on them, immediately with shell and shrapnel, and every shot tore gaps in their ranks as they exposed a slight flank to us. . . . The enemy's second line, into which we were pitching shell, came up to the support of the first line. . . . As each one advanced they received a more galling fire from our line of artillery. . . . The Sixth and Eighth New Jersey regiment marched past our rear in quick time to reinforce our left, where the enemy were driving our troops. . . . and the Seventh New Jersey was posted in our rear for support. About 4 o'clock a spherical case shot exploded to the right of the first caisson, killing one horse. . . . A fragment of shell disemboweled the nigh pole horse; another took off his fore leg. I was holding him by the bridle; the team started to run, made a fine "left about," dragging horse and me fifty yards to the rear. . . . Banks, Williams, Vandine and I replaced the pole which was broken, divested the dead horse of harness, and our farrier, Fairchild, brought up some spare horses to replace similar losses. We put harness on a pair and pulled the caisson to its place in line. . . .

Timm, a gunner, and Riley, No. 5, had hold of a handspike to direct the line of fire of their gun. . . . A shell plunged into the ground under the trail and exploded under their feet. The trail flopped up and threw them twenty feet in the air; they fell together; Riley was underneath, both covered with blood and dirt. Timm scrambled to his feet, wiped the dirt out of his eyes, and asked Riley if he was hurt. He said, "By Jiminey, I didn't think they could touch me without taking a limb, and now, damn 'em, they have taken half the meat I did have." The shell had sheared all the flesh from Riley's right hip clear to the bone. . . . Sergt. Clairville called on the drivers to take the place of those wounded; as they took vacant positions. Riley stood still like one dazed. Lieut. Simms yelled at him, "Riley, why the bloody hell don't you roll that gun by hand to the front?" Riley turned his wounded hip and thigh to the Lieutenant's view and said, "Lieutenant, if your hip was shot off like that, what the bloody hell would you do?" He was ordered to go to the hospital, and went away on one foot and two hands like a lame dog. Caleb Harrison took the place of the injured No. 1. The sponge bucket was broken and its contents spilled. He cursed the Rebels. The spare bucket was put in place, and what little water was in our canteens emptied into it, after which he sponged and rammed home the shell, and the fire of the gun was directed to our opponent and Bonnell pulled the lanyard. We all said, "Take that for Riley." I was sent with seven or eight canteens to the spring near the Trostle house to fill them. As I passed the supporting regiment a shell exploded over the line, killing or wounding seven or eight men. The canteens filled, I faced to the south. A grand but terrible picture met my view. On the road near by, the Fifth Corps was marching to the left. Our left and front was a sheet of flame. The air was dotted with little balloons of white smoke, showing where shells had burst, and sent their deadly messengers to the fighting lines below. From Longstreet's right, all along to our right as far as one could see, the enemy's artillery was actively engaged, as shown by the white steam-like clouds of smoke arising from their battery positions. To the left I could see the enemy driving our men up the sides of the Little Round Top, and was rejoiced to see them driven back again. The Fifth Corps, which was miles away when the battle began, were hurried to the front to reinforce us. When I got back to the guns all hands had a refreshing drink of water. Some of the men said, "My God, but that is good, this is hotter than hell here."

Some of the war's bloodiest fighting took place in the peach orchard, in a wheatfield nearby, and at Devil's Den and on Little Round Top. Desperately, furiously, the men of both armies fought in 92-degree heat. By 5:30 p.m. Battery B's ammunition began to run low, just at the time another fresh Confederate division joined the attack. Orderly Sergeant Galbraith was sent to the rear to find John Cronk, who six-mule team was loaded with extra rounds.

About 6 o'clock Cronk came up on a dead run. Under orders, we were ready to jump into his wagon and unload the boxes of ammunition. How he sung oaths to those mules to keep them quiet under that fire, where a hundred shells were exploding every minute, and the crackle of his whip was like a sharp skirmish fire. . . . In returning from gun to caisson a shell exploded over me. The concussion threw me to the ground, and for a short time I was unconscious. Martin Donohue was bending over me when I became conscious, tears from his eyes falling on my face, and as I bathed my eyelids he inserted the nozzle of his canteen between my lips, and said, "Mike, shure you're not kilt entirely, for 'tis I would be lonesome without you." When I returned to the gun, which I did slowly, I was somewhat benumbed from shock. The query was, "Were you hit hard?" "No." "Bully boy! Hurry up the ammunition lively now, and we will give them hell yet. You see the devils are gaining ground on our left." There was a break in our line 500 yards to the left. A crippled battery was leaving the Peach Orchard on the right. A brigade of the enemy, with six battle flags, moved across our front and formed line near the Rose house. They advanced against us under a galling fire. We had been throwing shell and shrapnel into them, but have nothing left but canister. They broke back and reformed at 450 yards. Timm, under Clairville's direction, fired a round of canister at the leading regiment, the colors fell, making a beautiful gap in their line, which was closed up, and on they came. Capt. Clark passed from gun to gun, animating and encouraging the men, as cool and calm as if it was a battery drill. Old Bill had a stick in his hand in which he cut a notch for every shot fired, grumbled at the slightest error, telling us to keep cool and keep our shirts on. We were getting too wild, and might lose Old Betsey, No. 1 gun. As I handed the next two canisters to Elias Campbell, each containing 76 balls, he said, "This is the stuff to feed them; 'tis good for them; feed it to their bellies, Timm; mow them down, Timm." And Timm aimed to hit them in the middle of their anatomy, and they fell like grass before a mower's scythe. Harrison, who had sponged after every shot and rammed every load since Bauer was hurt, said, "Damn them, we are paying off for Riley now." During this time the front of the Battery was almost a sheet of flame; the men at the guns fairly flew to their work. The guns themselves seemed full of life; dogs of war, nearly red hot; how they roared and thundered! Shells of the enemy's guns were shrieking overhead, or throwing up clouds of dust and dirt where they exploded, bullets were zipping from front and flank. Sergt. McChesney and Bob Stuart were wounded badly, but still staid to work their guns. Splinters were flying from gun carriages and wheels. Horses were being killed and wounded, and taken out of harness, as they fell, by their drivers. At every gun were wounded men, many too slight for the hospital. They staid until the last shot was fired, and then rode out on the guns. Every one's shirt was soaked with sweat, some with blood. All were grimed with powder smoke, and not a man but kept to his work. . . . Our canister fire was too much for the charging column. It threw it into great confusion, and all who were not killed and wounded changed direction to the right when about 200 yards distant, and disappeared, seeking shelter behind the slope of a hill on our left, near the wheat field, which had become a veritable crater of a volcano, a very whirlwind of battle. Rebel yells and Yankee cheers alternated rapidly, as either side gained an advantage or reinforcement. There was an incessant roar of musketry and artillery, a rapid movement of troops. Now blue, now gray, as they emerged from the woods and rocks, and charged recklessly into each other's ranks, with yells and shouts and cheers, which were heard above the sound of musketry and artillery. The wheat field was reaped with the harvest of death. In our front were over 120 dead from three South Carolina regiments. At the Rose house and barn were 200 more. The last round of canister was fired. . . . The Captain gave the orders to limber up and go to the rear. . . . The infantry on our flanks had fallen back. The enemy were half way through the Peach Orchard on our right flank; as the wheels of the limber struck the trail the lead team was hit. Higgins jumped out of the saddle and cut the traces, and the gun drove off with four horses. A Rebel yelled, "Halt, you Yankee sons of bitches; we want those guns!" Ennis yelled back, "Go to hell! We want to use them yet awhile." At that moment the remnant of the Sixty-third Pennsylvania, who were lying in a sunken road, rose up and poured a volley into their faces, causing them to halt.

Battery B bivouacked for the night near a farm house. "Before the drivers dismounted Capt. Clark called all to 'Attention,' and said: 'Boys, those of you who survive this war will have reason to be proud of this day's work. I ask you all to return thanks to God that he brought you safely out of this day's battle.'"[30]

At 1 p.m. on the third day of battle 150 Rebel guns opened fire on the center of Meade's line, strung along the top of Cemetery Ridge. The largest Confederate bombardment of the war was only the prelude: Two hours later close to 15,000 Rebel infantry, three solid ranks of men extending more than a mile flank to flank, flags flying in the soft breeze, charged the Union line, General George Pickett's all-Virginia division in the van. Gloucester County's William Haines, a private with the Twelfth New Jersey, was nearly killed by a Confederate shell that landed in the midst of Company F, just as it was preparing a hasty meal:

[The rebel shell] fell on the rock we were sitting on, and bursted, scattering the little balls it was filled with all around us, but they seemed to have but little force; one of them struck Sergeant White's canteen and dented it. . . .

In less than a minute the shot and shell were flying in all directions; the air was full of them. . . . We lay flat on the ground, but could not lay long in any one position, so we turn over on our backs, look up and trace the course of the shells; we could see a dark line flit across overhead and

others across this towards every point of the compass. . . . I almost trem-
ble yet when I think what an awful din it made, the shrieking shells
bursting everywhere and the solid shot tearing through the house and
barn on our right, cutting the limbs off the trees in our rear, and some
striking the stone wall that covered some of our company. How we
hugged the ground behind the hog pen, thinking it might stop a shot or
shell. I believe, in times like this, each individual thinks that every shot
he hears coming near him is going to hit him. I wondered that no more
of us were hurt. While this artillery battle was being fought, one of our
caissons blew up, near the left of our regiment, a great column of smoke
rising up several hundred feet. . . . This battle lasted about an hour and
a half; it stopped as suddenly as it started. What a relief to be able to get
on our feet and stretch ourselves: some of us may have thought the
battle of Gettysburg ended; but, "Look! do you see them coming?" was
the cry on every side. General Hays rode along in front of our line shouting, "They are coming, boys; we must whip them, and you men with
buck and ball, don't fire until they get to that fence;" pointing to the
fence along the Emmittsburg road. That act of General Hays' caused
every man to determine to do his part, and I think every man thought we
would whip them. Their lines had been formed and advanced quite a
distance to the front before the cannonading ceased. We had no time to
care for our wounded; W. H. Park was lying under our feet groaning
with pain; he had been hit with a stone out of the wall he lay behind; no
one wanted to carry him to the rear, for the rear had become a dangerous place; in fact, there was no rear, it was all front, and our attention
just then was centered on the advancing foe. As we looked, I think the
grandest sight I ever witnessed unfolded itself to our view, as the different lines came marching toward us, their bayonets glistening in the sun,
from right to left, as far as the eye could reach; but on they come, their
officers mounted, riding up and down their lines. . . . The lines looked to
be as straight as a line could be, and at an equal distance apart. Everything was quiet until they had advanced about half the distance, when
pandemonium seemed to be let loose among our artillery; the ground
fairly shook under us. From the Round Tops to Cemetery Hill, the cannon hurled forth death and destruction in the advancing lines; we could
see our shells burst in their lines, and it looked as though they had all
been cut down in that place, but they would close up the gap and come
on again. At last they are within range of the infantry . . . but we still hold
our fire, they soon reach the fence, their ranks thinned but their formation unbroken, and then the real tug of war commenced. Like a sheet of

fire the Twelfth New Jersey hurled the buck and ball at them; they climb
the fences, with their lines all broken; they come on in companies and
squads quite up to our lines (as many fell within twenty paces of us).

At last the firing ceases, the battle is over, and we have a chance to
look around. As the smoke lifted, what a horrible sight; dead and dying
everywhere, the ground almost covered with them; their wounded and
prisoners coming into our lines by the hundreds; some crawling on their
hands and knees, others using two muskets as crutches; they are no
longer our foes—the last drop of water or the last hard tack was freely
given to them. What had become of those rebel lines that had advanced
so bravely across the fields? The first line had been annihilated; the second was retreating, all broken and shattered, one-half left behind: the
third, falling back in good order. Now we have time to look to our own
company and sum up our casualties. Albright is dead, shot in the head;
W. H. Park still lay on the ground, but now he is sent to the hospital; all
the other wounded were able to care for themselves.[31]

Pickett's charge had been thrown back, and with it Southern hopes for a
victory on Union soil. As Lee withdrew his beaten forces from Pennsylvania, the news that the Rebels had been whipped electrified the North. The
Paterson Daily Guardian published an extra edition heralding Meade's triumph. "The anxiety of the public to obtain copies was unprecedented," reported the paper.

The rush when the doors were opened was like the charge of an army on
a small scale. . . . Boys in the street sold again at all prices, until the
whole town was flooded with the good news. In our churches the matter
was referred to by our pastors, and in several patriotic songs were sung
in the evening by the rejoicing congregations. Such a day of joy we have
not seen since the war commenced.[32]

New Brunswick's citizens poured into the streets on the evening of June 6,
marching through the town in a joyful procession "illuminated with
torches and lanterns, while roman candles, rockets and bombs burst into
the air continually."[33] Newark held a great mass meeting in Military Park
attended by "large numbers of citizens, including many ladies."[34] When
word reached New Jersey that Vicksburg had surrendered, many believed
the war was nearly over. "The Republic is saved!" proclaimed Jersey City's
American Standard. "Who can fail to pour out from a full heart, joyful
thanks and grateful praises to Almighty God."

For the first since the outbreak of the rebellion we begin to see day. Lee's grand army has been broken, if not annihilated; Vicksburg has fallen, and its garrison are prisoners of war; our armies in vast and concentrated force are converging upon the heart of the South; the main strength and support of the rebellion has been snapped like a broken reed, and nothing now is wanting but the final crushing blow, which in the name of mercy, humanity, peace and restored Union, we hope may not be long delayed. . . . One week ago we were trembling and despondent. Our enemy seemed irresistible. . . . We expected with calm apathy that Harrisburg and Baltimore would be occupied by the invading foe, and even feared to hear that the National Capital had been reduced to ashes. Since then this powerful army has been crushed to atoms, and its pride laid low; its threatening thousands now fill a nameless grave in a strange land.[35]

The dead lay thickly on the ground at Gettysburg, both blue and gray. "The scenes on the field of battle defy description," wrote one soldier. "Beginning on the right of the Union line, the dead bodies of the enemy . . . presented a harrowing spectacle. They were so close together that it was impossible to walk over the ground without carefully selecting a spot for each step, and the broken muskets, straps, belts, clothing and implements of warfare . . . presented a demoralizing spectacle." There were so many dead that it became impossible to bury them all, and hundreds were merely covered with earth where they had fallen.[36]

On the evening of July 6 a pretty twenty-three-year-old Quaker girl from Salem County, Cornelia Hancock, arrived on the battlefield with her brother-in-law, a Philadelphia doctor, and a contingent of nurses. She had no training, and had been rejected as a nurse, but she was determined to help. What she saw utterly appalled her.

We arrived in the town . . . three days after the last day of battle. . . . Every barn, church, and building of any size in Gettysburg had been converted into a temporary hospital. We went the same evening to one of the churches, where I saw for the first time what war meant. Hundreds of desperately wounded men were stretched out on boards laid across the high-backed pews as closely as they could be packed together. The boards were covered with straw. Thus elevated, these poor sufferers' faces, white and drawn with pain, were almost on a level with my own. I seemed to stand breast-high in a sea of anguish.

The townspeople of Gettysburg were in devoted attendance, and there were many from other villages and towns. The wounds of all had been dressed at least once, and some systematic care was already established. Too inexperienced to nurse, I went from one pallet to another with pencil, paper, and stamps in hand, and spent the rest of that night in writing letters from the soldiers to their families and friends. To many mothers, sisters, and wives I penned the last message of those who were soon to become the "beloved dead."

Learning that the wounded of the . . . 12th Regiment of New Jersey were in a Field Hospital about five miles outside of Gettysburg, we determined to go there early the next morning, expecting to find some familiar faces among the regiments of my native state. As we drew near our destination we began to realize that war has other horrors than the sufferings of the wounded or the desolation of the bereft. A sickening, overpowering, awful stench announced the presence of the unburied dead, on which the July sun was mercilessly shining, and at every step the air grew heavier and fouler, until it seemed to possess a palpable horrible density that could be seen and felt and cut with a knife. Not the presence of the dead bodies themselves, swollen and disfigured as they were, and lying in heaps on every side, was as awful to the spectator as that deadly, nauseating atmosphere which robbed the battlefield of its glory, the survivors of their victory, and the wounded of what little chance of life was left to them.

As we made our way to a little woods in which we were told was the Field Hospital we were seeking, the first sight that met our eyes was a collection of semi-conscious but still living human forms, all of whom had been shot through the head, and were considered hopeless. They were laid there to die and I hoped that they were indeed too near death to have consciousness. Yet many a groan came from them, and their limbs tossed and twitched. The few surgeons who were left in charge of the battlefield after the Union army had started in pursuit of Lee had begun their paralyzing task by sorting the dead from the dying, and the dying from those whose lives might be saved; hence the groups of prostrate, bleeding men laid together according to their wounds.

There was hardly a tent to be seen. Earth was the only available bed during those first hours after the battle. A long table stood in this woods and around it gathered a number of surgeons and attendants. This was the operating table, and for seven days it literally ran blood. A wagon stood near rapidly filling with amputated legs and arms; when wholly filled, this gruesome spectacle withdrew from sight and returned as soon as possible for another load. So appalling was the number of the wounded as yet unsuccored, so helpless seemed the few who were battling against tremendous odds to save life, and so overwhelming was the demand for any kind of aid that could be given quickly, that one's senses were benumbed by the awful responsibility that fell to the living. Action of a kind hitherto unknown and unheard of was needed here and existed here only. From the pallid countenances of the sufferers, their inarticulate cries, and the many evidences of physical exhaustion which were common to all of them, it was swiftly borne in upon us that nourishment was one of the pressing needs of the moment and that here we might be of service. Our party separated quickly, each intent on carrying out her own scheme of usefulness. No one paid the slightest attention to us, unusual as was the presence of half a dozen women on such a field; nor did anyone have time to give us orders or to answer questions. Wagons of bread and provisions were arriving and I helped myself to their stores. I sat down with a loaf in one hand and a jar of jelly in the other: it was not hospital diet but it was food, and a dozen poor fellows lying near me turned their eyes in piteous entreaty, anxiously watching my efforts to arrange a meal. There was not a spoon, knife, fork or plate to be had that day, and it seemed as if there was no more serious problem under Heaven than the task of dividing that too well-baked loaf into portions that could be swallowed by weak and dying men. I succeeded, however, in breaking it into small pieces, and spreading jelly over each with a stick. A shingle board made an excellent tray, and it was handed from one to another. I had the joy of seeing every morsel swallowed greedily by those whom I had prayed day and night I might be permitted to serve. An hour or so later, in another wagon, I found boxes of condensed milk and bottles of whiskey and brandy. It was an easy task to mix milk punches and to serve them from bottles and tin cans emptied of their former contents. I need not say that every hour brought an improvement in the situation, that trains from the North came pouring into Gettysburg laden with doctors, nurses, hospital supplies, tents, and all kinds of food and utensils: but that first day of my arrival . . . was a time that taxed the ingenuity and fortitude of the living as sorely as if we had been a party of shipwrecked mariners thrown upon a desert island.[37]

Later that summer soldiers in the Gettysburg hospitals had a medal struck for the young woman one grateful New Jersey cavalryman rightly called "the Florence Nightingale of America."

FOUR

"It Was a Godforsaken Place"

THE HOME FRONT

New Jersey was the only Free State to reject Abraham Lincoln in both the 1860 and 1864 presidential elections. He lost the state in 1860 by a margin of 62,800 to 58,000. Four years later George B. McClellan, twice-dismissed commander of the Army of the Potomac, defeated the President by 7,300 votes. Little wonder, then, that New Jersey was a source of anguish to Unionists and an inspiration to opponents of the administration across the nation. An Illinois politician speaking before a Newark Lincoln-Johnson rally in 1864 admitted that he had come to New Jersey despite warnings that "there were no Lincoln men there and it was a Godforsaken place." An angry *New York Tribune* once declared: "In no other Free State are disloyal utterances so frequent and so bold as in New Jersey." New Jersey's Copperhead press, led by the *Trenton Daily True American* and the *Newark Daily Journal,* denounced the Republicans, the president, and the war unsparingly. Lincoln was a frequent target of vilification: The *Somerset Messenger* called him "a Presidential pygmy"; a Bergen County newspaper labeled him "a backwoods buffoon . . . the father of all iniquity"; and the *Newark Daily Journal* continually referred to him as that "smutty joker."[1]

In fact, New Jersey was never disloyal to the Union—the number of brave soldiers sent to the front is evidence enough of that. Yet its image as a Copperhead state was widespread. In November 1863 an exasperated Republican newspaper, the *Somerset Unionist,* railed against the "senseless, unjust and ignorant criticism [that is] fulminated against New Jersey."[2] Writing two years after the war ended, John Y. Foster, the newspaper editor, remembered that "New Jersey . . . held up with steady hand the authority and power of the Government, faithfully fulfilling all the obligations laid upon her by the pressure of events."[3]

Still, there were many in New Jersey who vigorously opposed the war or the policies of the president or both. Many factors explain New Jersey's ambivalence. The state's prewar economy had been based largely upon

Southern markets: Newark manufacturers and Trenton merchants carried on an active trade with the slaveholding states; Jersey cereals and cider found a ready market below the Mason-Dixon line. Social as well as economic ties bound some Jerseyans to the South: Half the student body of Princeton College in 1860 called the South their home; hundreds of wealthy planters from Virginia, Maryland, and the Carolinas vacationed regularly at Jersey seacoast resorts. New Jersey's large free Black population had long been a source of friction. Alone among the Northern states, New Jersey permitted the capture of runaway slaves within her borders. New Jersey's proximity to New York City, a hotbed of Copperhead sentiments, and the sense of insecurity that had made tiny New Jersey a conservative champion of states' rights as early as the American Revolution, were among the varied elements that produced what some have called "the northernmost of the Border States."

The state was in the Democratic camp during the greater part of the war. Although Republican Charles S. Olden had been narrowly elected governor in 1859, both houses of the state legislature remained overwhelmingly Democratic until 1865. In 1863 Joel Parker, whose often contradictory positions infuriated Unionists, succeeded Olden in the governor's chair, defeating Republican Marcus L. Ward, the "soldiers' friend," by some 15,000 votes, up to then the largest majority won by any statewide candidate. While a large body of opinion opposed secession and supported Lincoln, New Jersey's Unionists were disorganized and politically ineffective throughout the war years. In perhaps no other Northern state was the conflict between supporters and opponents of the administration so bitter as in New Jersey.

The fierce tug of war between Republicans and Democrats was to continue until the end of the fighting, and beyond. In April 1865, when word came that Richmond had fallen to the Union army, the state legislature debated resolutions expressing New Jersey's thanks to Lincoln and the soldiers. The Democratic-controlled Assembly adopted the resolutions only after deleting all mention of Lincoln. When the State Senate took up a similar resolution, it refused to express its appreciation to the victorious army, sending the measure back to committee. Not until November of 1865 was New Jersey "redeemed," at least in the eyes of Unionists. Hoisting the double banner of reunion and the martyred president, the Republicans campaigned with an enthusiasm and confidence they had never shown before. On election day they were victorious, carrying both houses of the legislature and electing the governor. "God be praised," wrote one jubilant Republican to Governor-elect Ward after the ballots had been counted, "not so much, that Marcus L. Ward is elected Governor, as that the people of New Jersey, have at the 'eleventh hour,' returned from all manner of wickedness and declared themselves Loyal and true to the Union."[4]

In the November 1862 elections the Democrats swept the state, electing a governor, four of five members of Congress, and both branches of the legislature. The *Trenton True American*, which more than once called emancipation of the slaves a "most stupendous act of folly," could hardly contain its enthusiasm:

The people of New Jersey on Tuesday last recorded a verdict which cannot be mistaken or misunderstood. They have declared that the [Republican] party is guilty of violating the Constitution . . . ; that it is guilty of the intention to pervert the purpose of the war now prevailing, from its original intention of subduing the rebellion and restoring the Union as it was, into a war for the emancipation of the slaves in the Southern States.[5]

To "restore the Union as it was" meant nothing less than the preservation of slavery, and there were many in New Jersey who saw nothing wrong with that. Hackensack's *Bergen Democrat*, for one, condemned "the Abolitionized Republican party":

We suggest that the President himself take command of a division of darkies. It is time that the commander in chief took the field in person, and certainly no better chance will ever offer itself than the present. Let Secretary [of War] Stanton also buckle on his armor—he ought to be good for a captaincy, at least, in the Ethiopian Guards. If there should be any vacancies in the subordinate positions, there are a few negro worshippers in this town who might be spared with profit, and who ought to have some better chance of airing their loyalty than in talking and prating about the "glorious victories," &c. But there is not much danger of such men venturing their worthless skins upon the battlefield. Whilst they stay at home and denounce their neighbors as secessionists, they keep a bright lookout for some chance to cheat the government, and thus show their loyalty and devotion to the Union.[6]

Joel Parker, the Monmouth County lawyer elected governor in 1862, claimed that "Abolition and Secession are the authors of our calamity, and Abolition is the parent of Secession." In his inaugural address Parker expressed the hope that South and North could be reconciled on the basis of law.

We should not be afraid of peace—an honorable and permanent peace—whether it come to us by the exercise of power, or by the exercise of conciliation. It should be a peace on the basis of "the Union as it was," not a Union of states where parts are held in subjugation as conquered provinces. . . . It should be a peace founded on the submission of all to the rightful authority of the Government, and the guarantee of all their constitutional rights by the Government. It should be a peace bringing with it such unity as will have the Constitution for its foundation, and obedience to the law for its corner-stone.[7]

Parker's Republican opponents were quick to remind voters that the "laws" the governor so revered included those upholding slavery.

The Federal defeat at Fredericksburg, leaving in its wake 13,000 dead, wounded, and missing, horrified the people of New Jersey, and intensified the clamor for peace. But New Jersey's largest newspaper, the *Newark Daily Advertiser*, saw nothing but folly in what it called "the most senseless plea . . . [for] peace with the rebels."

It is scarcely to be supposed that those who counsel peace would favor the partition of the nation in twain—or would advocate the sundering of our Union into two or more distinct and independent sovereignties. It cannot be that any well meaning man who longs for peace would be willing to say to the authors of the doctrine of secession and the leaders of this infamous rebellion: "Let us agree to part in peace. Take you such and such States and we will take these others, and let the war cease." Peace at such a price would be bought far too dearly. It would be surrendering the principle on which our Government is based; would be robbing the nation of half its grandeur; would desecrate the Constitution; would sow the seed of interminable strife between the parts that agree to separate, and lead to endless anarchy among those that remained. And yet this is the certain, shameful, and disastrous result which must follow any other peace than that which is achieved by the armies of the Union. No other peace is possible but that which . . . shall be won on the battlefield.[8]

The year 1863 saw Copperhead influence in New Jersey at high tide. The blundering and bloodshed of Fredericksburg, the embarrassment of the Mud March, generally ineffectual efforts of the Union armies everywhere, all served to depress and anger the people. Even Lincoln was discouraged: "It appears to me the Almighty is against us," he told a friend in late

December 1862, "and I can hardly see a ray of hope." Early in February 1863 Clement L. Vallandigham, a former Ohio congressman who would later be arrested for treason, was invited to Newark by the city's Union Democratic Club. Speaking before "a multitudinous throng" that included the city's mayor and Democratic congressman, Vallandigham denounced the war, the Emancipation Proclamation, and what he called "the black torrent of abolitionism." "I want the Union as it was—part slave and part free," he declared to the cheering throng.[9]

A soldier in the Ninth Regiment called Vallandigham "Villain-damn-him." Newark's leading Republican newspaper, the *Daily Mercury*, was appalled by the whole affair:

The speaker of the evening—that eminent patriot C. L. Vallandigham—was . . . received with such marks of favor by the audience as removed all doubts of their hearty approval of the infamous opinions and character which have made this man so notorious. Probably nowhere in the loyal States could be gathered an audience, before which they could be proclaimed with such assurance of favor. . . . The nearer the speaker approached to open and avowed treason the greater the enthusiasm of his hearers. When he counselled resistance to the draft, even though lawfully ordered, the most vociferous applause evidenced how heartily the crowd sympathized with the speaker. . . . At the mention of "Stonewall Jackson" the patriots shouted with delight. . . . When the speaker asked, "Will you send out your sons again to the battle-field?" overwhelming, enthusiastic cries of "No, no!" "Never, never!" "God forbid!" "Not if I know myself!" &c came from all parts of the house. "Shall they be conscripted to carry on this war for two years more, and for the negro?" he asked, a tremendous outburst of yells, cheers, cries of "No, never!" "Let them try it!" "See them damned first!" "We defy them!" was the response. The whole affair needed only to have been transferred to Richmond to have been a perfect success.[10]

Flemington's Republican newspaper urged its readers not to be discouraged, to have faith that the Union could be restored. "Stand fast by the good old flag, and its cherished folds will surely float over a restored and regenerated nation!"

Sorrowfully do we realize the unwelcome fact that there are some among us whose hearts are not for the Union—who mourn over our victories and rejoice at our defeats. Our people are depressed by their evil bodings, and appalled by the boldness of their treason. Sometimes we think our nation is not worthy to be saved. We feel that if we are not true to the Union, Peace will never return to us. If we will not appreciate and cherish our liberties, we are not fit to enjoy them. . . . The army is fighting to regain the Union, and restore Peace. The Government is the protector and the supporter of the army in its great and holy work. We who are at home—who do not fight—MUST SUPPORT THE GOVERNMENT.[11]

After weeks of heated debate, on March 18, 1863, the Democratic-controlled state legislature passed the so-called Peace Resolutions, an extraordinary document that protested the emancipation of the slaves, the creation of West Virginia, the suspension of the writ of habeas corpus, and a war it said was waged "for the accomplishment of unconstitutional or partisan purposes." Declaring that New Jersey's willingness to supply troops was motivated by no animosity toward the South, the Democrats called for the appointment of peace commissioners to adopt a plan "by which the present civil war may be brought to a close."

The reaction of New Jersey's Unionists to the Peace Resolutions was nothing short of apoplectic. The state's leading Republican paper, the *Daily Mercury*, condemned "the insignificant and contemptable faction" in the legislature that had passed the resolutions.

It rests then with the Union men of this State . . . to light the fires of patriotism on every hill-top, and in every valley. Summon the children of the men of '76 to the redemption of their noble birth-land, and tell the world that New Jersey is not the lost and degraded creature which a miserable band of copperhead disloyalists would make her appear; but that still, as of old, her skirts are pure from taint of treason or cowardice, and her heart warm and loyal to the Union she helped to found, and which she loves with a love unsurpassed. Thirty thousand gallant sons of New Jersey are asserting this sentiment to-day, before the nation, and in the teeth of the foe. Let hundreds of thousands more from her iron-hills to the sandy marge of her ocean-washed counties take up the cry in thunder tones—New Jersey is loyal among the loyal.[12]

A correspondent of the *Sentinel of Freedom* contrasted "the patriotism of those who have offered up their lives on our battle-fields" to the disloyalists who remained behind:

While our soldiers in the field have added lustre to our name, politicians at home—the tools of demagogues of other States, have robbed us of our hard earned laurels, and for the time caused the very name of New Jersey to stink in the nostrils of patriotism. They have preached a crusade against the Government, instead of one against rebels. The Legislature of the State has insulted the nation by sending an avowed sympathizer with treason to the U.S. Senate. The copperheads have assembled in the capital of our State to inculcate treason and to advise resistance to the Government. They have invited the greatest advocate of treason, Vallandigham, to address them in the largest city in the State, and applauded him the loudest when he stabbed his country the deepest. . . . Shame where is thy blush . . .?

Desperately, madly have the copperheads of New Jersey attempted to rush the State into the maelstrom of secession and anarchy, but thanks to an all wise Providence, their very madness has been our salvation, and their attempts are producing a revulsion of sentiment which is destined to overwhelm these agitators and consign their names to lowest infamy. And the aroused patriotism of the sons of New Jersey will soon atone to the nation for the dishonor placed upon the State by the action of the copperheads—like rats they are fast deserting the sinking ship—which they had rigged to sail them into power.[13]

Most New Jersey soldiers reacted angrily to the Peace Resolutions. Wrote one cavalryman:

I am ashamed at the New Jersey House of Representatives for having passed those cowardly Peace Resolutions. I hope the people will not countenance them or the men who voted for them. I want peace, but am willing to have it on no terms but the whole Union of the States, one and inseparable. The laws of the General Government, under the Constitution, must be administered in every State of the Union, and traitors must lay down their arms before I am willing to talk of peace. This, with freedom for the black man, is just what I ask; nothing less will satisfy me. It is irritating enough to have enemies in front with arms in their hands; but worse—far worse—to have them behind, trying to embarrass the government and discourage the soldiers in the field, and also opposing enlistments and drafts.[14]

In the field the men of the Twenty-fourth Regiment cheered as one of its officers castigated "these traitors at home . . . [who] outstrip each other in their haste to throw themselves at the feet of the slave power."[15] Members of the Twenty-sixth Regiment, drawn up into a hollow square, denounced "with but five dissenting votes . . . the work of a set of false, cowardly and traitorous demagogues."[16] Officers of the Eleventh New Jersey pledged to "put forth every effort, endure every fatigue, and shrink from no danger, until, under the gracious guidance of a kind Providence, every armed rebel shall be conquered, and traitors at home shall quake with fear, as the proud emblem of our national independence shall assert its power from North to South, and crush beneath its powerful folds all who dared to assail its honor."[17]

The twin Union victories at Gettysburg and Vicksburg dampened the enthusiasm of New Jersey's Copperheads, although there was much life in them yet. Less than a week after Lee's retreat from Pennsylvania, Somerset County Copperheads rallied at Somerville. Reported the *Somerset Unionist*:

The Democratic mass meeting to which the "people" of Somerset County were invited, came off on Thursday last in this village. In point of numbers it was quite respectable, some six or eight hundred of all ages and sexes being present. The principal delegations from the country came from the upper townships, and numbered a score of wagons tolerably well-filled, and bearing banners and devices, the prevailing motto being PEACE. From the rear of one of these wagons hung a small secession flag, but which on entering the village was speedily put out of sight. This delegation cheered quite lustily for Jeff. Davis on passing the public school building. . . . A notable feature of the meeting was that as usual with gatherings of this sort, there was not one word of sympathy for the Government, or of condemnation of the rebels.[18]

The insatiable demands of the Union army for more manpower resulted in the Enrollment Act of 1863, which for the first time extended federal control to the recruitment process. The new law provided for draft boards in each congressional district, district provost marshals and enrollment officers whose job it was to identify draft-age men in their districts. If a man were drafted, he could provide a substitute, or pay a commutation fee of $300 that would exempt him from a particular draft. Opposition to the Enrollment Act was widespread, not only among Copperheads, who called the act unconstitutional, but also among workingmen who could not afford a substitute or pay the commutation fee. In March 1863 foreign-born workers at two plants in Jersey City were chased off the job by their fellow-employees:

A difficulty occurred yesterday between the employees at the Chemical Works in Jersey City, in consequence of some of the men refusing to

127

become naturalized citizens, in order to escape the draft. The other workmen, who are nearly all naturalized citizens, allege that the former have enjoyed the privileges and blessings of the country for a number of years, and consequently they should in common give their aid and assistance in support of the government. The men refused to take out their papers, when the loyal naturalized citizens expelled them from the premises. The proprietors of the works raised no objections to the proceedings, and the aliens will be under the necessity of becoming citizens, or seek employment elsewhere.[19]

The Union defeat at Chancellorsville, with the loss of nearly 17,000 men, undermined New Jersey's efforts to raise additional troops. Enrollment officials met with great resistance in Newark, where the city's working-class Irish population resented the law's obvious bias toward the well-off. When actual drafting began across the Hudson River in New York City on July 11, 1863, a full-scale riot broke out. A largely Irish mob rampaged through Manhattan's East Side for four days, setting fire to a colored orphanage, lynching a number of Blacks, wrecking draft offices, an armory, and the homes and offices of Republican officials. Nearly a hundred perished during the disorders. News of the New York riots triggered a reaction in Newark.

The excitement in this city yesterday afternoon and evening [July 13] on receipt of the news of the riotous resistance to the draft in New York, was intense. A crowd assembled around the bulletin boards of the newspaper offices, discussing the news and the conscription act and condemning the $300 exemption clause. . . . The discussions became warmer and warmer, and at last the crowd gave cheers for the New York conscripts, State rights, Vallandigham, Governors Seymour and Parker, Gen. Runyon, Mayor Bigelow and others, and groans for Lincoln, Greeley, Provost Marshal Miller, his guard, etc.

A man named Stainsbury made some remarks in favor of this exemption clause which were received with groans and hisses. The speaker was attacked and beaten, and took refuge in a cigar store, from which he escaped without any further injury. Between 9 and 10 o'clock [p.m.], the crowd having increased in numbers and getting restive from the want of occupation or something to arouse them, a rush was made for the *Mercury* office, and a half-crazy fellow was placed on a barrel by the excited mob, and made a harangue in opposition to the Conscript Act. Cries were made of "Down with the wheel," "We won't be drafted," "The wheel's broken," "Where are you, $300," etc. A cry was then made to mob the *Mercury* office and destroy the contents, and the infuriated crowd were with difficulty restrained from carrying their threats into execution. A demand was made that a flag be raised over the building, which, after some delay, was done by Officer Haury, who foresaw that conciliatory means only would be of avail in saving the building from destruction. Appeals were made to the excited crowd to withhold the hand of violence . . . while several of the members of the police force endeavored to quell the rising spirit of insurrection. For a time these efforts were successful, but soon a volley of stones was fired at the windows, while the outer doors of the *Mercury* office were forced open. Soon after the flag was run up the mob became pacified, and yielded to the appeals of the conservative citizens who counseled peace and quiet. We are informed that some water was thrown upon the crowd from the windows of the *Mercury* office or from the adjoining buildings, and this act exasperated them to the first demonstrations of violence.

Dispersing from this scene of disorder the rioters proceeded up Broad street to Fulton street, where angry and menacing demonstrations were made in front of the residence of Provost Marshal E. N. Miller. The mob, amid shouts of "Miller," "Hang him," etc., began to hurl stones against the doors and windows. The darkness of the night, the falling rain, and some dense shade trees interfered with their aim, and the damage was comparatively trifling. Alderman John Remer of the First Ward made his appearance and from the stoop of Mr. Miller's residence besought the crowd to disperse. Alderman Ball addressed them in the same strains, and by their united efforts succeeded in pacifying the mob and restraining them from further mischief.

Various threats were made against Mr. Miller, and had it not been for the timely intervention of Messrs. Ball and Remer, his residence would unquestionably have been destroyed. Mr. Miller effected his escape from the house by the back yard, and the apprehension of his family were at one time intense. . . . The mob appeared to have gathered quite promiscuously. It numbered from 1000 to 1500 persons, without organization or object, and having no ringleader.[20]

Newark's escape from anything worse than broken glass and shattered doors may have been due to the heavy downpour that dampened the mob's anger, the presence of several hundred newly returned veterans in the city, or just plain luck. Despite antidraft protests, all of them peaceful, in Bloomfield, Orange, Jersey City, Princeton, Morristown, and Hackensack, New Jersey eventually managed to raise its quota of enlisted men. There was no draft in the state in 1863.

Repeal of the commutation provision of the Enrollment Act in mid-1864 left draft-age men only three options: service, desertion, or hiring a substitute. The draft "has been the absorbing topic of the week," reported the *Morristown True Democratic Banner* on June 2, 1864.

There has been much skedaddling, we learn, from the mines and iron works of Rockaway Township. One of our town wags who happened in Hoboken as a train arrived with a party of skedaddlers on board with trunks, boxes, bags, etc., remarked in a loud voice to a friend—"Jim, Major Brown has fixed things alright at this ferry—No man crosses it without having his pass examined." The skedaddlers who were leaning towards the ferry, at once stopped, and then with alarmed looks, scattered in various directions, some going to the Jersey City Ferry.

Some of the wide-a-wakes who thought they were doing a big thing for their country when, with banner, torch, and cape, they paraded their fanaticism before the public, having been delightfully excited over the draft . . . seem at a loss to find epithets and curses deep enough to express their change of sentiment with, while pulling the hard earned dollars out of their pockets to obtain exemption. They have paid pretty dear for participating as showmen to Abe Lincoln. . . .

Chatham and Pequannoc have by this time got the substitutes they contracted for to fill their quotas. Other townships are taking measures to obtain substitutes also, and a number of associations have been formed to pay the exemption fees of those of its members who are drafted.[21]

Efforts to avoid the draft continued at a furious pace throughout 1864. The cost of substitutes fluctuated between $300 and $800, ex-Confederate prisoners were recruited and towns across the state raised bounty money by taxation or the sale of bonds to entice men into enlisting. In mid-year Monmouth County extended its bounty of $200 to black men, an apparently successful effort, and many cities sent agents to the battle fronts with satchels of greenbacks to entice veterans whose terms of service were about to expire. In Essex County a committee of the Board of Freeholders was put in charge of filling the county's quota and paying the bounty.

As a preliminary step [the Committee] have applied to Governor Parker to use his influence to obtain permission to raise a new regiment of one year men in this county. This will no doubt stimulate volunteering . . . as more or less excitement is always produced by the formation of new regiments, and many are induced to enlist through preference for a particular officer, while others are secured who have strong objections to being sent to veteran regiments, but who would volunteer if their comrades were as inexperienced as themselves. The Committee have also determined to take advantage of recruiting in the Rebel states, and have dispatched Colonel C. M. Zulick . . . to Alabama and Georgia, to secure all the colored recruits possible. If he is successful, he is to notify the Committee, and the necessary funds will be forwarded. . . .

There now remains but three weeks in which to complete this work, and unless a vigorous effort is made our quota will not be filled. The number required from the county is 2,349, and as there is no certainty that the agent despatched to the insurrectionary States will secure any colored recruits, the work at home should not be allowed to flag. The men will be raised—by volunteering if possible, by a draft if necessary—and there are so many arguments in favor of the former, that it is to be hoped that the latter mode will not be found necessary. We understand that Major Wm. W. Morris has been appointed recruiting agent for the city, and that he will open a tent immediately upon the park, while the funds will be disbursed by Mr. Baldwin. At Orange, a public meeting was held, on Saturday evening, to promote enlistments. Speeches were made, and a Committee appointed to solicit funds to carry on the work until the bonds of the town can be issued.[22]

Bounty jumpers, men who enlisted only to desert at the first opportunity, then enlist again under a different name, were commonplace. Three of them were caught in Morristown, reported *The Jerseyman* on June 18.

Three professional gentlemen engaged in the "substitute" business came to grief at the Provost Marshal's office in this Town on Wednesday night last. Their names are William Maxwell *alias* Milligan, George Wright and Alexander Paddow—all foreigners. Having got their price, been regularly mustered in, and quartered in the upper rooms of the office for the night, they suggested to Sergeant Wm. N. Busby, in the Invalid Corps, who was in charge, that $100 from each of them would be paid to him for arrangements in their escape. The Sergeant, being honest, communicated the proposition to Major Brown . . . and measures were promptly taken to test the disposition and purpose of these fellows, and to secure them. The Sergeant, under advice, pretended to fall in with the arrangement, took their $300, and instead of taking them out of the back door upon a lawful errand as they supposed, marched them right into the clutches of the Provost Marshal. They were immediately [put in irons] and taken to the Work House where they were kept overnight, and the next morning sent off to Trenton. Wright had a couple of hand cuff keys in his possession, which he was of course deprived of previous to his lodgment in jail, and is undoubtedly, if not an old offender in other crimes, at least a scientific operator in the "substitute" line; and the others, it is thought, were not wholly unknown to him before their adventure here. The Sergeant who resisted their bribes and blandishments deserves credit for his integrity and faithfulness.[23]

Edward N. Fuller, editor of the *Newark Daily Journal,* was the state's most influential voice in opposition to the war. On July 19, after President Lincoln issued his call for a half million additional men to suppress the rebellion, Fuller exploded in an editorial that was to lead to his arrest.

It will be seen that Mr. Lincoln has called for another half a million men. Those who desire to be butchered will please step forward at once. All others will stay at home and defy Old Abe and his minions to drag them from their families. We hope that the people of New Jersey will at once put their feet down and insist that not a man shall be forced out of the State to engage in the abolition butchery and swear to die at their own doors rather than march one step to fulfill the dictates of that mad revolutionary fanaticism, which has destroyed the best government the world ever saw, and would now butcher its remaining inhabitants to carry out a mere fanatical sentiment. This has gone far enough and *must be stopped.* Let the people rise as one man and demand that this wholesale murder shall cease.[24]

The next day, in another editorial, Fuller called Lincoln "a third-rate country lawyer" and a "blunderer, with the tone and air of a despot." Added Fuller: "When the draft shall come off, if it ever does, it is proposed that all leading Lincolnites shall be seized by the people, clothed in their master's uniform, presented with a musket, and marched to the nearest military camp to the tune of John Brown, and other patriotic songs." The *Trenton State Gazette and Republican* could stand no more:

So far as we have yet seen, every Democratic newspaper denounces the new call for men to reinforce our armies now in the field contending against an armed rebellion. All seem actuated by a fiendish purpose to stir up resistance and rebellion in the northern States, and thus aid the rebels, at the expense of civil strife in every neighborhood. They all agree in sentiment, and only differ in degree. Some are content with general denunciation . . . while others openly counsel resistance. In the latter class is the Newark Journal. . . .

We are friends of the liberty of the press, but that liberty should stop short of open incitement to violation of the laws and treason. The newspaper that should openly counsel wholesale murder and pillage, would soon be stopped, and we know of no code of law or morals that should cause the guardians of the law to longer suffer the publication of a paper that thus daringly urges its readers to commit treason which must unavoidably include murder, rapine and the wholesale catalogue of crime. We do not hesitate in saying that such a newspaper should be suppressed. It has, more than once, urged its followers to resistance, and longer forbearance in its case would be weakness. There is plainly a purpose on that part of a gang of reckless traitors in this State to array the State against the National Government. By this open declaration they must think their plans nearly ripe for execution. It is better to meet them now than to give them further time to strengthen their treason.[25]

Two other newspapers, the *Somerset Messenger* and the *Bergen Democrat*, wrote approvingly of Fuller's astonishing editorial, but it was copied by the press generally. Federal officials took action on July 21, arresting Fuller, charging him with counseling persons to resist the draft and inciting insurrection against the United States. Soon afterward, the editors of the *Somerset Messenger* and *Bergen Democrat* were likewise arrested. Fuller was unrepentant, saying later, "If this be treason, let it be treason." The course of the war, which now more clearly favored the North, soon rendered Fuller and his fellow Copperheads an irrelevancy. In the end, despite all the controversy, only a thousand or so New Jerseyans were actually drafted. Thousands of others, encouraged by bounties or hired as substitutes, served honorably in the ranks. As late as February 1865, however, there was still a need for manpower. The *Paterson Daily Press* viewed enlistment as a simple business proposition:

The price of substitutes has been run up enormously by the draft. The brokers demand $1,000 and upwards for 3 years men. Men in Paterson are asking $1,500 but they may as well understand first as last, that they won't get any such preposterous price. Few drafted men can, or will, submit to such a swindle. The fact is, and if it is not understood now, it will before long, that there are plenty of men to be had. Let but the fact become fairly understood—and it is a *fact*—that the war is nearly over, and plenty of men can be had for $500 to $600 for one year. Why, look at it for a moment! The strong probability is that the men now being called into the service will never see a battle-field. From present appearances there are veterans enough now at the front to wipe out the Rebellion in three months. . . . The man who enters service now, depositing his $600, $800 or $1,000 as the case may be, in the savings-bank, or investing it in U.S. securities, will come home in a few months with a snug little capital to commence business with, to buy him a house, or what not. *It is clearly the very best thing any young man without a family can now do to go into the service as a substitute.* He will never have such a chance again, as he has now.[26]

No sooner had the first regiments reached Washington in the spring of 1861 than it became obvious that the government had no plans for the health and comfort of the troops. The earliest organized movement in New Jersey for army relief took place in Newark on April 24, 1861, when the ladies of that city formed an association "for the purpose of preparing necessary comforts for the volunteers." Within two weeks ladies' aid societies existed in nearly all the larger cities and towns, and by the close of the year nearly every town in the state had its own relief association. Many originated within the churches, others were wholly spontaneous. The first organization for the relief of the families of volunteers sprang to life in Lambertville as early as April 1861, soon to be followed by similar efforts in Trenton, Mount Holly, Jersey City, Paterson, Newark, and all the large towns. By the end of the war millions of dollars had been raised to aid New Jersey's soldiers and their families. The work in Morristown was typical.

This celebration of the Fourth of July [1863] is for a purpose so humane—for the relief, by festival, of the widows and children whose misfortunes have been caused by the casualties of the war—that we must bespeak for it the earnest and conscientious patronage of the people of the county. The loss in Co. L, 27 Reg't. of some nineteen of the thirty-three out of this small township, who were drowned in the Cumberland River added to the losses by the ordinary casualties of the war seems to call for aid for the afflicted, upon the patriotic citizens of the county generally, and as a matter of duty.

The ladies of the Township of Rockaway are ever patriotic and vigilant; and are determined, in their festival purposed for the day, to greet all with such a reception as only the women of New Jersey, in their sympathies for their sisters in this heavy sorrow, and for the many orphans thus cast upon their charities, can and will tender.

Rockaway has thus been made to bear a large proportion of the county's burden of the war. Most of the dead have left helpless families—and the aid to be given at home must be by few. Come, therefore, men and women of Morris County and help to lighten the sorrows of many—wipe away tears, and cause at least one ray of sunshine, each of you, to shine in upon desolated homes, and you will feel happier in your remembrances of the nation's Holiday of 1863.

An oration by an eminent speaker, with the other customary observances of the day, with Beckers' Brass Band of Morristown, may be relied upon. Again we say, "To Rockaway on the Fourth of July!"[27]

Women in the town of Bergen (now part of Jersey City) were every bit as active as those elsewhere. According to a March 1863 report in the *American Standard*:

A number of patriotic ladies of the town of Bergen formed themselves into an association, last September, for the purpose of furnishing necessary comforts to our soldiers in the army. Since that time they have sent to the hospital at Newark, and to the sanitary commission at Washington, a large number of garments, suitable for the sick and wounded. . . . They have sent . . . a large box of clothing, which was delivered to the soldiers at camp Washington, and within the past fortnight they have sent . . . another large box, containing 109 pair of socks, sheets, knives and forks, tin plates, suitable reading matter and stationery. Since their organization they have collected, by subscription and the proceeds of the festival held on New Years day at the lecture room of the Presbyterian church, Bergen . . . the sum of $567.[28]

As Thanksgiving Day 1864 drew near, the North's women redoubled their efforts to insure that the men at the front would enjoy the holiday. The ladies of Jersey City raised $1,500 for the purchase of "cigars and tobacco for the soldiers and sailors." The citizens of Orange sent tomatoes "as sauce for Thanksgiving turkeys." Soldiers recuperating at Newark's Ward General Hospital, reported the *Paterson Daily Press* on November 18, were a special concern.

It is proposed by the ladies of New Jersey to furnish a thanksgiving dinner to the soldiers (nearly twelve hundred in number and nearly all Jerseymen) in the Ward U.S. general hospital at Newark. To this end they invite contributions from all sections of the state of poultry, meats, vegetables and fruit of all kinds, pies, cakes, jellies, preserves, butter, &c. As there are but few sick (nearly all being wounded) among the patients, they can relish and enjoy a hearty meal—and such it is proposed to give them. The several railroad and express companies have been requested to furnish free transportation to all donations for the above object. It is requested that poultry and meats, whenever practicable, be sent COOKED.[29]

On August 31, 1864, the National Democratic party nominated George B. McClellan, the former commander of the Army of the Potomac, as its candidate for president on a platform that pronounced the war a failure and demanded an immediate unconditional armistice to be followed by a peace conference. McClellan, who had taken up residence in West Orange in mid-1863, accepted his party's nomination but repudiated its platform. By the time the 1864 presidential campaign began in earnest, the tide of war had swung heavily to the North: In late August Union Admiral David Farragut's fleet seized Mobile Bay, the Confederacy's last major Gulf Coast port; on September 2 Sherman's army captured Atlanta, shattering Rebel morale, and by mid-October Confederates were finally cleared from the Shenandoah Valley. Encircling Petersburg, Grant's men were slowly tightening the noose around Richmond.

The 1864 campaign was a no-holds-barred affair, one of the hardest-fought within memory, and possibly one of the ugliest. Newspapers on both sides loosed a torrent of hyperbole upon the public. Typical of the Copperhead press, the *Bergen Democrat* denounced the Republicans as "monsters and barbarians" intent upon exterminating the South, killing half the men in the North and prolonging the war for thirty years. The pro-Lincoln *Trenton Daily State Gazette* said the election was "an issue between Union and Disunion, between Freedom and Slavery, between Democracy and Aristocracy."[30] The *Paterson Daily Press* claimed that "the great masses of the American people saw that their beloved land stood on the very brink of destruction, and felt in every pulse of their hearts, that upon the results of the political contest, this fall, alone depended the weal or woe of this great and glorious republic":

For some time previous to the late election business began to lag and in some parts of [Paterson] it almost ceased for want of encouragement. Men who were wont to measure calico by the yard threw their yard sticks aside and applied themselves with all their energies to the election of their favorite men. Everybody seemed to fall into the great political current as it swept over the land, bearing along with it every object that lay in its path. Lawyers left their briefs and Blackstone's lying on their shelves, neglected their cases and took to the political stump; clerks deserted their desks, allowing their accounts to take care of themselves, while they dabbled in the great whirlpool of political strife; blacksmiths left their forges, machinists forsook their files, chisels and hammers, and all as it were with one accord betook themselves to politics, and politics was the order of the day, the war for the time being utterly ignored except when it was needed for argument.[31]

Five days before the polls opened, Jersey City Unionists paraded through the city's downtown streets.

The largest and most successful torchlight procession that has ever been witnessed in Jersey City was that got up by the Unionists last night. In addition to torches and lamps, numbers of wagons, bearing flags, banners, devices, &c., were in the procession. The houses along the line of march were very generally illuminated and decorated with flags and lanterns, and as the procession moved along the street, it was accompanied by a continued blaze of fire-works.

About two hundred Paterson boys with torches took part in the demonstration. In passing through a section of Jersey City corresponding to [Paterson's] "Dublin," they were received by a crowd of fierce, ugly-looking hags and masculine Plug-Uglies, who began to throw stones into the procession. About a dozen of our men were struck. We have been shown a stone with which Mr. John Reid, the photographer, was hit on the head, making an ugly cut. It weighs a pound and a half. Our boys turned on their cowardly, heathenish assailants and smote them hip and thigh, cracking their pates in the most delicious manner and chasing several of them two or three blocks. The only way to carry conviction to the minds of those ruffians is by making an incision in the skull. Order was at length restored and the procession ended its march without further trouble.[32]

A day later, on November 4, a torch-lit procession of McClellan supporters marched through Trenton. As the parade crossed the tracks at South Warren Street the New York to Washington express steamed suddenly into view, its whistle blowing furiously. Stephen Tice, a signal-man stationed at the crossing, had inexplicably given the all-clear moments before the train smashed into a wagon carrying ladies from the Third Ward, injuring many severely. "The most painful and disgraceful part of the affair is yet to be related," reported the *Daily State Gazette*:

As soon as the nature of the accident was known by the crowd, a rush was made for the engineer and fireman of the train, who were fortunate enough to make their escape. After pelting the engine and some of the cars with stones, the excited crowd assaulted Mr. Tice, the signal-man, who was as blameless in the matter as any man in the town. Mr. Tice fled to his house and shut the door, but the infuriated crowd followed him, burst into his house, and beat him to death with clubs. Mrs. Tice and Mr. Tice's daughters pleaded with the mob for the life of their husband and father, but in vain. One ruffian snatched a tea-kettle from the stove and threw it with all his force at Mrs. Tice, but it fortunately missed her. The daughters made their escape from the back part of the house, but Mrs. Tice remained in the house, and saw her husband murdered. We understand on Saturday, that she had become a raving lunatic from the effects of this outrage.[33]

Most rallies were peaceful. In Woodbury, in Gloucester County, 4,000 enthusiastic Unionists turned out to cheer "a large number of young ladies, representing the several States, and dressed in the national colors [who] occupied seats on the platform."[34] But there was considerable violence, real or threatened, as the campaign reached a frenzied climax. A Republican orator who spoke for two hours at a Union meeting at Bound Brook, in Somerset County, wrote that his audience "came on the ground with lamps trimmed and burning."

Pickets were thrown out along the entire lines of the meeting to keep an eye upon the operations of "Moseby's men." Notice was given from the stand that the meeting had only a peaceful and patriotic mission, and that it would prove a dangerous operation to attempt to disturb it. We then commenced our address . . . to a throng of over two thousand listeners. . . . No attempt at disturbance was made. The adopted Democrats, or Moseby's men, with short pipes, pug-faces, and malignant countenances, hung around the outskirts of the meeting, giving a faint utterance occasionally to the Democratic rallying cry of "negar," but a wholesome dread of consequences kept them from any "peaceful" demonstrations of violence.[35]

New Jersey's soldiers in the field, barred by state law from casting absentee ballots, made their feelings known through the pages of the newspapers. A member of the Ninth New Jersey, stationed in North Carolina, wrote to the anti-Lincoln *Paterson Daily Register* on October 7:

Mr. Editor: We desire to express to you our extreme satisfaction at the straightforward and honest course you have taken in the nation's affairs since this war commenced, and when your much abused journal came out with the heading George B. McClellan and Pendleton, our satisfaction was unbounded. Now two-thirds of the brave old 9th are for Little Mac, and who the rest are for, matters but little. So it is all through the army, as far as my observation goes, and in the course of the past eventful campaign I have conversed with men from nearly a hundred different regiments on the subject, and in most cases they were in favor of the "Hero of Antietam." We are fully satisfied that under McClellan we can conquer a peace right speedily. We look forward to the day with longing hearts when misrule and corruption will have to give way to "Little Mac," Liberty, Union and Justice. All we ask of you at home is to put him into a position to clean out the filthy nuisance that has accumulated in Washington for the past four years. Little did our grandsires think that the Capitol their hands helped to rear would be used as a low comedy play house and Old Abe the clown.[36]

In fact, of the ballots cast by soldiers from states where absentee voting was allowed, fully two-thirds were for Lincoln, and there is no reason to believe that New Jersey's troops would have voted much differently. One soldier, "a consistent democrat all his life," spoke for the majority in a letter published in a Trenton paper:

I should think that the people, after witnessing the copperhead proceedings at Chicago, and reading McClellan's milk and water letters and speeches, could see that the sole aim of the party is to get the reins of government in their own hands. . . . From their dishonorable and villainous actions in the past, I think we should be able to judge of what they would do in the future, if the people should give them the power, which God grant they may not do. As to the army, I think if a fair vote was taken for the two candidates, Mac might possibly get two-tenths of the whole—I am sure not much more than that. We think the army has done too much for our cause and rights, has suffered too much, and that too many valuable lives have been sacrificed to relinquish all to a set of cowards, traitors that would disgrace us with a peace that would bring humiliation and shame upon every honest loyal Northern man—a peace that would bring everlasting disgrace upon every soldier that has raised his arm to defend and sustain the Union—that would make our wives and sisters blush for their friends in the country's army and navy. And for

what? Why, for the spoils of office they would do this. We cannot throw
to the winds all that has been done, now that victory is almost within our
grasp. No, never, and I earnestly hope that the people will sustain the
army a short time longer, and all will be well.[37]

On Election Day New Jersey once again followed its own unique course,
joining only Kentucky and Delaware in casting a majority for McClellan.
"New Jersey almost solitary and alone has done her duty nobly," declared
the *Morristown True Democratic Banner*.[38] The *Flemington Republican*,
however, saw the results in a different light. The election, it said, "decided
that the Nation shall live and Slavery shall die."[39] Republicans rejoiced in
Lincoln's national victory, hugely enjoying a clever satire that first appeared in the *Jersey City Times* and was quickly reprinted in Unionist papers across the state under the headline, "The Great Railroad Disaster":

We have to record the most extensive and fatal casualty ever known in
this country. On Tuesday morning, 8th inst., at an early hour a very large
train left Orange, New Jersey, *en route* for the White House, Washington, D.C., under the charge of chief engineer George B. McClellan. It
was expected to make the trip through in twelve hours. . . . All the copperheads in the country were passengers, besides a few innocent people
who had been deluded into taking an excursion trip by the offer of dead-
head tickets. Horatio Seymour of New York was conductor, assisted by
Franklin Pierce, C. L. Vallandigham and Joel Parker. . . . For convenience and comfort the passengers were classified in the cars; the fogies
under the charge of Robert C. Winthrop and Millard Fillmore, the short
boys under the charge of John Van Buren and Captain Rynders, the
mountebanks and minstrels led by Jack Rogers and Marble, editor of
the World, and the few clergymen marshaled by the very Rev. Chauncey
Burr and H. J. Vandyke. There were several cars that were to be attached to the train that did not make the connection—one from Canada,
with George N. Sanders, conductor, and a roomy one from New York,
filed with Governor Seymour's "friends" were both detained by the un-
warrantable interference of a man named Benjamin F. Butler, who came
to New York last week to "stop for a spell." The cars were gorgeously
decorated with such elegant mottoes as the following—"Butter has,"
"Abe Lincoln is a gorilla," "Little Mac's the boy," "Niggers for slaves,"
"We are coming, brother Jeff," "Let us change our base," "Here's your
spaniels for you, Massa Davis." They moved out of the Orange depot
gaily, to the tune of Dixie, tho' the engineer hesitated, when the final
moment of departure came, about stepping on the platform, and was at

last only got on board by a little expedient of Fernando Wood, who pulled him into his train backwards by his coat tail. Engineer McClellan was dressed in a full rig as a Major General, for which his Uncle Sam paid. He was very nervous and remarked that he should prefer a gunboat to ride on to such a locomotive. This engine was a new one, and it was built at Chicago last August, but on a plan designed by Benedict Arnold, and subsequently improved by Aaron Burr and John C. Calhoun. It was built to the order of Jeff Davis and bore the engaging name of "Cessation," which was adopted as a slight change from the original designation "Secession." It occasioned a good deal of remark that hardly any soldiers took passage on the train. There were some men named Grant, Sheridan, Hooker and Dix around, who very ungenerously expressed doubts as to the safety of the track and the ability of the engineer, and it is supposed this prejudiced the "blue coat" boys. Besides this the conductor of the train refused to have an American flag on the engine, and the soldiers have a stubborn feeling of prejudice on that subject. Notwithstanding these slight drawbacks, the train moved off, with the good wishes and cheers of all the rebel soldiers in Lee's army, all the British aristocrats, and the pirate Semmes and his friends. From all that can be learned from the incoherent talk of the few survivors of the sad catastrophe, it appears that there was trouble from the very start. The engineer and his fireman, Pendleton, quarreled about his firing up, and the conductors and the fare-takers were constantly giving contradictory orders to the brakeman and the nervous old gentlemen pulled frantically on the bell rope, giving the engineer no end of trouble. Just how the accident happened no one can tell now, but certain it is, that before the train got half-way through, there was a shocking smash-up.

The locomotive exploded, the cars were piled in fragments, the track torn up, and such a multitude of passengers fatally injured that it is doubtful if their names can ever be ascertained. Some assert that an old Illinois joker familiarly called Old Abe caused the disaster by putting a rail on the track; others that the fireman Pendleton let too much water out of the peace tank upon the fire in McClellan's boiler; others that Vallandigham ran the train off the track by dropping an "O.A.K." stick of timber under the wheels; still others, that the engineer was frightened by suddenly discovering "a nigger in his wood pile" on the tender, and overturned the locomotive by attempting to "change his base" too suddenly. Whatever be the cause, there is no doubt of the complete wreck of the whole train, and the sad fate of the excursionists. There are but slight fragments of the more distinguished persons that are recognizable. . . . Gov. Parker was badly bruised and lost his eye sight, so that he "can't see it" any more. Pendleton was pitched headlong into a nasty ditch, filled with secession mud, which choked him, and as for the engineer, he was blown so much higher than Gilderoy's kite, and was so minutely pulverized that there is no ocular proof that any such man ever existed.

The funeral of the excursionists will very soon be attended in Richmond, Va., by Jeff Davis and his cabinet, and it is currently reported that U. S. Grant may attend, not however in the character of a mourner. There will be no more trains run on this road as the company being made bankrupt by this calamity will immediately wind up its affairs. The Union line is however in good running order.[40]

---

1. *(top, left)* Major General Philip Kearny, killed at Chantilly, Virginia, September 1, 1862. From Joseph Atkinson, *History of Newark, N.J.* (Newark, 1878).

2. *(top, right)* Colonel Robert McAllister of the Eleventh New Jersey, brevetted major general "for gallant and meritorious services." Courtesy John W. Kuhl.

3. *(bottom, left)* Colonel Sir Percy Wyndham, First New Jersey Cavalry, wounded at Brandy Station, Virginia, June 1863.

4. *(bottom, right)* Colonel Hugh H. Janeway, First New Jersey Cavalry, killed in action at Amelia Springs, Virginia, April 5, 1865, just four days before Lee's surrender. From Samuel Toombs, *New Jersey Troops in the Gettysburg Campaign* (Orange, N.J., 1888).

5. *(top, left)* Colonel E. Burd Grubb, Twenty-third Regiment, in 1863, awarded the brevet rank of brigadier general for gallantry. From Camille Baquet, *History of the First Brigade*, New Jersey Volunteers (Trenton, 1910).

6. *(top, right)* Twenty-three-year-old James M. Weart of Jersey City, who enrolled on April 16, 1861, said to be the state's first volunteer. From Alexander McLean, *History of Jersey City, N.J.* (Jersey City, 1895).

7. *(bottom, left)* Brevet Major A. Judson Clark, Battery B, First New Jersey Light Artillery. Courtesy John W. Kuhl.

8. *(bottom, right)* First Lieutenant J. Madison Drake, Ninth New Jersey, prison escapee and Medal of Honor winner. Courtesy John W. Kuhl.

9. *(top)* Colonel Isaac M. Taylor, Second New Jersey, killed in action at Gaines' Mill, Virginia, June 1862. Courtesy John W. Kuhl.

10. *(bottom)* Lieutenant Colonel Virgil Broderick, First New Jersey Cavalry, killed in action at Brandy Station, Virginia, June 1863. Courtesy John W. Kuhl.

11. *(left)* Corporal George A. Berdan, Seventh New Jersey, promoted to second lieutenant, killed at Chancellorsville, May 3, 1863. Courtesy John W. Kuhl.

12. *(right)* Captain James McKiernan, Company G, Seventh New Jersey. Courtesy John W. Kuhl.

13. *(top)* Private Michael Hanifen, soldier and historian, Battery B, First New Jersey Light Artillery. Courtesy John W. Kuhl.

14. *(bottom)* John C. Patterson, first lieutenant, captain, major, and lieutenant colonel, Fourteenth New Jersey. Courtesy John W. Kuhl.

15. Major David Hatfield, First New Jersey, died of wounds suffered at Gaines'
Mill, Virginia, June 1862. Courtesy John W. Kuhl.

16. Ladies sewing for the soldiers, by Winslow Homer. From *Harper's Weekly*.

17. *(left)* Brigadier General George W. Taylor, First New Jersey Brigade, died of wounds suffered at Second Bull Run, August 1862. Courtesy John W. Kuhl.

18. *(right)* Major Henry W. Sawyer, First New Jersey Cavalry, captured at Brandy Station, Virginia, June 1863, whose death warrant was never carried out due to his wife's boldness. Courtesy John W. Kuhl.

19. *(left)* Sergeant Frederick Schaedel, Company D, Eleventh New Jersey, a native of Germany, wounded at Hatcher's Run, Virginia, March 1865.

20. *(right)* Private William S. Van Fleet, First New Jersey, who died of wounds suffered at Spotsylvania, Virginia, May 25, 1864. Courtesy Parsippany Historical and Preservation Society.

21. *(top)* Second Lieutenant Joseph Ferguson, First New Jersey, captured during the Battle of the Wilderness, May 1864. From Joseph Ferguson, *Life Struggles in Rebel Prisons* (Philadelphia, 1865).

22. *(bottom)* Camp Monmouth, the Tenth New Jersey's home on the outskirts of Washington, D.C., 1861–1862. Courtesy Special Collections and University Archives, Rutgers University Libraries.

23. Recruiting poster for Captain E. R. Pennington's company, Twelfth Regiment, U.S. Army, Spring 1864 (not to be confused with the Twelfth New Jersey Volunteers). Courtesy the Newark Public Library.

24. Ward General Hospital, Newark, New Jersey, by the end of the war one of the largest in the country. Courtesy the Newark Public Library.

FIVE

"Go in, Jersies, We Will Follow You!"

1864

Eighteen hundred sixty-four was the worst year of the war, the bloodiest of all, yet it was also the beginning of the end. Before the year was over, Southern dreams of nationhood lay in ruins, slavery was doomed, and Yankee arms triumphant. None of that was clear on March 4, when Newark's Copperhead newspaper, the *Daily Journal*, marked the third anniversary of Lincoln's inauguration with a stinging editorial:

Now to-day, three years after Mr. Lincoln's inauguration, after an enormous expenditure of money and an immense loss of life, the country is apparently farther from a settlement than ever, and the conquest of the South is still indefinitely postponed. Nothing has been gained by the war and the country is rapidly going to destruction. How long will the people of the North submit to this state of things? Will they not arise in their might and demand the cessation of civil strife?[1]

Less than a week later, as if in answer to his critics, Lincoln appointed U. S. Grant to the newly created rank of lieutenant general, giving him command of all of the Union armies. Now at last Lincoln, and the Union, had found a soldier capable of ending the war. Grant was in his mid forties, with a squint in his left eye, stooped shoulders, and a uniform that, charitably, tended toward the shabby. But his very plainness drew people to him—he was without "airs or falderols or highfalutin talk"—and his record on the battlefield—the victories at Forts Henry and Donelson, Vicksburg and Missionary Ridge—made it crystal clear that here was a man who could fight.

Grant's strategy to end the war, hopefully by the fall of 1864, was straightforward. Convinced that Union armies had "acted independently and without concert, like a balky team, no two ever pulling together," Grant worked out a plan to apply the whole weight of Northern resources and manpower remorselessly, concentrating forces against the principal

Confederate armies, wearing them down until there was no more life in them. As soon as those armies vanished, he reasoned, the rebellion would end. There were two Rebel armies that had to be put out of commission: The incomparable Army of Northern Virginia, commanded by Robert E. Lee, and the Army of Tennessee, now led by Joseph E. Johnston. Grant would go for Lee, William T. Sherman was to destroy Johnston's army.

Only three New Jersey regiments, the Thirteenth, Thirty-third, and Thirty-fifth, saw active duty under Sherman in the western theater of the war. The Thirteenth, a three-year regiment recruited mostly from Essex, Hudson, and Passaic counties, had already been bloodied at Antietam, Chancellorsville, and Gettysburg. The Thirty-third and Thirty-fifth were Zouave outfits, garbed in natty dark blue trousers, a short blue jacket trimmed in red, a crimson sash, and a blue French-style cap or "kepi." Their outlandish uniforms aside, the Zouaves proved to be every bit as battle-ready as the seasoned veterans of the Thirteenth.

Brimming with confidence, Sherman set out after Confederate general Joseph E. Johnston on May 4 with nearly 100,000 men. Sherman's goal was to annihilate Johnston's army and seize Atlanta, a critical transportation center that was second only to Richmond as a source of supplies and munitions for the South's armies. Sherman's men pushed southeast into Georgia along the line of the Western & Atlantic Railroad, clashing with Johnston's troops at Dalton, Resaca, Allatoona Pass, Dallas, and the Kennesaw Mountains. Each time the Yankees managed to outflank the increasingly desperate Rebels, and gradually, inexorably, Sherman's men closed in on Atlanta.

The Thirty-third New Jersey, assigned to the XXth Corps, collided with the Confederates at Resaca, where Johnston had deployed his men on a ridge blocking Sherman's path. When Southern artillery opened a deadly fire, the bluecoats were ordered to take the guns "at all hazards." With two New York regiments the Thirty-third attacked the Rebel battery, braving a hail of lead that cost the Jerseymen nearly one hundred casualties. The *Paterson Daily Press* printed Corporal Marvin Denniston's account:

We left Lookout valley on the 4th [of May,] and marched all the week, early and late. My feet were sore, and it was awfully hot. I threw away my overcoat, woolen blanket, zouave jacket, and everything I did not need. I cannot tell you the plan of the battle, but I can tell you of myself. . . . We came up to the rebels; they were on a range of hills, strongly fortified. Our brigade was marched to the highest point. One regiment had gone ahead of us, and we could hear a shot now and then. Our regiment was sent forward; we went to the foot of the hill and unslung our knapsacks. Company B was deployed first, and then the whole regiment as skirmishers, and we start up; it was stony and steep. I thought I never could go, but soon the firing commenced, and our captain was shot the first one, in the leg, which has since been taken off. Our company was on the extreme right, and I went nearly to the top before I saw a rebel. I was half bent, with my gun at a trail, when I saw a man step from behind a tree and raise his gun. I fell to the ground as soon as I could, and the ball struck not six inches from my side. I tell you, I cannot express my feelings at that moment. We kept up a fire for some twenty minutes, dodging from one tree to another, expecting to get a ball every minute. . . . Every once in a while some of our boys would scream out "I am wounded."

Our division all marched up, heavy firing going on at the same time. Then we were drawn up in a line in the woods. There were three or four lines ahead of us, and we all made a rush, yelling and hooting, guns roaring, bullets singing and whizzing amongst us. Here was another hill to ascend, and when the lines ahead of us reached the top, they lay down: but our colonel would not let us, and we rushed right over them, the men hollering "Go in, Jersies, we will follow you!" Over the hill, down the hollow, up another hill, we drove the rebels; but there we had to stop. Oh! What a dreadful volley they poured into us! We had to drop and lie still, and didn't I hug the ground close? There we lay amongst the dead and wounded. The rebels made a rush on our flank, but were repulsed. We stayed on the hill until dark and the firing had stopped. They came to the top of the hill and fired into us again. We could not see them. Many of us started down the hill, and I did not stop till I got behind a log; but [we] were formed again, and went up. It was a lovely moonlight night, and one of our bands was playing "Yankee Doodle." About 12 o'clock the fight commenced. Our men made a rush on their batteries and took them. . . .

The rebels skedaddled that night, and we have been after them all this week; they are not far ahead now. . . . They have burned bridges as they went and we have waded some, and one we came across in two flat boats. Gen. Geary stood on the bank when we came over and said, "Come on, Jersies, only two corps between Lee and Richmond." He was in front of us looking at us when we laid in line of battle, the bullets coming like hail. . . . We take the railroad and repair it as we go along. Our cavalry scour the country, and we forage, kill chickens, pigs, calves and everything we got hold of. Nobody but women left.[2]

With Sherman's forces closing in on Atlanta, Confederate President Jefferson Davis, long dissatisfied with Johnston's performance, replaced him with the more aggressive John Bell Hood. The XXth Corps crossed the Chatahoochee River on July 17 and two days later Peach Tree Creek, less than five miles from Georgia's capital. On the following day the Thirty-third was ordered forward 500 yards to prepare gun emplacements on a small rise. Suddenly a swarm of Alabama graybacks shouting the Rebel yell came crashing through the trees.

About 3 p.m. the Division skirmishers having seized a hill some 400 or 500 yards in advance of the main line, which it was important to hold, General Geary sent for the . . . 33rd. The Regiment . . . was ordered to fortify the position and to support the skirmish line; preparations were also to be made to plant a battery. The Regiment had scarcely reached the position, and had not yet stacked its arms when a heavy volley was poured upon the skirmishers in advance; the woods in front—apparently deserted—were filled with heavy lines of the enemy, rapidly advancing, with cheers and yells; in an instant they were upon the Regiment, delivering a heavy fire. The advance line halted for a moment, but only to swing down the ravine on the right, passing to the right and rear of the Regiment, pouring in a heavy fire from those quarters. Simultaneously dense masses of the enemy were rapidly approaching on the left. The 33rd stood firing defiantly, braving overwhelming numbers; and not until the rebels were so close as to order the surrender of the Regimental colors, did Colonel Fourrat give the orders to "fall back fighting."

The moment the regiment commenced to retire, the rebels with a loud exultant cheer, rushed in upon it, sweeping, almost over-trampling, the men back to the main line. The impetus of the enemy's charge was terrible; almost completely surrounding the Regiment, his lines dashed upon the main line seemingly instantaneously with the arrival of the Regiment. The dense masses of the enemy[,] covering the front of the entire Corps, bore down upon our lines, unprotected by any completed works, and it was only by the most desperate fighting and obstinacy that the Corps was saved from annihilation. Charging in the old "Stonewall Jackson" style, and fighting as they have never fought in Georgia before, advancing in all the pomp of war, banners waving, swords and muskets glistening, the enemy was confident of overwhelming our lines; but the Corps of Joe Hooker was not to be swept away without a struggle and fighting as ever; dark closed in upon a defeated and discomfited foe, who fell back abandoning his dead, torn and bleeding.

Regimental losses at Peach Tree Creek were heavy, seventy-two killed, wounded, and missing. Worse, the regimental colors were lost.

With deepest regret but without shame or sense of disgrace I write, the 33rd in the fight of the 20th lost the regimental colors presented by the State. After the command had been given to fall back, the color-bearer and color-guard halted, evidently supposing an order to that effect had been given. Surrounded as they were by the enemy, this delay was fatal; separated from the rest of the command and overpowered, the bearer of the regimental colors were captured and the flag that had waved triumphantly and proudly on the hard-fought fields of the campaign fell into the hands of the enemy. One color-bearer is missing, one of the color-guard is killed, and two wounded and missing. Lost, not through cowardice but overpowered. The Thirty-third feels its loss, but it feels no disgrace—its 13 officers and 221 men killed or wounded or languishing in Southern prisons are pledges of its bravery—it is proud of its bravery and does not feel that this has been one whit tarnished.[3]

Hood's furious attacks on the Union armies slowed but did not stop the Yankee advance. On the evening of September 1 Hood's exhausted men evacuated Atlanta, blowing up carloads of ammunition. The next day, as a jubilant Sherman was telegraphing the news to Washington—"Atlanta is ours," he wired, "and fairly won!"—the bluecoats raised the Stars and Stripes over city hall.

In mid-November Sherman's army left the smoking ruins of Atlanta behind, launching their epic march through Georgia to the sea. With a force of 62,000 of his best soldiers, Sherman cut a fifty-mile-wide swath of destruction through the heartland of the Confederacy, leaving in his wake wrecked railroads, burned depots, plantation houses looted, and farms stripped bare. Boldly cutting all communications with the North, the triumphant Yankees plunged into the Georgia pinelands, moving ten to fifteen miles a day, avoiding battle with the weakened Rebels, thoroughly enjoying what one troop admitted was "a gay old campaign." A month later Sherman linked up with the Federal fleet in Savannah harbor and, on December 22 entered the city, sending a jaunty telegram to Lincoln: "I beg to present you, as a Christmas gift, the city of Savannah."

"The mystery is solved," wrote a member of the Thirteenth Regiment, "and Sherman's grand army, after a march of over 300 miles through the heart of the South, has at last halted . . . behind the city of Savannah." He continued:

The 20th Army Corps . . . left the ruins of Atlanta on the 15th day of November, after having destroyed a greater part of the once "Queen City" of the South. All the public buildings, including the Georgia State Rail-

147

road depots, rolling mill, and machine shops, were leveled with the ground; some of these were splendid specimens of workmanship . . . and no little amount of labor was requisite to demolish them, which was done with the use of battering rams. . . . The railroads leading from the city were all torn up, the ties burnt and rails burnt and twisted, rendering them altogether unserviceable.

Leaving the smoking ruins of the city in our rear, our course lay along the Augusta Railroad to the village of Decatur, thence around the base of Stone Mountain, destroying the railroad as we advanced. The next town in our advance was that of Social Circle, a small but pleasant railroad station on the Augusta road. Here commenced in earnest "foraging for supplies," and from the amount of provisions daily gathered by the troops, it was plain that the South was not in a starving condition. Corn, pork, sweet potatoes, fowls of all descriptions, butter, eggs, honey, &c., came flowing in, in such quantities as would have delighted the eyes and heart of an epicure. The good people expecting us along, made preparations, by burying their provisions, for our reception with empty larders, but the quick-scented Yankees soon discovered the hiding place, and the good things were brought to light. . . .

From here we marched to Milledgeville, the State Capital. Here, for the first time in our line of march, matters looked as though an attack, or resistance to our further advance might be expected, but the defenses of city were found to be deserted, and the city was formally surrendered, our corps marching in with drums beating and colors flying about 3 o'clock on the afternoon of the 22d of November. As you enter the town, on your left you notice the State Penitentiary, which contained at the time of our occupation a large number of convicts, who were let loose, and the prison destroyed by our troops. Farther up to the left may be seen the Executive mansion, a dark, sombre looking place, somewhat the worse from time and neglect. This, with the capital and depot, were all destroyed. Farther along was the State Arsenal, a brick structure, containing large quantities of powder, a few firearms, and large numbers of lances and large knives, some 18 inches in length, which were destined to hack the entire Yankee nation into mince meat.

After a short rest . . . we left on the 24th, once more shaping our course for the coast. Sandersonville, the next in course, was not entered without a struggle, a portion of [Confederate] cavalry disputing our advance. Here the 13th New Jersey again distinguished themselves. Deploying as skirmishers, they charged upon the rebel lines, driving them through and beyond the town. Sandersonville, being the county seat of

Washington County, of course contained a Court House and jail—to be destroyed.

After leaving Sandersonville, the country grew more swampy and less populous and wealthy, consequently foraging became less profitable. Our course from here lay . . . through a forest of immense pine trees, with an occasional small plantation to vary the scene. Our way became considerably impeded through here from the seemingly bottomless swamps which cross the roads at short intervals, and across which the rebels had felled trees to obstruct our progress.

Upon arriving in our present position [on an island in the river opposite Savannah], foraging having given out and our supply of breadstuffs having become exhausted, the question of supplies began to force itself upon us in a rather unpleasant manner. Luckily we found upon the river banks two or three rice mills in running order, with a large supply of rice in the hull on hand. These, manned by the negroes, were set in motion. . . .

When the order was read to the troops, publishing the fact of communications being established with the fleet, they sent up such a shout as must have sent terror to the hearts of the rebels in our front. Then the glorious news, 21 tons of *mail* for Sherman's army arrived. . . . Then, when [the mail] was received and distributed, to see the cheering, smiling faces everywhere, for all seemed to have one letter at least, while others, more lucky, had all they could read for an hour perhaps. Then the papers with the news; the confirmation of the success of the Union ticket, and the home news. . . .

Yesterday I saw a collection of negroes . . . that had joined us since leaving Atlanta. There were some 900 grown persons in the group, besides innumerable pickaninnies, and these of all shapes, and almost every hue and color, from the seemingly pure Circassian blood to the genuine African of late importation. Judge what must have been the number of slaves who have left their masters to follow the uncertain fortune of the Yankee army during this strange and mysterious campaign.[4]

Sherman's march through Georgia was but one of several coordinated moves by Grant to break up the Confederate armies and bring the war to an end before 1864 was over. Nathaniel Bank's Army of the Gulf was ordered to capture Mobile, then push northward to prevent Rebel forces in Alabama from threatening Sherman. Union troops in the Shenandoah Valley were to threaten Lee's communications and tie down its defenders, preventing them from reinforcing Lee. The Army of the James, commanded by Benjamin Butler, was to advance up the James River, threatening the Confederate capital from the south. Meantime Grant, with a force nearly twice that of Lee, would cross the Rapidan River and turn the Confederate army's right flank, forcing a battle that, given the North's superiority in men and material, might well grind up Lee's army and open the road to Richmond.

Just after midnight on May 4, 1864, units of the Army of the Potomac began crossing the Rapidan in two columns, hoping to move through a six-teen-square-mile tract of marsh and scrub woods known locally as The Wilderness. A rapid movement would put Union forces on Lee's right flank, in open meadows where Grant's superior forces could outmaneuver the enemy. Shortly after sun-up, after studying scouting reports that the Federals were on the march, Lee sent three corps eastward to intercept them. Fewer in numbers but more familiar with the terrain, the Confeder-ates crashed into the bluecoats as they marched along narrow roads through the tangled thickets. Savage fighting surged back and forth through the underbrush, as friendly units fired on each other by mistake, regiments marched blindly in a haze of gunsmoke and the stubby pines and dry needles caught fire, threatening to cremate the thousands of in-jured soldiers from both sides lying on the blood-soaked ground. In three days of murderous combat, over 27,000 men were dead, injured, or miss-ing in action.

The Fifteenth New Jersey, assigned to Colonel Emory Upton's brigade, was posted on a small hillock in the woods. It was a little past noon when the regiment was ordered into The Wilderness, wrote Chaplain Alanson Haines:

We formed in line of battle, and began to march through the jagged pines, as we were able; keeping as good a front as the thicket would per-mit. Across some open ground we double-quicked. . . . On the advance was a wooded hill. The Fifteenth was ordered . . . to take a position upon it, to fill a gap. . . . Here we were established, while at times the conflict raged around us and in our front, the remainder of that day and the day following. . . . It was impossible to see the enemy; and though we peered into the thick woods, we were fighting invisible foemen. We soon began intrenching. Our men scraped the stones and earth before them as best they could, until spades were brought. All the time the enemy were sending a shower of bullets over and past us. It would at times lessen, then start again afresh. We lay, on the crest of the hill, stooping low as every fusilade swept over. . . . We replied by occasional volleys, but could not see what damage we inflicted. We were screened by bushes on our front. The enemy before was screened in the same manner. Between the two lay an open, cleared flat, of small extent, through which passed the Orange pike.

After a time two or three pieces of artillery were directed upon us. The shells flew over our heads at a lively rate. The trees rattled and the branches fell; but though we bowed our heads low to the ground and knew not what was to follow, no man left his place. Captain John H. Vanderveer, of Company E, had his hand shattered by a piece of shell, and was wounded in the throat by a bullet. . . . On the right and far off to the left the musketry continued to roll in a heavy continuous roar. One volley, just at dark, commenced far away on the right, possibly two miles off, and came rolling down the line, like thunder, until opposite us, when it stopped, our regiment, and one or two that joined up, having orders not to fire until the enemy appeared in front, which they did not do. In the excitement it was no easy matter to restrain the ardor of our regiment, and keep the men steady. All night we lay with arms in our hands, drawing a volley every few moments from the rebel skirmishers a few yards off. This made us lie low and kept us in constant wakefulness. The dead were lying thick about us and some wounded in a field to our left, between the lines, crying out for water, and to be carried off.

Before dawn on May 6 the men of the Fifteenth were put on the alert, mindful of a possible daybreak attack:

Volleys were fired from either side, then the noises died down, with only an occasional shot from rebel sharpshooters, as some man exposed himself. Just at sunrise Captain Ellis Hamilton, Company F, stood up and walked in front along the picket line, and thus became a mark for one of the rebel riflemen posted in a tree. He was struck by a ball which passed through both thighs. . . .

At length, an hour after sunrise, as we were, ourselves, advancing to assault, the roar of artillery and musketry on the right announced that the enemy had assailed. Soon the combat approached, and swept by our regimental front, and so on to the left. It was vehement for a time, but presently died down, and the morning was only disturbed by occasional discharges of artillery and scattered firing of riflemen and shots on the picket line. Leonard Decker, of Company D, was killed. A piece of shell passed under his arm, tearing away the elbow, and making a great hole in his side. We carried him, bleeding, a little to the rear, but he died a few hours later. We buried him in a shallow grave behind our line. . . . The unburied dead were numerous. The bodies were black and swollen, and were becoming quite offensive. At one time the woods took fire, and scorched and burned, among the wounded and the dead, but the flames were soon extinguished. . . . The flames ran in our rear, and the smoke and heat added very much to our discomfort. . . .

As the sun was setting we expected the terrific firing of the evening before to begin again, only more loud, from the number of pieces of artillery which had been brought into position. It came as we expected. The enemy . . . made a fierce attack a little to our right. For a time it threatened to sweep away the right wing of the army. . . .

We could see the line to the right of us giving way. It did as far as the Fifth Maine and Fifth Wisconsin Regiments, who joined our immediate right, but they and our own were as steady as ever. In front of us some of our sharpshooters were posted, and they could hear Confederate officers trying to get their men to charge, but in vain. They could not be forced in upon our position, over the flat and up our crest. As the right above us was turned, bullets came flying in from our rear, and then, indeed, it became a trying time. Our division hospital was captured, and with it some of our officers' luggage. A panic was started among the attendants, and they made off in great haste, throwing away much of the property consigned to their care.

The First New Jersey Brigade suffered considerably. The Tenth Regiment was in this disorder, and thrown into confusion, and lost nearly an entire company in prisoners. Its commander, Colonel Ryerson, had rallied his men, and made them lie down upon a new line he had determined to hold. A sharp fire starting up again, some of his men began to run from the position. He rose upon one knee, shouting to them to come back. At that moment he received a bullet shot, which pierced the bugle upon his cap and fractured his skull. He was carried to a log cabin in the rear. . . .

Haines, Dr. Hall, and another regimental chaplain were standing near the brigade hospital when the Rebels attacked.

Almost at the first volley Seymour's brigade broke and ran. Nothing remained for us but to move out of the rush of the fugitives, and before the hail of bullets that came whistling by our ears. Soon Shaler's brigade also broke, and added to the confusion. We gathered up all our things and went over the nearest rise of ground, where we knew there was no immediate danger. The rush of disorganized soldiers was great. We began to call upon the men to rally. The cry was taken up through the crowding mass as they flocked by; but, though line officers and men shouted "Rally, boys! Rally, boys!" they were one and all hurrying away, and the cry only seemed to redouble their speed. A color-sergeant of a New York regiment came up to where we stood, with his colors, and joined the cry with, "Rally round these colors, boys!" But in vain; they paused but for a moment, and still swept by. So we went to the next roll of land, the color-sergeant keeping with us. Here he called lustily, "Rally here, around these colors." Seizing the non-commissioned officers as they came up, I made a dozen men gather around the flag, and appealed to some officers to stay with us, and show a little courage. I told them I knew there were troops enough in front with their lines unbroken, and we might know the enemy were already checked and being driven, from the sound of the discharges. We gathered some hundred men in a short time. I made them lie down, and was obeyed by all to whom I spoke—as they called me Colonel. Dr. Hall had his horse, and mounting him, rode back and forth, stopping all he could, until we had nearly a regiment made up of fugitives from many. General Wright rode up, and dashed ahead into the front. I thought the retreat was certainly checked at this point; but the enemy opened fire with two guns, and sent their shells bursting over our heads. Then all control over our assemblage was gone. The enemy ceased to advance, and the conflict turned off to the right; but our panic-stricken men took to their heels and deserted us. General Wright rode back hastily, and soon brought a reserve, composed of the One Hundred and Sixth New York and the Fourteenth New Jersey Regiments, who came up in order, and threw themselves under the brow of the hill.

In the midst of the battle Haines and his companions decided to try to rejoin the Fifteenth.

Stragglers from the Tenth and Second [New Jersey regiments] reported great losses, and fierce assaults upon their regiments, but knew nothing of the Fifteenth. We started down the path through the woods, and soon reached the ground which was strewn with dead and wounded troops from both sides. The wounded begged for help, but we stopped only once to examine a man who cried he was bleeding to death. . . . In the dusk we soon lost ourselves in the thicket, and knew not but that we were running upon the enemy. We were debating whether to return, when our movements were quickened by some unexpected volleys in close vicinity. We lost our way entirely; but a kind Providence at last brought us to the pickets of the Union line. We were forced to abandon the idea of reaching our regiment, the attempt seeming almost hopeless.

We feared, too, that they were prisoners, surrounded and overwhelmed by superior numbers. Lieutenant-Colonel Hall, of the Fourteenth, invited us to join him for the night; but he soon received orders to move, and we went with his regiment. At midnight we came upon some stragglers from the brigade, and found our lost hospital attendants. . . . At 2 A. M. Upton's brigade passed, and, to our joy, with the Fifteenth bringing up the rear.

I called out, "Colonel Penrose!" and he answered, "All right, Chaplain." He said that they had held their position on the knoll until after 9 o'clock; and, though the firing had been very heavy on his front, his losses were almost nothing. Lieutenant-Colonel Campbell remained behind, to bring off the rear pickets. My own horse was said to be captured, so I mounted Colonel Campbell's, and we rode a distance through a thicket, tearing our clothes and scratching our faces, and, an hour later, lay down on the ground, where we remained until daybreak.[5]

John Bacon Hoffman of Shiloh, in Cumberland County, a private in the Tenth New Jersey, was among the thirty-eight casualties the regiment suffered in the Battle of the Wilderness. But Hoffman was one of the lucky ones: Captured by the Confederates, he was liberated a few days later by Sheridan's cavalry.

On Wednesday, May 4th, morning at four o'clock the whole Brigade and all of the army of the army of the Potomac took up its line of march. We marched all day. It was very hot and dusty. We crossed the Rapidan River on pontoons. At three o'clock we stopped for dinner then resumed our march and encamped at night, tired, sore, dirty and hungry. Early in the A.M. we resumed our march on the plank road and were soon on the battle ground of the Wilderness. We were in the second line of the battle supporting the advance. In the afternoon I was among those who were detailed to work on the breastworks and the sharp shooters were picking at us all the time.

Ten o'clock that night we left the place and marched all night to where our batteries could support us. We threw up breastworks in the morning and held them until night. That was Saturday night, May 7th. We again left them at night and marched all night and past noon, Sunday, when we reached the battle ground near Chancellorsville. We were allowed a few minutes to make coffee and then went in and laid on our faces in the second line of battle for some time. The grape and canister cutting the trees around us at fearful rate. Finally we were ordered forward to relieve the front lines, passed them and charged across an open field or meadow under a galling fire. Many of our boys fell. We went on and soon came into the woods again within a few yards of the rebel breastworks. The balls flew around us with fearful rapidity. Our officers feared that our own men were in front of us and ordered us to cease firing. We obeyed and no fire was returned.

Some of the regiments and part of ours took the alarm and fell back. But there were some of us who would not fall back without the order and in a few minutes we found the rebels had flanked and surrounded us entire. We were only a few and two or three who refused to surrender were quickly shot down. So we had to surrender, were quickly disarmed and marched to the rear of the rebel works, where we lay all night under guard, without a mouthful to eat. We had all of us left our knapsacks in the rear when we went into the engagement and there the rebels took my haversack and canteen. . . .

The next Monday our captors marched us about 25 miles still with nothing to eat. They treated us very kindly, however, and said they would give us if they had it; but had nothing for themselves and I think it was so. Virginia is destitute of provision. They were marching us to Beaver Dam Station from where we were to take the cars for Richmond. We were within half a mile of the station, at about sunset when all at once, one of the guards in the rear shouted out, "The Yanks are coming."

Our guards, numbering about thirty, put spurs to their horses and flew pursued by Sheridan's Cavalry which came down the road like a whirlwind; a whole Brigade of them. So we were rescued. They captured two trains of cars at the station, loaded with provision for Lee's army; such things as smoked meat, hard tack, meal, sugar, coffee, etc. The Cavalry men took what they wanted and so did we. Then the torch was applied and trains, buildings, provisions and all were burned. . . . In the morning we started with the Cavalry. We were on foot and so had to march pretty fast and get along as best as we could but preferred that to being taken as prisoners again as we should have been had we fallen to the rear. . . . From that time until this morning, we have been following up the Cavalry for our lives and hard marching it has been. Our provisions soon ran out and we had to live on what little we could forage as we went along. At one time we were within two miles of Richmond and actually within the outside line of its fortifications. We all expected to be taken again but the Cavalry cut its way through and of course we went along with them.[6]

Under McClellan, Burnside, and Hooker, the Army of the Potomac had fought the Rebels, often valiantly, then regardless of the outcome returned to its base to rest and refit. Not so under Grant. With barely enough time to

catch its breath, the Yankee army was ordered south again, this time toward Spotsylvania, a small crossroads village. Grant's plan was to force Lee to retreat or fight. For the men in the ranks it was a turning point in the war. "Our spirits rose," recalled one veteran. "The men began to sing." For the next eleven months, until the Confederates lay down their arms at Appomattox Court House, the Army of the Potomac kept up a relentless pressure on the enemy.

At Spotsylvania the Rebels built the strongest fieldworks of the war, with trenches, breastworks, artillery emplacements, and a cleared field of fire in front of their first line of defense, felled trees designed to entangle the attackers. Grant tried to flank the Rebel line and smash through it, leading to twelve days of the most vicious fighting seen so far in the war. The Fifteenth New Jersey was in the thick of the battle, its casualty list of 272 men killed, wounded, and missing exceeded only by one other Union regiment. On May 8 the regiment was ordered to charge the Rebel works.

The Fifteenth at once moved gallantly forward, charging at double-quick, but without firing a gun—the enemy also reserving his fire. Soon, the assailants, reaching a marsh, were exposed to an enfilading fire, which swept their ranks in three directions, but though whole companies seemed to melt away, the gallant Jerseymen plunged straight forward through the soft, spongy marsh, forced their way through the fallen timber and over every obstacle until they mounted the crest and standing on the parapets fired on the rebels in their own ditches. So pitiless was the assailing fire that the enemy speedily gave way, and had the Fifteenth been properly supported, or in greater numbers, the victory must have been complete. But now, back in the woods, a drum beat the assembly, and perceiving the weakness of the attacking force, the rebels rallied from all sides to beat back the meagre remnant of the brave little regiment. Thus overwhelmed, the Fifteenth slowly fell back, having lost in all one hundred and one men; but it had performed one of the most gallant achievements of the campaign. . . . The Tenth Regiment, which was sent in about the same time as the Fifteenth, participating in the charge on the front, scattered very soon after becoming engaged—Lieutenant-Colonel Tay, however, leading forward three or four companies until they came up to the works, when he, Captain Snowden and several other officers and a large number of men, after maintaining a short, unequal contest, were forced to surrender.

For the next three days the Fifteenth skirmished with the enemy. On May 12 "hostilities were renewed with unsparing violence" when the First Jersey Brigade was sent forward to attack the same Rebel works it had as-saulted on May 10.

Few charges of this memorable campaign were more difficult, or more grandly executed than that made at this time by the Jersey Brigade. They had not only to force their way through a pine thicket, and then forming, dash across an open space, but to do so in the face of a deadly concentrated fire which no ordinary line could resist. But the Jerseymen were equal to the occasion. Bidding his men reserve their fire until they saw the foe and knew that every shot would tell, Colonel Penrose steadily pushed forward the brave command. A thousand men soon lay lifeless, or wounded and bleeding, upon the ground, but still the line swept on. The Fifteenth, dashing through the abattis before the rebel works, swept over a portion of the breastworks, which for a time they stoutly held, driving out the rebels, or bayonetting those who tena-ciously clung to the position. Some threw down their muskets and lifted their hands in token of surrender and lay crouching in the ditch, only, however, to resume their weapons when their captors were more hardly pressed. Lieutenant Justice, of whom Colonel Campbell said, "He was to-day as brave as a lion," as he rose on the breastwork, waving his sword and shouting to his company, was shot by one of these skulking rebels, who was in turn run through with the bayonet by a man of Company A. Captain Walker was shot through the head at the first exposure to the enemy's fire. Captain Shimer was killed. Lieutenant Vanvoy was wounded, and while moving to the rear, was again struck and expired in a few moments. Captain Van Blarcom received several terrible wounds, but survived with the loss of a leg. Lieutenant Fowler was wounded and captured. . . .

The tenure of the salient was brief. The line to the right and left was broken, and an enfilading fire from a long distance on the right, swept through the thin ranks. The enemy had an inner line of breastworks from which he poured a deadly fire. It was impossible to hold the cap-tured bank so long as it was swept by the works yet untaken. Accord-ingly, the regiment fell back, and when Colonel Campbell gathered his shattered battalion, only seventy-five were found. . . .

So fierce was the incessant shower of bullets that the bodies of the dead were riddled, and great trees cut away a few feet from the ground. Within the salient the dead were literally piled in heaps, and the com-batants fought over a mound of their dead comrades. Few points, if any, on the broad theater of the war witnessed greater carnage than this. Forty bodies, or near one-fifth of the whole regiment, lay on the breastwork, in the ditch or the narrow, open space in front. Numbers had crawled away to expire in the woods, and others were carried to the hospital, there to have their sufferings prolonged for a few days more, and then expire.[7]

Private James Mangan, Company D, who lost his arm in the savagery and was captured, lay a few feet from D Company's captain, James Walker, after both were shot:

Captain Walker fell, pierced with several bullets. About the same time, my right arm was broken below the elbow, and my shoulder pierced by a bullet that laid me out in the trench, with nothing but a bank of earth between me and the enemy. I spoke to the Captain, but he was dead. Close by me lay a comrade whose leg was broken. He could load his musket, but could not get at his caps. So I capped his gun for him several times, and whenever a rebel showed his head he fired at him. We thought we were "gone" anyhow, and so agreed to sell our lives as dearly as possible. And we kept on in this way until he (my comrade) was killed by a ball through the head.[8]

A Confederate strong point known forever afterward as the "Bloody Angle" was the scene of some of the most desperate fighting of the war. Corporal John Beech of the Fourth New Jersey won the Medal of Honor for his heroism that day.

As we arrived on the field the Johnnies were rallying. . . . Our Brigade was halted and almost immediately the command came "right-face," "forward double-quick," "march," and on the run we went about a quarter of a mile towards the right and came to halt in front of an angle in the works which were protected by an abatis of fallen trees. As we were double-quicking, a bullet sped through our ranks and Andrew Broughton of our company fell mortally wounded. . . . We formed rapidly, and almost immediately the command was given to charge.

With a cheer we bounded forward, pushing and pulling away the abatis, and on to, and over the breastworks some of us went. Pierson (of my company) and I mounted the breastworks together, and as we did so, I heard the fatal bullet, as Pierson clapped his hand to his side and started to the rear. Those of us who passed over the breastworks and into the clearing received a murderous fire . . . from the enemy advancing through the clearing, and we had to beat a hasty retreat back to the works, but the Johnnies were right on top of us and captured several of our regiment. . . . The Confederates now advanced until close to the works. Brigade after brigade was brought up around the spot and the fighting became desperate. As I recrossed the breastworks, a section of the battery was being brought into position [and] some of my regiment had to make way for them. Horses and men began to go down before they were in position. My regiment, pretty well mixed up in getting through the abatis had halted and were lying down, firing. The fire was getting murderous and the enemy was preparing for a charge. The battery was well up to the works, and was suffering severely. Seeing the condition of affairs, I laid my musket down and appealed to Captain King . . . to tell some of the men to get up and help work those guns, and I started to serve ammunition. At this time there were but four rounds of canister left, after which we used shell. The battery was charged by a Mississippi Brigade who reached the works, but could get no further. Bullets were flying like hail stones, and with three men, we had to abandon the guns.[9]

May 12 was a fateful day for the Eleventh New Jersey as well. A cold rain began to fall as the Second Corps charged a salient in the Rebel breastworks, a charge that would split Lee's army in two at a cost to the Eleventh of 70 of the 200 men engaged. "As we moved forward," wrote Thomas Marbaker, the regimental historian, "orders were given to make as little noise as possible."

As soon as [the men] struck . . . open ground they gave voice to a cheer, which was answered by a volley of musketry and two cannon shots. The line now moved rapidly forward, and, before the enemy could recover, had swept over the works, capturing four thousand prisoners, twenty pieces of artillery, with their caissons and horses, thirty colors, a quantity of small arms, together with [two rebel generals]. But the battle was not to be so easily won as this initial success would seem to indicate. We pressed forward to the second line of works, but they had been strongly manned, and the advance was checked.

The position captured was of the utmost importance to Lee, and he rapidly threw forward reinforcements . . . and then ensued one of the most desperate struggles of the war. The Union forces were pushed back and the enemy again occupied the interior of the works, but the Union troops clung desperately to their face and could not be dislodged. At the point occupied by the Eleventh Regiment, the reverse side of the salient, offered but little protection from the fire of the enemy's works on the hill, consequently our men moved a little to the left where a sharp descent in the ground running from and forming an acute angle with the salient offered some protection. For some distance to the left of where our line joined the works the enemy occupied one side and we the other. Our line under the brow of the hill opened fire over the top of the works so soon as formed. This was our only safety, for when our fire slackened for a moment the enemy would rise from behind the works and pour a destructive fire into our ranks along the foot of the hill. Our forces at this point was not less than ten ranks in depth. The enemy brought up their reinforcements under cover of the woods in the rear. Many of them, either ignorant of our position or over-anxious to single out an officer, would raise their heads above the works and fall back dead. Our fire was mainly kept up by those in the rear loading their pieces and passing them up to the front ranks. A great portion of the enemy's fire was of a random character, although many of our men were hit by shots fired through the crevices of the logs and holes in the earth-works. Frequently their muskets could be seen with the barrels resting on top of the logs and the stock in a forked stick, the gun was then fired without exposing the hand. No doubt many of our men were struck by these shots, and invariably in the head. Lieutenant-Colonel Schoonover was slightly wounded under the ear by one of these shots. Occasionally during the day the enemy would display a regimental flag above the works, but the staff would be almost instantly cut off by our bullets. Their works at this point were constructed with traverses a few yards apart. Several times a white flag was shown above the works, and as soon as our fire would slacken, the men, evidently between two of these traverses, would jump over and surrender. At one time the men to the left of where the white flag was displayed discovered the movement too soon for us, and for our own safety we were compelled to open fire before all of them were safely over, and a number fell back into their own lines pierced by the bullets of friends and foes. The fire was kept up until nearly midnight, when it ceased, and the entire line fell into our hands after fourteen hours of constant fighting.[10]

The fighting on May 12 was some of the most horrific of the war, a frenzy of killing that ended only when Lee ordered the exhausted Confederate survivors to fall back to a new line a half mile in the rear. Next morning the "Bloody Angle" contained only corpses. Wrote Colonel John Schoonover:

I went over the works at daylight the next morning, and the sight was one not easily forgotten. In the ditches between the traverses I counted two hundred and fifty dead, mostly shot in the head, and in some places they lay three and four deep. I only recollect finding one wounded man there. He was sitting erect, his eyes completely closed, and seemed in great agony. A short distance in the rear of the rebel works I noticed two rebel colonels lying side by side, while their horses lay near them. The evidence of the continued fire at this point during the day and part of the night was everywhere apparent. The trees near the works were stripped of their foliage, and looked as though an army of locusts had passed during the night. The brush between the lines was cut and torn into shreds, and the fallen bodies of men and horses lay there with the flesh shot and torn from the bones. The peculiar whirring sound of a flying ramrod was frequently heard during the day. I noticed two of these that had fastened themselves in the oak trees near by. While the great number of the enemy's dead and the terrible effects of our fire upon the logs composing the breastworks attested the general accuracy of our fire, the absence of the foliage from the top of the tallest trees made it evident that during a battle there is much random firing. There is a large percentage of men in actual battle who load carefully, aim deliberately and shoot to kill. On the other hand, it is not an uncommon thing for a soldier, amidst the excitement of battle, to load his gun, shut his eyes and fire in the air straight over his head.[11]

From May 5 through May 12 the Army of the Potomac lost some 32,000 men killed, wounded, and missing, a total greater than that of any other week of the war. Fifteenth Regiment chaplain Alanson Haines did his best to succor the wounded and dying:

With Doctor Hall . . . I found a place in the rear—a little hollow with green grass and a spring of water—where we made hasty preparations for receiving the coming wounded. Those that could walk soon began to find their way in of themselves, and some few were helped in by their comrades as soon as the charge was over and a portion withdrawn. It was a terrible thing to lay some of our best and truest men in a long row on the blankets, waiting their turn for the Surgeon's care. Some came with body wounds, and arms shattered, and hands dangling. With the hospital attendants, I began ripping the clothes and dressing the wounds of the slightly wounded, while Doctor Hall attended the more dangerous cases. At ten o'clock, with the drum corps, I sought the regiment to take off any of our wounded we could find. On my way, I met some men carrying Orderly Sergeant Martin Van Gilder, of Hamburg, mortally wounded, in a blanket. With his hand all blood he seized mine, saying, "Chaplain, I am going. Tell my wife I am happy."[12]

William S. Van Fleet, a twenty-eight-year-old schoolmaster from Parsippany, joined the First New Jersey on January 5, 1864. The Wilderness and Spotsylvania were his first and only battles. "I received your letter last Friday night," he wrote his wife, Anna, a day or so before the army began its march toward The Wilderness. "I was on picket at the time."

I was glad to hear from you that you were well. . . . I expect we will soon be on the move and when we do move I expect that it will not be long before we go right into battle. When we do get on the move I don't suppose that I will be able to write so often. I have written nearly every week since I have been here. I should like to see you all but that is impossible now. I hope that I may be spared to see you all again but God's will be done. I don't fear death. If I should not see you again on earth, I pray that we may meet in heaven above. . . . Love to all and a kiss for my little girls.

Severely wounded at Spotsylvania, Van Fleet would die on May 25 at the Federal hospital at Fredericksburg. "I will tell you of the death of your son, the best I can remember," wrote a comrade to Van Fleet's grieving father:

I went to the hospital in Fredericksburg the 14th; he was there at that time in great distress; he was wounded in the cavity of the knee and on the 21st, I think, his leg was amputated above the knee; before this I wrote a letter to his wife at his request. He was brought back beside me after his leg was off. He was in good spirits and his stump did as well as could be expected. It became corrupt with maggots, but the Doctor got them all out again and he looked well in the face. I was talking to him at times all the day before he died; did what I could for him. . . . He ate a good dinner of potatoes and beef the day before he died. It seemed to me that he was conscious of his position for he talked to me a great deal on religion. I think he told me he was a member of a church. He seemed to be happy and calm. I think he gave his heart to God, [and] not knowing what the result of his limb [surgery] may be, said he wanted to see his wife and friends. I shall tell you something I did not tell you in my first letter, that is, the night he died the bandage broke loose and he bled to death. I heard him screaming as the last drop of blood was leaving him. I called the nurse but he could not be found until your son was a corpse. Had the doctor been in the ward he could have taken up the artery and sewn him. He was buried to the left of the city and a head board with his name and his regiment on, and you can find it easy enough, but you can't move him till October.[13]

"I propose to fight it out on this line if it takes all summer," declared Grant in a dispatch sent to Washington on the day before the Bloody Angle, and he meant it. Instead of disengaging, Grant replenished his depleted ranks with additional regiments drawn from the defenses of Washington. Southward again went the Federal army, assaulting Lee's lines and maneuvering to turn his right flank. Crossing the North Anna River, the bluecoats moved toward Cold Harbor, a dusty crossroads less than six miles northeast of Richmond.

Never before had the nation seen fighting such as this. Rebel and Yankee forces remained in close contact, as bluecoat and grayback probed each other's lines. On June 1 the Sixth Corps was ordered to assault the entrenched Rebel lines defending the approaches to Cold Harbor. Three companies of the Fourteenth New Jersey, led by Captain John C. Patterson, breached the enemy defenses. With the captain in the lead, 14 Jerseymen captured 166 Rebel soldiers. Wrote Patterson:

We moved out from our position at Crump's Creek on the evening of May 31st, marching all the night in the direction of Cold Harbor, and reaching there a little past twelve o'clock, pm. [On] June lst, we were immediately formed in line, and our corps (Sixth) ordered to get ready for a charge. The bugle sounded at about a quarter to five o'clock, p. m., and we dashed forward, my company on the right. We suffered severely, but getting through a slough we were soon upon the enemy, leaping the works, and putting him to route. I being on the right directed the movement. We pursued the rebels some sixty paces beyond their works, when I ordered a halt, finding that we were alone. I then formed the line, and passing to the left, found that we were broken from the rest of the regiment; I then faced left, and moved off obliquely to rejoin the rest of the regiment to the left and rear. In moving along the enemy's works, I found the cause of the break in the regiment to be a bend in the works. As we sprang on the works, just at the bend, we saw the enemy in pretty strong force just above the bend firing at the rest of my regiment. I immediately called to the men to follow me, but the noise of battle, I suppose, prevented my call being heard. I then called for volunteers, and in answer fourteen brave boys sprang over the works, led by young Rodman M. Clark. I ordered the boys to fire a volley into the rebels as they stood packed together, which they did, and the most of them threw down their arms. At this point young Clark displayed great gallantry, dashing in among the rebs and commencing to disarm them. Some of them still kept firing at us, but all the while we were disarming others. I ran up to the one I judged to be a superior officer, and placing my pistol at his head, told him if he did not have his men stop firing I would shoot him, whereupon he ordered them to cease. Before they did so, however, one scamp fired at me so closely that I felt the heat of the explosion in my face. The rebel officer proved to be a Major. I ordered him to pass to the rear, and then proceeded, assisted by young Clark and the other boys, to secure as many prisoners as possible—our time being short, as we were feeling the fire of rebel reinforcements. In about ten to fifteen minutes, I secured and turned over to the Provost Marshal one hundred and sixty-six men, including one Major, three Captains and three Lieutenants. I had one man killed and one badly wounded.[14]

By now both armies were bloodied and exhausted. The Rebels were hungry as well, this Grant knew from prisoners captured during the last four weeks of constant fighting, and their morale was slipping. A final blow at the Confederate troops manning the lines at Cold Harbor, he thought, would drive them toward Richmond and perhaps annihilate them. But Lee's Army of Northern Virginia was far from finished, and the Yankee troops had nearly run out of steam. A massive assault ordered by Grant on June 3 resulted in 7,000 Union casualties, with no ground gained. "I regret this assault more than any one I have ever ordered," wrote Grant that evening.

The Twelfth Regiment, raised in the southern part of the state, had been decimated in the campaign from The Wilderness to Cold Harbor, with a total strength now of only 100 men. Forty-one had been killed, 212 wounded, and 15 missing since the army crossed the Rapidan. The attack on June 3 brought them within 150 yards of the enemy's positions but they could advance no further. Corporal William P. Haines of Company F remembered Cold Harbor as "one of the dreariest, bloodiest, most unsatisfactory of our whole list of battles."

Our faces were drawn and pinched from excitement and exposure; our clothing ragged and dirty; our scant rations were neither stimulating nor nourishing; and our ranks were so terribly thinned out, that the whole regiment only took up the space of a company, and the few who were left were not very hungry for more fighting. After a very hot and dusty all-night march, we halted at a little cross-road house, just at sunrise, June 2d. The smiling slaves soon gathered around us, and, in answer to our questions, told us, " Dis yar is Cold Harbor, boss," though why so called, we never found out, as it is far inland. We were completely tired out with our twenty-four hours' march, and were asleep almost as soon as we struck the ground; but after resting for an hour or more, we were moved up in line of battle, and the rebel bullets from an unseen foe in

the bushes ahead of us, began to sing their familiar music in our ears.
We halted at a fence, which we soon tore down, piled up, and covered
with dirt, for a slight breastwork; and lay behind this the rest of the day
and night. . . .

In the advance of the skirmishers, next morning at daylight, as we
were working our way through the thick bushes, we saw a rebel soldier
at the foot of a big tree ahead of us, and as he seemed disinclined to
move at the invitation of our rifles, we made a run for him, and found he
was cold and stiff, having been killed by our cavalry the day before. In
his haversack we found a small loaf of corn bread, one end of which was
soaked with his blood, but as Johnny cake was a great luxury to us, we
cut off the damp end and breakfasted on the rest, first rolling him out, so
we could get back of the tree for a few minutes' rest. Then we advanced
to the edge of the open field, the main line came up somewhat broken,
and we re-formed for the charge. While doing this, a rebel shell passed
right lengthwise of our line, about two feet from the ground, and so
close that it seemed to knock down almost every man in the regiment,
just by the force of its wind, and Captain McComb, who was commanding the regiment that morning, and standing facing us, one step in front,
had his leg completely torn off, and soon bled to death. We started in on
this charge fully determined to either drive them back or die; but the
Fifth Corps troops, which connected on our right, failed to be ready and
did not move, and as we rushed across the field and little orchard our
flank was in air, and the rebel batteries began to rake our line endways
with grape and canister, and by the time we reached their main line,
fully one-half of that charging column of three brigades were stretched
out on the ground; and as the rebels very pointedly refused to vacate, we
hurriedly fell back, gathering up the wounded as we ran, and sought
shelter in the edge of the woods, and back of the same tree from which
we had rolled the dead rebel a few minutes before. Here we held our
position; the axes and shovels were brought in by the engineers; and we
cut and rolled up logs for a slight breastwork, right in plain sight of the
rebels, not over two hundred yards in front of us. And whilst at this work
Joseph Jones received a bullet in the abdomen, which caused his death a
few days later. We held this light line all day, and as soon as it was dark
we went to work like beavers, and at daylight next morning we had a fine
trench and a bank of earth in front of us, three feet high and ten feet
thick, with a head-log on top, raised just high enough to get our muskets
under. Here we spent eight days, in comparative safety, while at the
front; but the open level ground in the rear made the duty of bringing
up supplies very dangerous.

Samuel Iredell and Isaac Schlichter were detailed on the morning of June 4th to go to the rear for rations. Sam was hit on the head by a spent ball, which stunned him badly. Isaac was shot through the body and died a few days later, after the shortest service of any man in the company. A new recruit, he spent but one night in our ranks, and received his death-wound in the morning. . . . The other companies had about the same casualties, so that three officers and ninety two men were all that were left in the line of that grand old regiment which marched from Woodbury less than two years before with one thousand men. A hole in the earthwork and a shallow ditch made safer communication with our skirmish line; and ditches and trenches in the rear concealed our fires and gave safety in preparing our meals. One comrade, of Company A, dug a cave, wherein he built his fire and made his coffee under ground, a hole serving as a chimney. We held this position for eight days, in hopes that the rebels would get tired of waiting and come over and make us a friendly visit, as we had called on them the first day, and in common courtesy they should return the call; but they were not sociable, only on two of the nights, when they opened on us with their batteries and gave us a lively serenade of shell and balls, during which and whilst lying low behind our earthworks, I felt something heavy strike the ground by my side, and by the flash of the guns I saw what I was confident was a smoking shell, which I grabbed up and threw as far as possible to the rear, fully expecting it to burst in my hands, which it luckily failed to do. Next morning, when we looked for that shell, we found an almost round knot, or wart, that a passing cannon ball had knocked off a large tree in our front, and our imagination had transformed it into a smoking shell and set our hair a-la-pompadour. We saw our sharpshooters play a neat trick on some of the rebel sharpshooters, who kept up a damaging fire on anyone who showed up near a big tree just in the rear of our line. They had killed one and wounded two more, when two of Berdan's men (one an Indian) came up; but they could not locate the fatal rebel, so they took positions about twenty yards apart and told us to hold up a cap on a ramrod, so that it looked like a head peeping over the earthworks, when the rebel promptly put a bullet through it. By the smoke of his gun our sharpshooters saw where he was—near a small tree on higher ground, quite a distance back from their line of battle—and as soon as our men got their telescope rifles set for the distance, our cap took another look over, got another bullet, and that rebel laid down to rest; another took his place, with the same result; and the third one soon followed the other two—to the hospital or cemetery—and no more shots came from that position.

The dead lay on this field, between our lines, unburied until June 7th (four days), in that hot sun, until the stench became unbearable, when a truce was agreed upon. Both sides sent out parties to bury their dead, and for two hours not a shot was fired, though no one was allowed out in front but the burial parties. We ran about on top of our breastworks, and laughed and talked with the saucy rebels like the best of friends, and James Mosey went over and swapped coffee for tobacco with one of them; but just as the two hours were up, the bugle sounded the recall. They shouted, "Get down, Yanks!" and in less than a minute it was certain death to show a head on either side. A few nights after this we very quietly slipped off and left them listening to the music of one of our brass bands, put there on purpose to amuse them, while we were rapidly moving off by the left flank towards the James River and Petersburg. They never knew we were gone until 9 o'clock the next morning, when we were many miles away, laughing to think how nicely we had given them the slip.[15]

The First New Jersey, mustered in for three years on May 21, 1861, was beyond its term of service when the Federal army reached Cold Harbor. On June 7 the Jersey Brigade was ordered to charge the Rebel lines. First Regiment Color Sergeant Charles A. Pettie had a narrow escape:

At about 9 A.M., an aide from some general at headquarters came rushing over and cried "Charge." Some of the boys said our time has expired, others said it was not a proper order, not being given to us by our commander. A few of us, however, jumped over the little earthwork and charged. I had gone about half the distance to the rebel line and found myself alone. Just then a charge of canister struck the earth a short distance in front of me, throwing the coarse gravel in my face and eyes, blinding me for probably two hours or more. I fell on my face, knowing that every move could be seen by the rebels, and lay quiet. When I regained my sight and noticed the condition of the soil (coarse gravel which had been ploughed), I began burrowing myself in the soil by slowly pushing the earth away from my head and body. When sufficiently protected, I took my tin plate, using it as a shovel, and finally had quite a good protection from the shots which were coming in both directions.

I had to wait for an opportune moment to rush back to our line, expecting darkness to cause a lull in the firing. I intended, if the rebels charged, to take my chance and fly for our line. Shortly after dark a charge was made by a brigade of Union troops on the left, which was repulsed. Then the entire rebel line fired rapidly, making a continued whiz of bullets over my head. The firing gradually ceased, and I made a run for our line at such speed that I fell headlong, colors and all, inside the earthworks, on top of the boys I had left early in the morning. The next morning we left the front to return to Trenton to be mustered out of service.[16]

Grant's failure to break the Confederate lines at Cold Harbor was as much due to the exhaustion of the Army of the Potomac as to the intricate intrenchments built by Lee's men. On the night of June 12–13, screened by cavalry, the Yankees slipped away from the battlefield, crossed the James River, and marched toward Petersburg, a vital rail center twenty miles south of Richmond. Only 2,500 Confederates manned the formidable defenses of the city as the bluecoats approached, but missed opportunities delayed the arrival of the bulk of the Union army until June 18. By the time Grant's men got into position, the greater part of Lee's troops had arrived to defend the city. After a series of futile assaults, Grant settled in for a siege that would last ten months.

Thus ended a seven-week campaign that for its ferocity was unmatched in the annals of the Civil War. More than 65,000 Union soldiers had been killed, wounded, or were missing since the crossing of the Rapidan. The Democrats at home denounced Grant as a "butcher." Even the most patriotic Unionists were dismayed. "What is all this struggling and fighting for," wrote the wife of one Yankee general. "What advancement of mankind to compensate for the present horrible calamities?" Lincoln himself conceded that this "terrible war" had "carried mourning to almost every home, until it can almost be said that 'the heavens are hung in black.' "

Fredericksburg, Belle Plain, and Washington were crowded with Federal wounded, tens of thousands of them. "This is a city of hospitals," wrote a Union doctor from Fredericksburg to the *Newark Daily Advertiser* on May 16:

Every church and store, and nearly all the dwellings are occupied for hospital uses. Trains of ambulances, crowded with wounded, throng the streets, and hundreds of heavy army wagons, with similar ghastly loads, pass to and fro at all hours of the day and night. Yesterday, there were at least 10,000 wounded collected at this point, and this number was probably increased by arrivals during the night from the battle field a few miles away. Many of the wounds are only slight, but it is remarkable how large a proportion of them are wounds of the arms and particularly of the right arm. In the hospital to which Dr. Ward and myself were assigned, at least one-third of all the wounded had been struck in the arms. . . .

The number of wounded New Jersey soldiers now here is quite large, but they are so scattered that it is impossible to gather a list. Yesterday I found a member of the 13th Regiment lying in the street, with two horrible wounds in his bowels and his arm in splints. He had dropped down right in the glare of the sun, exhausted, and but for timely help must have died. Stimulants were provided, his wounds dressed, a stretcher obtained, and he was carried to a hospital, where he will probably die. His name is Stephen Kidd, and he belongs in Woodstown, Salem County. We also found in hospital a member of the 15th Regiment— Silas Strawbridge, from Morristown—who had received a ball in his left hand. All our regiments have behaved magnificently, and we feel a pride in saying here that we are Jerseymen.[17]

A member of Morris County's Sanitary Commission visited Washington in mid-May, sharing his observations with the readers of Morristown's Unionist paper, *The Jerseyman*:

We have spent a day in the hospitals of the city, among those wounded in the great battles of last week. It is hard, at our quiet homes in Morris County, to realise what war is; but here, in these vast hospitals filled with many thousands of brave, patriotic wounded soldiers, one can realise it to its fullest extent.

We first called at Mount Pleasant Hospital, where we found the drummer boy belonging to the company that went from this town last January. His first words were: "Did you know my brother was killed." How sad he looked. A few weeks ago we saw him in the camp, when he said his father had died a few days before, and he went on to tell me who had been killed and who had been wounded. As he expressed himself, most all were gone. He gave a deep sigh, and said it was a dreadful battle. He has not yet recovered from the shock his young mind had received in the eight days' fight. Said he: "My drum is gone, and I have lost everything I had. But," he said, "I think the end of the war is near at hand; we whipped them."

Passing out of Mount Pleasant Hospital we went over to Carver Hospital, capable of holding thousands of wounded men. There were some there also from our town and county, and many from other parts of New Jersey. In this hospital were numbers severely wounded. One young man, about twenty-five years of age, had just had an amputation performed just below the knee. He was the picture of meekness and manly patience. A kind lady was there feeding him with something she had brought for him. He looked up at her, and smiling pleasantly remarked, "How cool and nice it is!" There is room for much of that kind of work here. I met Mrs. Lincoln and another lady passing through the wards, doing deeds of kindness, and cheering the hearts of the wounded. . . .

When in Baltimore, a few days ago, we saw a number of Belle Island prisoners recently exchanged. It is hard to realise that human beings could have received such treatment at the hands of civilized people. As one remarked, "They tried to kill us by giving us poor food, and so little of it that it would not sustain us." The mind of some of them was almost gone, and they looked like idiots; nothing but skin and bones; some with feet and legs gone, having been frozen last winter. A day of retribution will come for those southern barbarians. The Lord grant it may come soon![18]

The Thirty-seventh New Jersey, the state's only one-hundred-day regiment, was mustered in on June 23, 1864, and shipped to City Point, Virginia, a small community eight miles east of Petersburg that would soon be transformed into the nerve center of Grant's operations. "The personnel of the regiment was not altogether encouraging," wrote one observer of the men recruited for what was promised to be only garrison duty.

The medical examination was by no means searching, and as a result there were many with only one eye; several with less fingers than the regulations allowed; a few, long since past the age at which military service terminates; and scores of mere boys from fifteen years of age upwards. As a detachment were working in the woods, near Bermuda Hundred, several huge Vermonters passing by, stopped; and, after looking at the youthful faces with some amazement as well as amusement, inquired who they were, to which the response was given, "Thirty-seventh New Jersey." "Oh!" said the questioner, "I thought it was some school-house broke loose"—to the disgust and mortification of the "boys."[19]

The men of the Thirty-seventh spent much of their time at City Point unloading military supplies.

We have been here just one week and it seems four, the days are so long and so much is done each day. Many in the Regiment are complaining with the diarrhea caused by the change of climate, water, hardships, etc. Our food is mainly hard tack and coffee. Hard Tack is like a large and thick square soda-cracker, without any soda in it. They are hard but when softened in coffee are not bad to take. I know they are good when we are very hungry, which is the usual case with me. When fried in ham-fat after being soaked in water they taste like fritters and form one of the luxuries of camp life. The coffee is good, but too much of it is not conducive to health. We can get of the Division Commissary butter, bread, ham, pickles and many other luxuries. The suttlers sell condensed milk at 40 cents a can, cheese 40 cents a pound and very poor at that, canned fruits $1 per can, and other things in proportion.

Our campaign promises to be no holiday work. One company is detached at the landing of Point of Rocks, unloading steamers; two others are on the extreme front on picket duty, and about 300 per day are detailed to work on fortifications on James River, marching three miles each way to and from their work. . . . From our work we can see obstructions in the river, the monitors and other vessels of our fleet, and from the signal tower the rebel rams can be seen.

This is the dirtiest country we ever saw. The fine white dust makes one so dirty that there is no use to try to keep clean. Shoulder straps, dress coats and everything else of that kind, except on dress parade and inspection, is played out. My dress coat looks as though it had seen three years service. The way we do is to dress as little as possible, shirt and trousers, with slouch hat, being enough, looking more like a pirate than anything else. . . .

The water in the James is delightfully soft and pleasant for bathing, and we enjoy it as often as possible. We are here for *work* and must not be over-nice about appearance. When we return we will look like veterans. . . .

Flies are the greatest nuisance in the day time, and prevent even taking an afternoon nap. When you eat your meals they hover over your victuals and almost into your mouth. When you light a candle, the moths and millers almost put it out and quite put *you* out, and finally a species of large black bug about half an inch long, like what we call at home pinch bugs, invite themselves to stay with us all night, and in the morning maybe half a dozen of these amiable social creatures will be found in the blankets when they are shaken. But these things are quite appropriate and don't trouble any one. One of our boys found two in his pocket yesterday. Musquitoes, thank Providence, are not found here. If they were they would be a half foot long. . . .

Some of the officers and men have grumbled much at our . . . hardships, but we should remember that we came by *volition*, and not compulsion and shall do our duty. Notwithstanding the extreme youth of the regiment they work like *veterans*, and though overworked all the time, are as cheery as possible. Old soldiers say that the work they do would break down a regiment of larger and older men twice as fast.[20]

Mastery of Virginia's fertile Shenandoah Valley was crucial to Grant's plan to grind down and destroy the Confederate armies. Less than sixty miles west of the nation's capital, the valley was an important source of foodstuffs for the Rebel armies and their animals. More importantly, it not only provided Lee with a direct invasion route into Maryland and Pennsylvania but also flanked any Union movement toward Richmond. Federal attempts in the spring of 1864 to gain control of the Shenandoah Valley came to naught. In June Lee ordered General Jubal Early and 15,000 of his best soldiers into the valley to draw off pressure from the besieged Confederates at Petersburg. Early's unexpected appearance northwest of Washington threw the city into a panic. To protect the capital, the Sixth Corps was ordered out of the Petersburg lines.

On July 8 advance elements of the Sixth Corps, including the Fourteenth New Jersey, reached the banks of the Monocacy River, forty-five miles west of Baltimore. The next day Early's men attacked. Union General Lew Wallace, in command of the improvised Federal army entrenched behind the river, knew his 5,000-man force was too small to defeat the Confederates but strong enough to gain time. "I made up my mind to fight," he said later. Early's forces struck first at Wallace's left flank, where the Fourteenth was posted. In fierce fighting, the Union soldiers repulsed charge after Rebel charge until late afternoon when a final, massive Confederate assault broke the Federal lines. Wallace ordered a withdrawal toward Baltimore. At a cost of nearly 1,300 casualties, Wallace's men had gained a vital twenty-four hours—time that allowed Federal forces to assemble at Washington in such numbers that Early, who came within four miles of the White House, at last had no choice but to turn away from the nation's capital.

For the Fourteenth, it was to be their finest hour.

The . . . Fourteenth . . . arrived at Frederick City on the morning of Friday. During the night . . . the city was evacuated and our forces fell back to the left side of the Monocacy river, to a position commanding the railroad bridge. Skirmishers had been thrown out facing the city, from which direction the enemy were expected. About 9 A.M., the enemy, who had forded the river some distance above, appeared in their rear, emerging from a covert of woods and advancing in strong line of battle, preceded by the usual skirmish line. Their advance was . . . a beautiful

172

sight, over a dozen battle flags waving defiantly, and the men eager with the expectation of soon destroying the "one hundred days' men" they had been told alone withstood them. On commanding eminences on either side of the river, they had their batteries in position. The Fourteenth stubbornly held their ground until the first line of the rebel advance was almost entirely destroyed. Meanwhile, our troops suffered greatly, especially in officers, and it became evident that owning to the overwhelming force of the rebels, their position could not be held, and they were ordered to fall back toward the Baltimore pike. Early in the action Lt. Col. Hall, commanding the Fourteenth, was wounded, and the command devolved upon the senior Captain, and it is a remarkable fact that each captain in his turn was either killed or wounded while in command of the regiment. . . . Our forces fell back to Monrovia, eight miles from the Junction, the rebels pursuing them a short distance. . . .

The color bearers of the Fourteenth were shot down four times during the fight. Sergt. Wm. B. Cottrell was the first to fall. Corporal Bryant and Corporal Silvers in turn took them, and each in turn fell, severely wounded, when Tommy Ryan, Co. H, caught them up and bore them bravely, until he too received a rebel bullet. The colors, though torn and ragged, are still in possession of the regiment.

While Capt. Harris, after being wounded in the shoulder, was being carried off in an ambulance, a rebel took deliberate aim and shot him through the leg, inflicting a more painful and dangerous wound than the first. . . .

While Corporal Clark lay upon the field seriously wounded, a rebel got behind him and used him as a breast work, firing over him so closely that the powder burnt his face. A Union soldier fired at the rebel and killed him; the ball grazed Clark's face and perforated the rim of his hat. . . . A trench 90 feet in length by measurement in front of the old camp ground of the Fourteenth is filled with the dead bodies of Union soldiers.[21]

The Fourteenth entered the fight with a combat strength of about 270 men, over fifty percent of whom would be killed, wounded, or captured. All of the regiment's officers, except two, were killed or wounded in the fighting at Monocacy Junction.

On August 7, 1864, Grant placed General Philip Sheridan in command of the Army of the Shenandoah, with orders to destroy Early's forces in the valley. Less than six weeks later 30,000 Federals under Sheridan's command attacked Rebel troops on the outskirts of Winchester, bringing on a twelve-hour battle that ended in a Confederate rout, the first time in the valley that a Rebel army had been driven from the field in defeat. Lieutenant Fred Farrier of the Tenth New Jersey, although wounded, lived to tell the story:

Although the wound in my breast is very painful, and I have little use of my left arm, yet I think I will be all right again ere long, and now endeavor to give you a little sketch of our past week's work. On Monday morning at 3 o'clock, we received orders to pack up (I was on picket) and move off, which we did along the Berryville pike. When we arrived at Berryville we heard our cavalry and flying artillery skirmishing at the Oppequm creek, but we did not think the Johnnies would make a stand there, although they had a good position. But they had works built there to prevent our crossing the creek. Our cavalry took them by surprise.... Our batteries opened on the rebs and fired at will for about fifteen minutes, which is all the rest we had had after a forced march of 9 miles.... We advanced in three lines of battle over a clear field nearly three fourths of a mile, and drove in their skirmishers.

They gave us spherical case and shell until we got within about 300 yards of them, and then they gave us grape and canister which cut our lines so that they had to break. Our brigade was on the second line. We laid down, and let the first line run over us, and they were rallied in front of the third line. Then our line advanced. We went close up to their works, driving the rebs line before us, but we had to fall back to form our line again. We formed under their fire and gave a yell and back went Johnnies to their works. We laid down to rest a few minutes, loading and firing at their batteries to keep them from working. We advanced again and gained more ground, and took another rest. Then we gave a yell (Sheridan passed in the rear of our line under their fire and said, "Give it to them boys, we have got them where we want them now") and off we started and got close to their batteries, and away they went. We fired a volley at them and they returned it at that time. I fell. A Minnie ball struck me in the left breast. The ball, passing through my coat, vest, and shirt, and struck the bone and flattened them, leaving the ball just level with the skin. After I came to my senses a little, I unbuttoned my coat, and not feeling anything, was going after the company again but soon felt such a pain that I could not go, so I went to the rear, and the doctor examined my wound. He found the ball, took it out, washed out the hole and put some plaster on it, and told me to go to the division hospital. But I could see our boys driving the rebs near Winchester, and I could not go to any hospital. It appeared as if the excitement kept me up, but I started for our boys on a double quick. But they and the Johnnies ran too fast for me.

When I got up to Winchester I could not go up any further on the run, so I took a short cut to the Strasburg road, with several of our men, and we met some Johnnies that could not run fast enough. We had got in a corn field and our boys let them have a few shots. They threw up their hats to surrender, but not until their 2d Lieut. and two men were killed. They said they surrendered before we fired on them, but we did not care for that. We took them prisoners. I took two of the prisoners and made them carry off one of our wounded men that lay on the field.

We took them back to Winchester and then we found our troops (infantry) which had given up the chase. The cavalry went after the flying Johnnies, every man seeming to be for himself, divisions all mixed up. . . . Then Sheridan came and told us that "we had them." And we did, for such a skedaddle I never saw. . . . Our loss was very heavy, for the field was covered with dead and wounded. Ours and theirs all lay together where we had charged twice.

The infantry remained at Winchester all night, and at day-break next morning we started after them and marched 17 miles. But they had made a stand at Strasburg, and that was a strong position, and we could not attack them right away, but we formed three lines of battle at night and built breast-works to fall back into in case of a repulse, and it was fixed at 3 o'clock next afternoon to storm. It looked doubtful about taking it, for it is a small gap in the mountain, and to look at it you would think that 5,000 men could keep back 25,000. . . . But our boys were in such good spirits, and the Johnnies so disheartened that they thought they had better give up. We charged up very steep hills but their fire did not take much effect. They held their works until we got close up to them, and you may know how they were hurried when I tell you that they had their horses hitched to the caissons and did not have time to limber up their guns. They left guns, caissons and horses for us. We tried to turn the guns on them, but our boys were so close to them we could not fire without hitting them, and off we went after them. They only got away two guns that were held in reserve, but they abandoned one of them on the road. They burned their wagons and ambulances. The infantry gave up the chase, and the cavalry started after them with their flying artillery, but it was now dark, and they had to travel very careful. . . .

We remained all night, and at day break we were off again, and they had made a stand at Mount Jackson. We got there about 10 o'clock, and shelled the woods, and then threw out our skirmishers until we had formed three lines of battle, and the bugle sounded. . . . That was a pretty sight—three army corps in battle lines, on a plain field. The rebs shelled us as we advanced with one piece of artillery, but they soon started off again and we broke our lines and marched up the valley in eighteen columns, and at New Market they attempted to make another stand, but our whole army made up three battle lines in less than ten minutes. They marched up so that they could wheel into lines of battle, which would reach nearly across the valley, and our cavalry finished our lines on the flanks. It appeared to frighten the rebs for they skedaddled again, and we after them. We shelled them all the way until dark. If it had been morning we would have had their whole wagon train, for we could see it, and shell it every hill they would go over, and the wagons that was hit they would set fire to. . . .

I do not think that we will pursue them any further, as our rations are out, and our wagon train is not up here yet. I don't think we would keep up communications, as all the people through here are secesh. . . . Some of the citizens of this town have just cut one of our soldier's throats and taken $340 from him. He belongs to the 15th N. J. Vols.[22]

Winchester bloodied Early's army, as did a second equally severe defeat at Fisher's Hill, but although much of the Shenandoah Valley was now in Union hands, the Confederates still had fight in them. On October 19 they crossed Cedar Creek, catching the tenting Federals by surprise and nearly routing them in turn. But by early morning, as Phil Sheridan galloped furiously back to the lines, the Union defenses stiffened. At 4 p.m. he ordered his men to charge: "Follow me!" he shouted. "We'll sleep in the old camp tonight!" And follow him they did, smashing through the Rebel lines and chasing the shattered Confederate army back to New Market. Early's army was finished and the valley at last free of graybacks. Captain John C. Patterson's letter to the *Ocean Emblem*, published in Toms River, told of Fourteenth Regiment's part in the battle:

We have again passed through the order of battle, and through the mercy of God I am unhurt—but many have fallen. We had a very hard fight—and at first quite disastrous to us; the enemy getting in our rear . . . during the night, and commencing a sharp attack just at daylight, overwhelming the pickets . . . , capturing quite a number of them, and drove them from their position in disorder, capturing some of our artillery, and then swung around so as to strike us; we resisted their attack for some time but our commander saw that it was useless to try to hold our position, and we fell back beyond the town of Middletown, forming a new line.

The enemy pressed us closely. . . . Gen. Sheridan rode along the line, and the boys cheered him with a yell that I've no doubt grated on the ears of the rebels. He told us there would be a different face on matters before 4 o'clock p.m., and we believed him. At about a quarter to 3 o'clock the order was *forward* along the whole line, and it was forward. It was but a few minutes before the enemy were in full retreat and in a few minutes a perfect rout—and such a rout—our cavalry dashed in at just the right time, and completed the panic begun. The infantry column halted at our position of the morning, but the cavalry dashed on into Strasburgh, and there the rebels had got into a perfect jam with the wagon train, ambulances, artillery, and almost everything. They had become elated with the morning successes, and brought up everything. Our cavalry recaptured all the artillery we had lost in the morning, (12 to 13 pieces) and more besides—between fifty and sixty pieces. I counted myself just fifty pieces of artillery, one hundred and nine ambulances, over sixty (U.S.) baggage wagons, and four hundred horses and mules; two or three thousand prisoners, and nine battle-flags at Gen. Sheridan's headquarters. Our cavalry chased them beyond Woodstock, a distance of nineteen miles; they threw away everything that would impede their flight. I also saw six to seven thousand muskets, and there was more to come in; it is the most complete defeat of the rebels they ever experienced in this valley, and I might say during the war. . . . It proved their victory of the morning to be a dear one to them. . . . Another hard blow has been struck for our flag, our Government, and for the right, but not without loss to us. . . . The loss of our regiment is thirty-six killed and wounded.[23]

Sherman's capture of Atlanta on September 2, coupled with Sheridan's splendid victory at Cedar Creek on October 19, cast a pall of gloom over what remained of the Confederacy. In the North there was an impending sense that the war, and its seemingly unending lists of casualties, was nearing an end. Meanwhile, in the trenches before Petersburg, the Federal troops soldiered on, enduring the mud and monotony, with long periods of idleness broken by furious assaults that served to tighten the Union noose around the city. In October Grant sent 43,000 men westerly to cut the Boydton Plank Road and Southside Railroad, two of Lee's remaining links to the outside world. The Second New Jersey Brigade, now led by Colonel Robert McAllister, longtime commander of the Eleventh New Jersey, moved out on October 26, only to be surprised the next day by Rebels led by General A. P. Hill. Fighting in an area of "dense wilderness, miry swamps and pine thickets," both sides became disoriented. The Union line collapsed and McAllister's brigade, including the Seventh, Eighth, Eleventh, and Twelfth New Jersey regiments, found itself assailed on all sides. "At 3:30 a.m. October 27th, we resumed our march," wrote McAllister to his wife, Ellen.

We . . . [met] but little or no opposition, until we reached the Boydton Plank Road within a mile of the Southside Railroad. Here the enemy showed themselves in greate force. The cavalry struck the Plank Road to the left of the infantry and swung around, with the aid of Genl. Egan's division. The Plank Road was now in our possession.

At this time I was bringing up the rear. The head of my Brigade had reached the field where we were massing. One regiment had turned in to the massing line, quite close to the plank road, when an aide came to me from Genl. Meade . . . and orders that I should stop and defend the rear—that the enemy were coming up in that direction. I halted, road [sic] back, and found Genl. Meade and staff coming up. The General directed me to throw a line across the road, put pickets far out, and send a company to reconnoiter. . . . The cavalry firing now ceased in our rear, and we could find nothing of the enemy. But there was heavy firing in our front and shells flying all around and bursting among us without doing any damage. I was now ordered forward and passed in the field spoken of. Genl. Egan had now advanced up the plank road a considerable distance—about one mile. I had just got my Brigade all in the field when I received an order to report to Genl. Egan, as he was nearly out of ammunition. . . . He had driven the enemy before him and had taken the hill on this side of the stream and held all up to it. . . .

Genl. Egan's division was along this front in rifle pitts captured from the enemy and facing the last hill. . . . The two Brigades of my own Division lay along the plank road, swinging around to the rear. . . . I marched up the plank road with about 2,000 muskets and reported to Genl. Egan without having a shot fired at me. He ordered me to form two lines of battle on the crest of this hill facing the enemy on the opposit hill. . . . Genl. Egan informed me that he wanted me to cross the narrow bridge and the stream and take the opposit hill from the enemy. I was then ordered to extend my left with the rear line of battle, making but one line. I had just completed this, preparatory to taking the opposit hill, when we were all surprised at the roar of musketry and artillery in our rear. The two Brigades of my Division under Genl. Mott were attacked. Our ambulances and artillery were all exposed and liable to be captured.

These had to be protected. These Brigades had to change front and fight the enemy on the very road we had just come in on. This left our rear and the plank road exposed, and the enemy pushed right up towards us on the hill. A few minutes more and we could be surrounded.

The enemy's artillery and musketry poured in upon us on every side. Our communication with the ballance of the 2nd Corps was entirely cut off; and what was worst than all, a connection had not been made between the 5th and 2nd Corps. We had secured the road, and the 5th Corps was to have connected with us. This they failed to do. The enemy's column passed through the gap thus left. And what was still worse, we had no ammunition except sixty rounds to a man in the cartridge boxes and on the persons of the men. We were to have received a new supply of ammunition along the lines from the 5th Corps, but the want of a connection prevented this.

You now understand our critical condition. Cut off from the ballance of our own Corps, as well as the 5th, were Egan's small division and my Brigade, nearly as large as his division, but 3/4 of them new men, some of which had never fired a gun and had had but very little drill.

The enemy, flushed with apparent victory, ran madly forward and captured one piece of artillery. Balls, shells, and musketry rolled in upon us from every side. It was enough to shake the courage of our old veterans. Genl. Egan ordered me to about face and charge the enemy. I gave the order, and off on the charge we went—down the hill, through the hazel brush and swamp. We met the enemy, drove them back pell mell, and captured over 100 prisoners. We met a heavy fire from two brigades in our rear (of which we knew nothing). This and the enemy's fire on my left—now the right—were too severe for my new troops. My line faltered and broke as we rose up the hill on the opposit side. But on recrossing the swamp, I reformed them again. The enemy, encouraged by our falling back, re-attacked. My men opened on them with a terrific fire and drove them back once more. The day was ours. Our communication was opened and the enemy passed from our rear. The artillery lost was recaptured. . . .

This charge not only saved Egan's division and my Brigade, but saved the Corps. . . . The darkness of the night closed in around us. A few pickets firing, an occasional shot, was all that was left of the sound of battle. Stillness reigned throughout the field. The rain poured down rapidly. The men lay down on the cold, wet ground and fell fast asleep.

On the plank road stood two houses. Here our wounded were carried—those that were taken back. With an aide I road and called to see them. In one house were 50 men from my Brigade. They were badly wounded, many of them mortally. In another house were about a dozen men. Poor fellows. They would take me by the hand and say, "Colonel, did I do my duty?"

"Yes! Yes!" I would reply. "You did it nobly. You did it nobly."

They would say, "I fought for my country, and I die for my country."

Oh, how my heart thrilled for these poor, dying soldiers! They were far from home and friends; and they were soon to be left in the hands of the enemy, for our ambulances were but few and all full. The ambulances could not make a second trip, and our part of the battlefield was so far in the advance—right in on the enemy.

Only one Surgeon made his appearance at these hospital houses. There were no nurses, no chaplains, no consolation, no relief. There was hardly a candle to light up the rooms even while we were there to see the wounded. . . .

I shall never forget that day or that battle—surrounded on all sides, cut off from the ballance of our Corps, no connection with the 5th Corps. The victorious yells of the Rebels sounded in our ears. Our fate seemed to be sealed without a hope of escape. It was a time of suspence and doubt. But add to all this what was still worse: some of Genl. Egan's men were about out of ammunition and none could be had. There was not a spade or shovel to throw up breastworks. But God put it in our hearts to work on and trust in Him. We charged down the hill; the enemy became panic-stricken and gave way. We rushed on and received the enemy's front and flank fire. We wavered and fell back. The enemy took courage and followed. We reformed and rolled in the musketry upon them. They faltered and retreated. The day was ours, and we were masters of the field.[24]

McAllister's success in extricating his men from what one member of the Eleventh called "this circle of death" earned him the brevet rank of brigadier general "for gallant and distinguished service at the battle of Boydton Plank Road."

Although its lines at Petersburg still held, by December 1864 the Confederacy itself was, to all intents and purposes, reduced to little more than the Carolinas and the southern tip of Virginia. On December 7 the Second New Jersey Brigade, now composed of the Eleventh and much-reduced elements of the Seventh and Eighth Regiments, as well as troops from New York and Massachusetts, turned away from the siege lines and south toward North Carolina on an expedition to destroy Confederate communications. With the South's fortunes on the wane, the Jerseymen encountered little opposition as they tore through the countryside, wrote Thomas Marbaker, then a nineteen-year-old sergeant:

Half-past six o'clock on the morning of December 7th found our division in motion, with our faces turned southward. . . . We soon struck the Jerusalem plank-road, and turned toward North Carolina. We had not marched many miles before it began to rain heavily, making the marching extremely tiresome. The march was a very rapid one, and the halts few and short. Heavily-loaded as the troops were with blankets, overcoats and the extra clothing necessary in winter, the rapid marching told heavily upon them, and the roadway was soon lined with stragglers. Others, in their efforts to keep up with their comrades, lightened their loads by throwing away overcoats and blankets, articles which they could illy spare. At one point in particular it seemed to me that for hundreds of yards the roadsides were covered with such impedimenta thrown away by the troops in our front. It was surely a rich harvest for the ill-clad Southern bushwackers, who were skulking in swamps and thickets awaiting our passage and an opportunity to shoot down and rob some foot-sore straggler.

Just after dark we crossed the Nottaway river on pontoons and bivouacked on the southern bank. We had marched a distance of twenty miles through rain and mud, and the order to bivouac was a welcome one. The evening brought a cessation of the rain, the clouds broke away and the stars began to look down upon a weary and wet lot of soldiers. Camp-fires were lit and soon the fragrant aroma of coffee—that panacea for many a soldier's ills—perfumed the evening air. Then pipes for those who smoked, and rest upon the sodden ground. . . .

On the morning of December 8th the roll was called long before the break of day, and at half-past six the column was again in motion. All the troops comprising the expedition had crossed the evening previous, except the stragglers, who were picked up by the cavalry that had followed to the river, and by them taken back to camp to prevent their being captured by the enemy. The day turned out warm and pleasant, overcoats were at a discount, and, as before, many thoughtlessly threw them away—an act which they very much regretted before the expedition reached camp again.

The country through which we were then passing seemed to be fertile and well tilled, but the same condition prevailed that was found in so many parts of the South through which Union troops passed. It seemed to be populated only by women, children and negroes. If a white man was seen, it was a specimen too old and decrepit to take to the shelter of the swamp and thickets. This condition did not prevail because there were no able bodied white men in the country (as many of our poor stragglers found to their sorrow), but because with guns in their hands they were lying in hiding, waiting until the column should pass beyond hearing, that they might pick off unwary stragglers and rob the bodies even to nakedness. Many murders of this kind were perpetrated, of which we knew nothing until the return-march revealed them. . . .

After a long, hard march we neared Jewett's Station, on the Weldon railroad, where we learned that our cavalry had already burned the station, cut the telegraph and were busy tearing up the railroad. We bivouacked for the night to be ready for a hard day's work on the morrow. The weather had changed again and the north wind was bringing with it frost and ice. Large camp-fires were lit and the night passed as comfortably as the circumstances would permit.

The boys were astir very early on the morning of the ninth, for the weather had grown so cold during the night that it was impossible to obtain much sleep, the only comfort to be had being around the camp-fires. Daylight was awaited with impatience, but with its coming we fell in line and marched down the railroad until we reached the track not yet destroyed. The cavalry had been at the work of destruction on the afternoon of the 8th, but, owing to their method of working, their progress had not been very rapid. Their plan was to pry the rails loose from the sleepers (which, owing to a lack of proper tools, was rather difficult), then lift the sleepers from their beds and put them in piles to be burned. General McAllister introduced a quicker . . . method of accomplishing the same result. Although his business had been that of building railroads, he yet seemed to be well versed in the art of destroying them. The brigade was deployed in single file on one side of the road, a man to each tie; then commands were given not known in military tactics, and not taught at West Point. First, the command was, "Take hold," when every man would bend over and grasp the end of a tie; then would follow the command, "Lift up," and in a few moments the railroad would be lying upside down. The strain incident to the turning would so loosen the spikes that the removal of the rails became much easier. After the separation of rails and sleepers the latter would be piled up and set on fire. The rails would then be placed across the burning sleepers, with the ends projecting. As the center became heated the ends would bend to the ground, thus making it impossible to use them again without being sent to the mill to be straightened. Oftentimes the heated rails would be taken and twisted around trees and telegraph poles. It was heavy work, but was thoroughly enjoyed by most of the men, and some-times quite a rivalry would exist as to who could put the most crooks in a heated rail. When the destruction of one section was completed we would move to another, and so the work went on until nine o'clock in the evening, when we were ordered to bivouac for the night, and were told that the object of the expedition had been accomplished and that at day-light we would begin our return march.

The Eleventh was now approaching the North Carolina border, destroying the railroad as it advanced.

On the outward march the rights of private property had been re-spected, at least by the officers and men of our division. That there was some plundering I have no doubt, for among large bodies of men there will always be found some who recognize no law but the law of might, and who, despite orders and the strictest discipline, will find ways of ap-propriating anything they think will be useful to themselves. . . .

The night of the 9th came cold and wet—rain, snow and sleet made sleep almost impossible, and, as on the previous night, the boys spent most of their time around the blazing camp-fires. We were bivouacked in a woods, and morning revealed the trees decked in crystals of ice. Early morning of the 10th found us in motion, with our faces once more turned northward. . . . We were quite a distance in the enemy's country, cut loose from all communication with the main army, and it was ex-pected that the enemy would try to prevent our return and that we would have to fight our way through. Preparations were made accord-ingly; flankers were thrown well out and every precaution taken to pre-vent a surprise. . . .

The night of the 10th was bitterly cold, and it was the fortune of the Eleventh to bivouac on the crest of a wind-swept hill; but the writer does not remember any cold winter's night during his term of service when he slept more snugly and comfortably than he did on that same cold night of December 10th, '64. He, with four or five comrades, was fortunate enough to secure the lee side of a log for a bed-chamber. After scraping together what leaves we could (we did not pitch any tents), we pooled our blankets, overcoats and tents and made a family bed. It was the writer's good luck to get a central position, where (with the possible exception of the tip of his nose) the cold could not reach him. Judging from the restlessness of those on the outer sides of the bed, they were not quite so comfortable.

Early on the morning of the 11th we were again on the move toward

Sussex Court House. The roads were solid in the early morning, but the heightening sun soon brought about the same conditions that had prevailed the day before. During the previous day we had heard frequent rumors of Union soldiers being found murdered and stripped along the way, but we, as a regiment, had had no ocular proof of their truth. We had not gone far on the way on the morning of the 11th, when word was brought that six or seven dead bodies were lying close together in the woods, not far from the line of march. General McAllister and a number of others went to view them. It was a pitiful sight; from all appearances they had been stripped and made to kneel in a circle, then shot—murdered in cold blood. What else could it be called but murder? After proof of such murders, committed not by the regular soldiery of the South, but by the so-called home-guards, who, hidden in swamp and thicket, like beasts of prey, lay in wait for the unsuspecting straggler . . . , is it any wonder that the remainder of our homeward march should have been lit by the flames of burning stacks and barns!

Shortly after dawn on the morning of December 12 the troops reached their old campground. Sergeant Marbaker was astonished by the desperate longing for freedom of the Blacks they had encountered on the railroad raid.

If there was any one among us who still entertained the idea that the Southern blacks were perfectly contented with the conditions of slavery, this Weldon railroad raid was well calculated to dispel it. From nearly every plantation passed they came in squads to join the line of march. Willingly turning their backs upon the only homes their lives had known, joyfully cutting loose from all the associations that under other conditions humanity is so loth to sever, they came with smiling faces and cheerful shouts to take refuge beneath the folds of our flag, recognizing, as if by intuition, that its broad stripes and glittering stars were the symbols of liberty and equality. . . .

On our way out, a group came hastening from a distant farm-house. It consisted of father, mother and a number of children. As they took their places along the highway, ready to join the column that was to lead them to the land of promise, they discovered that one daughter had been left behind. The father, fearful that he would be detained if he returned for her, tearfully implored some one to go. One of General McAllister's aids rode up to the house, and, getting the child, brought it to the father. His thankfulness was unbounded, and the happy family, now united, gave voice to many expressions of gratitude. Colonel Price, of the Seventh New Jersey . . . had them placed in a baggagewaggon.

On our return march, when passing a plantation . . . a group of seventeen [blacks] came hastening across the fields to join the Union column. They had heard of our approach, and upon seeing the stars and stripes floating in the breeze they gathered their household goods and hastened to its protecting folds. They were of all sizes and almost every hue. One, a girl of about sixteen, was very pretty and showed but little trace of negro blood; another, a year or so older, was very dark, but each called the same woman mother. Although the weather was cold enough to make the need of heavy clothing felt, these poor people were very thinly clad, the girls having on light summer clothing and only a threadbare shawl to add its protection. There were also two small children, but in the excitement of flight one had been forgotten. The older and darker of the two girls mentioned dropped her bundle and started back, saying that she would carry the child herself rather than it should be left behind. She soon returned, bearing it with her, but in an almost nude condition, its bare legs being exposed to the biting winter air. The mother carried the youngest, the daughter mentioned the next, and, though some of the party were barefooted, with smiling faces they trudged along the half frozen highway beside the Union soldiers. A stream was reached which had to be forded. This caused a dilemma, but members of McAllister's staff, taking the youngest upon their horses in front, carried them safely over, and the happy party went on rejoicing. It was a laughable sight to see those men of many battles carrying in their arms those woolly-headed pickaninnies, but it was an act that did credit to their humanity.[25]

SIX

"Exhausted, Starved, Emaciated, Dying"

IMPRISONMENT AND ESCAPE

Neither the North nor the South had a single prison camp capable of holding more than a handful of men when the war broke out, and no plans to build any. The Confederates hoped to leave the Union peacefully, the Federal government expected quick victory after a campaign that might last at most a few months Lacking prison facilities, field commanders took it upon themselves to release captured soldiers on parole, that is, on their oath not to take up arms again. Exchanges often took place on the battlefield itself, or within a few days after the fighting ended.

As the months passed, both sides took an increasing number of prisoners. Early on, factories, warehouses, and county jails were pressed into use. Later, the North set up a string of camps to house the nearly 220,000 Rebel soldiers captured during four years of warfare. Barely able to feed, clothe, and house its own soldiers let alone the 200,000 Federal prisoners eventually taken by its armies, the South pressed for a formal system of prisoner exchange. Despite misgivings by the North that any such agreement would imply recognition of the Confederate government, by July 1862 arrangements had been worked out for exchanges between armies: a private for a private, sixty privates for a commanding general. The system collapsed ten months later after the Rebels threatened to execute or re-enslave captured Blacks who wore the Federal uniform. When some of the more than 30,000 soldiers paroled after the capture of Vicksburg in July 1863 were found in uniform again, exchanges were halted. General Grant was strongly against the exchange of prisoners, writing, "Every man we hold, when released on parole or otherwise, becomes an active soldier against us. . . . If a system of exchanges liberates all prisoners taken, we will have to fight on until the whole South is exterminated." Wholesale exchanges did not resume again until December 1864, when thousands of sick and wounded prisoners were released from captivity.

Prison camps, both North and South, were dreadful places, with inadequate shelter, minimal sanitation, poor food, and rampant sickness and death. On the whole Southern prisons were no worse than their Northern counterparts, with the notorious exception of Andersonville, in southwest Georgia. There, some 33,000 prisoners were herded into a twenty-six-acre stockade with a three-acre swamp at its center. During the year it was in use as a prison, more than 12,000 Federal soldiers perished there and 43,000 cases of disease or wounds were reported. Little wonder that its commandant, Captain Henry Wirz, was the only Confederate official hanged after the war ended.

There are no reliable estimates of the number of New Jersey soldiers either imprisoned or dying while in captivity. Five thousand or more Jerseymen were probably captured by the enemy and perhaps of that number, nearly a thousand may have died in prison, hundreds of them at Andersonville.

John J. Bray, quartermaster sergeant of Company L, First New Jersey Cavalry, was captured while on picket duty at Warrenton, Virginia. Held at Richmond's Pemberton Factory Prison for two months, he escaped on January 10, 1864, and later rejoined his unit. While on furlough Bray wrote a lighthearted account of his escape for *Harper's Monthly*. Bray died at Newark's Ward Army Hospital on April 4, 1865.

On the night of November 12, 1863, we were suddenly surrounded by a band of Mosby's roughriders, and before we knew it were taken prisoners, the darkness enabling the assailants to come upon us unobserved. We did not enjoy the prospect of a protracted imprisonment in Richmond which we knew would be our fate; but there was no door of escape, and we submitted as gracefully as we could.

Our captors, though rough and shaggy fellows, were by no means the savages they have sometimes been painted; on the contrary they treated us kindly, respecting all our rights as prisoners, not even appropriating any of our effects, as it would have been natural for them as guerrillas, to have done. We were, of course, put under guard and were disarmed; but we were not altogether excluded from the chat of the camp to which we were carried. . . .

In the morning, under an armed escort, we set out on foot for Richmond. . . . At Sperryville, where we were handed over to the 4th Virginia Cavalry, we had a taste of the "chivalrous" manners of the true Virginian. These cavalrymen, representing probably the First Families, the moment we were placed under their control, helped themselves unceremoniously to our caps and overcoats, and, regardless of common decency and humanity, attempted even to take our blankets, notwithstanding we were shivering with cold and suffering greatly from exposure. In this intention, however, they were finally restrained by their officers, who had yet some scruples of conscience remaining, and for the rest of the way we continued in the enjoyment of the little protection the blankets could give us.

We arrived in Richmond on the 17th and were at once conducted to the "Pemberton Factory Prison," where we had a speedy introduction to all the repellent features of prison life. The prison is a building twenty-five by one hundred feet, four stories high, occupied originally as a tobacco manufactory, but appropriated for the last two years to its present use. Each floor contained 280 prisoners, making 1,120 in all in this single building. The building was filthy to the last degree; there was not a clean spot anywhere; the hold of a slave ship could not have been more offensive. The mere appearance of the place was enough to sicken sensitive stomachs. Some of the prisoners who had been exhausted by their long journey did faint upon entering their quarters. As to myself I had become hardened to the utmost rigors of camp life; two years or more in the saddle had effectually emptied me of all refinements of smell or taste, and as a consequence I got along in my new situation with comparatively little inconvenience.

Of course there was little amusement, sitting day after day on the floor of our prison and looking into one another's faces like so many gaping imbeciles. Isolated from the world, hardly permitted to look from our small windows into the next street without, we could only find within ourselves the diversion we needed, and our thought was far too monotonous to suggest any variety of entertainment.

We had one amusement, however, which somewhat relieved the daily monotony, and that was "skirmishing." This was an indiscriminate scuffle, in which every man received a thorough shaking, all entering into the "engagement" with the zest of country boys into a husking frolic, but all in good humor and for a benevolent and proper sanitary purpose. The object of this wholesale scrimmage was the rout and dispersion of the vermin which moved upon us in dense and threatening columns at every opportunity, surrounding us, assailing us, actually, at times, "occupying, holding and possessing" our persons. But for the scrimmaging in which we indulged, and the "demoralization" thereby of the vermin forces, many of us would have been inevitably overcome, and probably carried out piecemeal at the keyholes, or dragged bodily to the dens of the persecutors.

Our food was of much better quality than we had expected to receive, but the quantity was anything but satisfactory. Each man received daily a half loaf of bread, the loaf being no larger than an old-fashioned country "rusk," a piece of fresh meat about two inches square, and a pint of bean soup, all without salt, not a morsel of which was seen in the prison. The food was obtained every morning by a detail of our own men under a sergeant, who, with pails and tubs were marched down into the yard and there furnished the allowance for the floor to which they belonged by the cooks in charge.

Occasionally some of the men, by the sale of their clothing, obtained a little money with which they were able through the guards to purchase articles outside, thus reinforcing their strength and making up for deficiencies in the regular supplies. On one or two occasions I indulged myself in this way, once selling my cavalry boots, for which I received seventy-five dollars in Rebel money, and at another time disposing of a threadbare, dirty blanket for twenty-five dollars, the guards eagerly purchasing in both instances, and seeming to imagine that they had made excellent bargains.

After a month in prison, Bray decided to escape.

I broached the subject to my comrades, suggesting that we had better act in concert; but they regarded the risk as too great, and unanimously declined to unite in the undertaking, some of them even endeavoring to dissuade me from my purpose. But my resolution was fixed; I longed to be free again, and to fill the saddle I knew to be waiting me in the ranks of the gallant First. Many things, however, had to be considered, and many preliminaries arranged before it was possible to attempt the execution of my purpose, at least with any hope of success. The first thing necessary was to possess myself of a Rebel uniform, which would enable me to pass the guards. So one day, just after we had received a batch of new clothing from our Government, I said banteringly to Ross, the officer having charge of our floor, "Ross, how will you trade coats? Mine is brand new, but I must have some money, you know; so if you'll trade right, I'm on hand for a bargain."

Ross was a good-natured, easy fellow, and particularly ragged, having scarcely a whole garment in his entire wardrobe. Of course he was only too anxious to trade, and we soon struck up a bargain, Ross agreeing to give me his coat for mine and thirty dollars to boot. Thus I secured a grey coat, a necessary part of the disguise in which I intended to escape.

Some days after, on the pretense that I was out of funds, I bantered Ross to trade pantaloons, offering mine, which were new, for his old ones and ten dollars in money. He knew that the prisoners often obtained in this way the means of purchasing supplies, and my offer therefore excited no suspicion. He at once closed with my offer, and making the exchange on the spot, I became, to all appearances, a Rebel soldier, having a suit of grey exactly like those of the guards.

The day after this transaction I determined, if possible, to put my plan in execution. Accordingly when the men passed down into the yard to draw their rations I went with them, resolved to seize any opportunity that offered to get away. But my time had not yet come. Every avenue of escape was guarded; sentinels stood at all the gates with vigilant eyes; and I was obliged to return to my quarters, still a prisoner, but still firmly set in my purpose.

A circumstance which happened on the same day served to confirm me in my determination. One of the tyrants in charge of the prison—they were all despots in their way—except Ross and one or two others—threatened, because of some caper of the men, to starve us in punishment, heaping upon me especially all sorts of abuse. Having something of Yankee grit in my nature, I resented the insult, telling the fellow I would throw him out of the window unless he at once desisted. The coward at once reported me to headquarters, no doubt with many exaggerations as to my offense, and a few hours after I was removed to Libby Prison for punishment. This consisted of "bucking and gagging," a process by no means calculated to inspire one with admiration for Rebel tenderness or humanity. Tying my hands together with strong cords about the wrists, my persecutors drew the arms thus united down over my knees, where they were securely pinioned; my mouth was then gagged, and having been placed on the floor, I was left for eight hours to my fate.

Of course, in such a predicament, it was impossible to sit, and to lie down was equally inconvenient. Aside from the suffering, one could not resist a feeling of humiliation mingled with anger that he should be made to occupy so ridiculous a position. . . . My punishment ended at last, and I went back to my prison only more intent than before on getting away. The next day I again attempted to put my scheme into execution, but was again unsuccessful. On Sunday morning, January 10, I made my final attempt. Arranging necessary preliminaries with a comrade, I passed down stairs with the detail sent for provisions, wearing my blanket, and keeping as much as possible under cover of those whom I was about to leave. Reaching the yard which was filled with Rebel soldiers, I suddenly, upon a favorable opportunity, slipped the blanket from my shoulders to those of my chum, and, stepping quickly into the throng, stood, to all appearances, a Rebel, having precisely their uniform, and looking as dirty and ragged as the worst of them.

But I was not yet free. The point now was to get out of the yard. To do this it was necessary to pass the sentinels standing at the gates, all of which were thus guarded. My wits, however, difficult as I knew my enterprise to be, did not desert me. With an air of unconcern, whistling "Bonnie Blue Flag," I sauntered slowly toward the nearest gate, paused a moment as I neared it, to laugh with the rest at some joke of one of the guards; then, abstractedly and with deliberate pace, as if passing in and out had been so customary an affair with me as to make any formal recognition of the sentinels unnecessary, passed out.

That my heart throbbed painfully under my waistcoat; that I expected every moment to hear the summons, "Halt" you need not be told. An age of feeling was crowded into that moment. But I passed out unchallenged. Whether it was that my nonchalant air put the sentinels off their guard, or that they were for the moment absorbed in the joke at which all the soldiers were laughing, I can not tell; nor does it matter. I was free; the whole world was before me; and my whole being was aglow with that thought. . . .

The sun was at its meridian as I passed the prison gate. In an hour I had struck the line of the Chickahominy Railroad. The weather was bitterly cold and the ground covered with snow; but I thought of nothing, cared for nothing but effecting my escape. Of course the utmost vigilance was necessary as the whole Peninsula was full of pickets, mostly mounted. While, therefore, pressing forward with all the rapidity possible under the circumstances, I kept my eyes on constant duty, scanning closely every marsh and thicket lest some enemy should unexpectedly appear and arrest my flight. No enemy that day, however, passed my path, though I frequently saw cavalry patrols in the distance, causing me to seek the shelter for a time of some friendly tree or fence.

At eleven o'clock that night I was within nine miles of New Kent Court House, having traveled a distance of twenty-one miles since noon. After nightfall the stars formed my only guide, and, having quitted the line of the railroad, I very naturally lost some of my reckoning. Besides, for the last few miles my strength had rapidly failed me, and much as I desired to get on I found that it would be impossible to continue. My feet were sore, my legs weak and limp, and withal I was chilled through and through, having neither blanket nor overcoat to protect me from the keen, piercing wind. Accordingly, utterly exhausted at last, I dropped upon the snow in the swamp, and in a moment was fast asleep.

When I awoke at last, with a stinging pain in my hands and feet, it was daylight. I endeavored to rise, but for a time was unable to do so. My feet were like lumps of ice, my face smarted with pain, my hands were red and without feeling; I had barely escaped freezing to death.

After considerable effort, however, I got upon my feet, and with slow
and difficult motion, and appetite clamoring for food, resumed my journey. As the blood in my veins warmed and strength returned I increased
my pace, going in a northeasterly direction, seeking an outlet from the
swamp in which I had spent the night.

After a while, as I was pursuing my devious way, a Negro suddenly
confronted me. Whence he came, I knew not; I only knew that he stood
before me with a look of inquiry in his eyes as much as to say, "Who are
you, sir?" I was, of course, startled; but I remembered that I wore a
Rebel uniform and met him accordingly. But he was not to be deceived.

"Yer can't come dat game on dis chile," he said, with a sparkle in his
eye; "I know yer, sar; you'se is a Yankee pris'ner 'scaped from Richmon'."
Then, as if to reassure me, he hurriedly added, "But, Lor' bless yer,
massa, I won't tell on yer; I'se real glad yer got away."

I saw in a moment the fellow could be trusted. I have never seen a
Negro yet, in this war, who could not be trusted by the Union soldier;
and so I unbosomed myself to him at once, telling him the whole story of
my escape, that I had lost my way, that I had not eaten a morsel of food
in twenty-four hours, and that if he could help me in any way I would be
more indebted than I could describe. "Dis chil' glad to help yer," he
replied in a tone of real pleasure and with a bright look in his eyes, and
at once started off at a rapid pace, leading me across the fields, a distance of four miles, to the house of another Negro to whom he explained
my situation and wishes. Here I was given something to eat, both the
man and woman treating me with the greatest kindness; and after a
short rest again started out, this time with my host as guide, for the main
road from which I had wandered. This was soon reached, and parting
from my black friend I pushed on, keeping the road as nearly as I could.

The road was thick with pickets and scouts and I was obliged at almost every turn to dodge aside to avoid discovery. For miles I succeeded
in "flanking" all I met; but at last a sharp bend in the road brought me
within twenty-five feet of a soldier on horseback looking squarely toward
me. How my heart leaped at the sight!

"Who are you?" was the instant salute; but without stopping to answer I leaped into the swamp and plunged into the depths of underbrush which overran it. My leap was followed by a shot from the soldier's
pistol, the ball whistling shrilly over but fortunately missing its mark. As
if determined not to be balked, the soldier dismounted from horse, and
for two hours hunted for me in the swamp, often passing close to my retreat, and keeping me in constant trepidation lest I should be discovered. But Providence again favored me; the scout tired at last in his vain

search and moved away, and I once more started for the Canaan of my hopes.

All that day I traveled on, dodging pickets, hiding in the swamps, lying under thickets, wading through bogs and water, until night again found me exhausted and incapable of going any farther. But I was not to be permitted to sleep without one more fright. Making my way in deep darkness through the underbrush, crackling the brittle twigs under my feet, a "What's that?" uttered in a sharp, strong voice, suddenly warned me of danger. A moment after I heard men talking, the words "Spy" and "Yankee" being conspicuous in their discussion. Then, crouching down, I heard them moving to and fro all around me and once one of the number passed so close to where I lay that I could hear him breathe. For an hour or more they kept up their search, discussing among themselves the probable cause of alarm, when, apparently concluding that they had been unnecessarily startled, they abandoned the field and left me to my thoughts. For some time after their departure, however, I did not dare to stir, not knowing at what moment they might return; or how near they might be to my retreat. But fatigue overcame me, and finding a soft place I threw myself on the ground, and pulling over me such leaves and brush as I could reach, very soon found oblivion in sleep.

Two days after his escape Bray reached the outskirts of Union-occupied Williamsburg, north of the James River.

It was a long time, however, before I could make up my mind, after I saw the lights of the town, whether it was the place I sought. My many escapes had made me unduly cautious; I had come so far and suffered so much and had so much to fear from capture and return to prison, that I felt it would be terrible now that the Promised Land was in sight, all by a want of vigilance or premature discovery of myself to the pickets. Consequently I determined if possible, to get through the lines into the village without discovery and I had nearly succeeded when a sharp challenge brought me to a halt. Again, however, the darkness favored me, and though an immediate hunt was instituted, I once more escaped, this time from our own pickets.

At length, quiet having been restored, I managed to creep through, and shortly after was in the village. Seeing a light in the window of a large building on the principal street, I cautiously crept up, designing to peer into the apparently occupied room, and learn from the uniforms of the occupants whether I was really among friends or foes. I had reached the window, and was raising my head to look in, when suddenly, a hand was laid heavily on my shoulder and a loud voice exclaimed: "Hello, here! Who is this? A spy?" I started as if a ball had struck me. Was I again a prisoner, or was this the grasp of a friend deceived by my uniform. But instinct was true and I answered at once, "I'm a Union soldier escaped from Richmond."

That was enough. Before I knew it I was inside the room, which proved to be the headquarters of the post commandant. An armchair was placed before the fire and I was thrust into it; my shoes were drawn off, and I was as cozy as kindly hands could make me.[1]

Shot in the hip during the Battle of the Wilderness, First Sergeant Pierson M. Walton of Company H, First New Jersey, was captured only to escape three weeks later. He described his adventures in a letter to his parents dated June 2, 1864:

I take this opportunity of writing a few lines to let you know how I am getting along and where I have been. On the 4th of May, we broke camp and crossed the Rapidan River at Germania Ford, and took the road to the Wilderness. On the 5th our regiment engaged the enemy nearly all day with a loss of ten officers, and 110 men. We were still under fire on the 6th until nearly night. When the enemy made a charge on our right flank, and I was shot through the loins, the ball entering above the left hip, and passing around the back bone coming out above the right hip, making nothing but a flesh wound.

The enemy held the ground when I fell and I was taken to a field hospital one mile from Robison tavern on the road to Fredericksburg and for 3 or 4 days was very weak from loss of blood, but after that I gained strength very fast. As soon as we became able to walk we were sent to Orange Court House, a distance of 20 miles, and thence south by way of Lynchburg; on the 29th . . . the Doctor wanted me to go [to a prison camp]. I put on a long face and was let off with the understanding that I must go next time. I then determined to make my escape so about 9 o'clock on the morning of the 29th I left the hospital going toward Fredericksburg and passing the rebel pickets near Chancellorsville by crawling between them in a sort of a gulley.

When I struck the road about two miles below Chancellorsville on the road to Fredericksburg, I then found that the rebel scouts were in the town, and our force had vacated. Then I left the road striking the Rappahanock River four miles above Banks Ford. I made a raft by lashing two small logs together with a piece of grape vine, crossing the river in safety and skirting the river bank down to the Ford, and halting for the night. In the morning, after dressing my wound, I started for Belle Plain Landing on the Potomac, getting my breakfast with a family by the name of Blake. After crossing the railroad the country was much infested with rebel scouts. I managed to escape all but one and he, being a gentleman, after examining my wound, bade me Godspeed, and told me to keep out of the way of the rest of the scouts, which advice I followed, and arrived at the river about 2 P. M. and tried to make signals to attract the attention of some passing vessel.

Failing in this, and seeing the scouts on the distant hills, I constructed a raft of plank and crossed the mouth of the Potomac creek to Windmill Point and skirting the river banks until I reached Aquia Creek Landing, when I spent some time in trying to attract the notice of the passing vessels, but in vain, as the river was four miles wide at this point. There being a large gang plank on the wharf, such as is used in steamers, I determined to launch this and cross the river or get to the channel and get picked up by some vessel. After working over one hour, I got my raft afloat, and seeing the scouts along the edge of the roads I shoved off, with a piece of board for an oar, at about 6 P.M., and had made nearly the Maryland shore when I heard the puffing of a steamer, and I made signals and stood for the channel. As soon as she came up to me she hove to and lowered a boat and took me aboard, where, when I told my tale, some could hardly believe me, but some of our men being on board soon proved my identity and where I was missing.

The doctor soon examined my wound and dressed it, and handed me in charge of the steward, who soon showed me some water to have a wash and what was equally agreeable a good drink of old brandy and a good meal included, something I had not enjoyed for some time, but the excitement that had kept me up was fast dying out and I was fast becoming helpless, but a good night's rest soon refreshed me and in the morning we made Alexandria, it being a hospital steamer. I was sent to this hospital and as soon as I get over my severe trip I will be north. Give my love to all the family.[2]

Captain Lewis Van Blarcom of the Fifteenth New Jersey was shot in the leg at the Battle of Spotsylvania Court House on May 18, 1864. After Confederate surgeons amputated his shattered limb, Van Blarcom was taken to Richmond's Libby Prison, a three-story brick warehouse converted into a prison for Federal officers, where he was held for four months.

The series of conflicts known as the battle of Spottsylvania commenced on Sunday afternoon, May 8th, 1864. . . . We reached the rebel position about noon; were first formed in line of battle in an open field, and then marched to the left and filed into a wood almost at right angles to our first position. In front of us, across an open space about one hundred yards in width, upon a wooded eminence, the rebels were apparently posted, proved by the dangerous frequency of rifle bullets from that direction. Just before sundown General Warren rode up in full uniform and stopped at a short distance from where I was and inquired, "Where is the commander of this regiment?" Col. Penrose responded, "I am." Warren then said, "I ordered this brigade into action an hour ago. Colonel, form your brigade and charge; I want to develop that hill." In five minutes we were in motion. Upon emerging from the wood we encountered a sharp skirmish fire, which was kept up during our advance across the open space, with little effect, however. Upon reaching the top of the hill we found the rebels in strong position about a hundred feet from its verge, behind hastily constructed works composed of earth and logs. They opened on us with disastrous effect, firing by ranks. At the second discharge, I fell, my left leg shattered above the knee with a rifle bullet. I turned, crawled back over the edge of the hill to get out of the line of fire. When I stopped I saw our men just entering the wood from which we charged, took out my knife, cut my pantaloons where the bullet had struck me to learn whether I was bleeding or not, as I had a tourniquet in my pocket, found there was no bleeding. Shortly a rebel appeared behind a bush a few feet above me and called out, "You are an officer, surrender." I said, "My leg is broken; go back and get some men and carry me off." In a few minutes four men appeared with a stretcher and called out to me to crawl along the side of the hill behind some bushes near by, as where I lay was in sight of our sharpshooters. I dragged myself to the place indicated, was placed upon the stretcher and carried to the rear of the rebel line. . . . As I lay upon the stretcher the rebels gathered about me, and a lieutenant inquired where I was hurt, and remarked that as I would probably have no further use for my sword he would like to have it. I said, "certainly," and unclasped the belt and handed it to him. He coolly unbuckled his old straps, threw down his sabre and buckled mine on. The blade was a fine one, that my company had presented me but a short time before. A moment after, as I lay upon the stretcher, a little fellow came up to me and said, "Haven't you got something to give me?" I handed him a book, which he received with thanks, and I told him if he would get my cap which fell from my head when I fell, I would give him my watch. He started off and in a few minutes returned with it, and the exchange was made. I lay there all night under a pine tree. [The rebel] Colonel . . . treated me very kindly;

furnished me with two blankets, and directed me to command his orderly in case I wanted anything through the night, his tent being near by.
The next morning I was carried to the rear a couple of miles, to the field
hospital of the division, located in a planter's yard. Four surgeons were
in attendance. They gave me the option to direct amputation or resection. The oldest surgeon present said, "Young man, we will do as you say,
but you had better have that leg taken off. We can perform a resection,
but your leg will be shortened four inches; will not be as useful to you as
an artificial leg, and you will have only about one chance in ten to live."
I decided upon amputation. I lay in that yard under some boards near a
fence, with, in my judgment, skillful surgical attendance, with a man
specially detailed to wait upon me, until the 19th. . . . On the 19th I was
placed in a big wagon and carried, much of the distance over corduroy
roads, to Guiney's Station, and there put in a box car and taken to Richmond, arriving there on Sunday morning, May 22d. . . .

**Van Blarcom was carried by ambulance through the crowded streets of
Richmond from the railroad depot to Libby Prison. So exhausted was he
that he did little but sleep for the next three days.**

I hardly raised my head until the morning of the Wednesday following.
Then felt much stronger, and looking around I encountered a familiar
face not over ten feet distant, in the person of Colonel Ed. Cook. He
looked at me carelessly and turned away; I said: "Ed., don't you know
me?" He sprang up, and called out in a voice that could be heard all over
the ward: "Lew. Van Blarcom, you look as though you had been sick
three months." The Colonel remained in the ward about a week, and I
ascribe my improvement from that hour much to his encouraging and
vivacious talk. He told me all about his capture in the Dahlgren raid, and
how he came to be in the hospital department of the prison; that a few
mornings before he had told the rebel surgeon, a Dr. Franklin, that he
was sick; that the doctor grunted out, the best thing he could prescribe
for him would be a rope; that he responded, he would prefer a ham. It
turned out that Cook had the measles, and hence his transfer to the hospital. I remained in the prison till the 12th of September following.
There were on the average about one hundred wounded officers in the
ward. Scarcely a morning came that from one to five were not carried
out dead. I lay next the wall near a window. There were six beds in that
row, and during the time four officers died thereon. The surgical attendance was good, and the attendants were our men brought from Belle
Isle. The rations were dealt out but once per day, consisting of a piece of

corn bread, two inches by three, about an inch thick, a spoonful of brown sugar, half a pint of buttermilk, and the same amount of black pea-soup, with an occasional suggestion of meat in it. The vegetable, called pea, was a cross between the bean and the pea, infested with insects in all stages of development, from the maggot to the fly. We would skim off the maggots, and, if a few whole peas remained after eating the soup, and the head of a fly protruded from any of them, we would remove it, being careful to save the pea. Occasionally we would have two or three small tomatoes or potatoes. Bread and potatoes could be bought by those who had the money. A four-ounce loaf of bread at one dollar Confederate money. I sold my overcoat and vest for eight dollars Confederate money, and bought eight of such loaves of bread. Some of the attendants had money; how obtained we did not inquire; most probably taken from the bodies of the dead. Lieutenant Horn, who occupied a bed next to mine, conceived the idea of borrowing money from attendants, which we did, on the basis of giving our note for one dollar, for two dollars Confederate money. One George Dehoof, if living, now holds my note for over thirty dollars borrowed in that way. I remember a Massachusetts lieutenant sold his gold watch for nine hundred dollars, and invested twenty dollars of it in the purchase of a water-melon, on which a few of us had a rare treat. Our time was occupied much the same daily, smoking, talking and reading. Reading matter was furnished in abundance—newspapers, books and pamphlets. . . .

Religious services were held every Sunday, usually by captured Chaplains of our own regiments. For a few Sundays the exercises were conducted by Dr. McCabe, reported to have come from Baltimore. He was evidently a man of much ability, but could not repress his secession proclivities. On the last Sunday he preached he took occasion to commend the action of the Southern people in precipitating the war. On the instant no further attention was given to his discourse, and a greater part of his audience began talking among themselves. That was the last we saw of Dr. McCabe. After the Presidential nominations there was much discussion among us concerning the political situation. Though mostly Republicans, we were solid McClellan men, and solely for the selfish reason that we did not approve the policy of the Administration on the question of the exchange and parole of prisoners. At that time General B. F. Butler was the Federal Commissary of prisoners, and General Ould the Confederate. We fully understood that the Confederates were willing to exchange on parole, and that General Butler refused, for the alleged reason that the Confederate Government would not regard the conditions of the parole, and would get able-bodied men to increase their ranks, and the Federals would get diseased, half-starved men in return. That consideration weighed but little with us, and we held the Administration responsible for our continued imprisonment. However, in September arrangements to parole were agreed upon; we were released, and, doubtless, all forgot the above-mentioned grievance, and voted for Lincoln. I signed my parole on the morning of the 12th day of September, 1864. . . . It was worth some privation to experience my feelings of exaltation when, on crutches, I went out of the door through which I had been carried over four months before, and was placed in an ambulance in waiting. . . . At the landing . . . near the Tredagar Works, we were transferred to an old steamboat . . . and soon were steaming down the river. The boat hauled up to what was called neutral ground, near the Dutch Gap Canal. I managed, with the aid of a stout deck hand, to get on the leading ambulance. . . . We were driven across, where we found the steamer New York . . . which we boarded. An hour after, we were called on the upper deck, and found a table with ample room for all, loaded with sandwiches and other good things. We arranged ourselves around it; scarcely a word was said, but a good deal of eating was done—being the first square meal we had had for months.[3]

Severely wounded at the Battle of Brandy Station on June 9, 1863, Captain Henry W. Sawyer of Cape May was also taken to Libby Prison, where a fate worse than incarceration awaited him. During the summer of 1863 all of New Jersey followed his story as it played out in the newspapers.

[On] . . . the 6th of July . . . all the captains among the prisoners were summoned by General Winder from their quarters into a lower room of the prison. No exchanges having taken place, the men generally supposed that they were to be paroled and sent home. But no such good fortune awaited them. Instead of receiving an order for their release, they were informed that an order had been issued by the Rebel War Department, directing that two captains should be selected by lot from among the prisoners, to be shot in retaliation for the execution by General Burnside of two Rebel officers, who had been detected in recruiting within the Union lines. The consternation occasioned by this announcement may be imagined. They had hoped for release, and here was an order which in a moment clouded the whole prospect. Escape of course was impossible; the drawing was inevitable. After being formed in a hollow square, a slip of paper, with the name of each man written upon it, and carefully folded up, was deposited in a box, whereupon Captain Turner informed the men that they might select whom they pleased to draw the names, the first two names drawn to indicate the men to be shot.

Captain Sawyer, who alone seemed to retain his self-possession, suggested that one of the chaplains be appointed. Three of the chaplains were called down from an upper room, and the Rev. Mr. Brown, of the Sixth Maryland, accepting the task, amid a silence almost deathlike, the drawing commenced. The first name taken out of the box was that of Captain Henry Washington Sawyer, of the Second New Jersey Cavalry, and the second that of Captain Flynn, of the Fifty-first Indiana. When the names were read out, reported the *Richmond Dispatch,* "Sawyer heard it with no apparent emotion, remarking that some one had to be drawn, and he could stand it as well as any one else. Flynn was very white and much depressed." The drawing over, the prisoners were returned to their quarters, the condemned, meanwhile, proceeding under guard to the headquarters of General Winder. Here they were warned not to delude themselves with any hope of escape, as retaliation must be and would be inflicted, it being added that the execution would positively take place on the 14th, eight days hence. Sawyer, however, desperate as the situation seemed, did not despair, but reflecting that if by any means his situation could be brought to the knowledge of the Government, he might still be rescued, he asked permission to write to his wife, which being granted on condition that the authorities should read the letter, he immediately wrote the following . . . :

My Dear Wife: I am under the necessity of informing you that my prospect looks dark. This morning, all the captains now prisoners at the Libby military prison, drew lots for two to be executed. It fell to my lot. Myself and Captain Flynn, of the Fifty-first Indiana Infantry, will be executed for two captains executed by Burnside.

The Provost-General, J. H. Winder, assures me that the Secretary of War of the Southern Confederacy, will permit yourself and my dear children to visit me before I am executed. You will be permitted to bring an attendance. Captain Whilldin, or uncle W. W. Ware, or Dan, had better come with you. My situation is hard to be borne, and I cannot think of dying without seeing you and the children. You will be allowed to return without molestation to your home. I am resigned to whatever is in store for me, with the consolation that I die without having committed any crime. I have no trial, no jury, nor am I charged with any crime, but it fell to my lot. You will proceed to Washington. My Government will give you transportation to Fortress Monroe, and you will get here by a flag of truce, and return the same way. Bring with you a shirt for me.

It will be necessary for you to preserve this letter, to bring evidence at Washington of my condition. My pay is due me from the 1st of March, which you are entitled to. . . . My dear wife— the fortune of war has put me in this position. If I must die, a sacrifice to my country, with God's will I must submit; only let me see you once more, and I will die becoming a man and an officer; but for God's sake do not disappoint me. Write to me as soon as you get this, and go to Captain Whilldin; he will advise you what to do.

I have done nothing to deserve this penalty. But you must submit to your fate. It will be no disgrace to myself, you, or the children; but you may point with pride and say, "I give my husband;" my children will have the consolation to say, "I was made an orphan for my country." God will provide for you, never fear. Oh! it is hard to leave you thus. I wish the ball that passed through my head in the last battle would have done its work; but it was not to be so. My mind is somewhat influenced, for it has come so suddenly on me. Write to me as soon as you get this: leave your letter open and I will get it. Direct my name and rank, by way of Fortress Monroe. Farewell! Farewell! and hope it is all for the best. I remain yours until death.

According to the *Richmond Dispatch,* "Sawyer wrote a letter home, and read it aloud to the detective standing near. Upon coming to the last part of it, saying, "Farewell, my dear wife, farewell, my children, farewell, mother," he begged those standing by to excuse him, and, turning aside, burst into tears. . . .

After penning this letter . . . , Sawyer and his companion were returned to prison, where they were placed in close confinement in a dungeon under ground. Here they were fed on corn-bread and water, the dungeon being so damp that their clothing mildewed. The 14th came at last, but still they remained unmolested. Sawyer had estimated aright; his letter had saved him from the Rebel clutch. Immediately upon receiving it, his true-hearted wife hastened to lay the matter before influential friends, and these at once proceeding to Washington, presented the case to the President and Secretary of War, who, without delay, directed that General Lee, son of General Robert E. Lee, and General Winder, son of the rebel Provost-Marshall-General, then prisoners in our hands, should be placed in close confinement as hostages—General

Butler being at the same time ordered to notify the Confederate Government that immediately upon receiving information, authentic or otherwise, of the execution of Sawyer and Flynn, he should proceed to execute Winder and Lee. This action, prompt and unmistakable, and the more significant, perhaps, to the enemy, because of General Butler's known resolution of purpose, produced the desired effect. Sawyer and Flynn were not executed. After remaining twenty-one days in the dungeon to which they were consigned, they were relieved and placed on the same footing as other prisoners. Still, however, the Richmond papers vehemently insisted that the execution must and would take place, and the fate of the condemned remained for some time longer a matter of speculation and doubt. But the days lengthened into weeks; the winter passed, and at length, in March, 1864, the prison doors were opened, Sawyer being exchanged for General Lee.[4]

Corporal Edgar H. Trelease of Newark, a member of the Eleventh Regiment, experienced first-hand the horrors of Andersonville, the infamous camp for enlisted men. A Union soldier had a better statistical chance of surviving the Battle of Gettysburg than getting out of Andersonville alive.

My introduction into the living death at Andersonville occurred on the 7th of July [1864], and I remained in its clutch until the 22nd of October following. In all that period not one gleam of comfort illuminated the misery of our bondage. The camp embraced thirty acres, surrounded by a stockade twelve feet high. Here during the month of August 30,000 prisoners were crowded together like cattle, for the most part without any shelter whatever from the heat or frequent rains. At night, during rainy weather, they lay on the ground in groups, remaining thus until morning, wet to the skin, and with no fire to dry their scanty clothing. Occasionally the days were intensely hot, followed by rainy nights, inducing necessarily sickness among all except the more robust, the want of proper food predisposing the system to disease. The daily fare consisted of less than a pint of meal, four spoonfuls of rice, three spoonfuls of beans, and two ounces of bacon; sometimes, however, only a part of these articles were received, and then in a damaged state. A favorite dish consisted in taking a pint of meal, mixing it with water, and making it into dumplings about the size of an egg, which were boiled with pieces of bacon of the size of marbles until they floated on the top of the soup thus made. Then taking out the dumplings, we cut them open and poured in the soup—having thus a dish which to us was a luxury, though in other times we would not have insulted our palates by offering them such a "mess." Sometimes we made coffee by burning pieces of corn-bread, and boiling it in tin cups, drinking the product, of course, without either sugar or milk. At other times, in the absence of other food, we dug up roots and ate them.

There being no sanitary regulations in the camp and no proper medical provisions, sickness and death were inevitable accompaniments of our imprisonment. Thousands of the prisoners were so afflicted with scurvy that their limbs were ready to drop from their bodies. I have seen the maggots scooped out by the handfuls from the sores of these suffer-ers. I have seen others, mere skeletons, wasted by disease, dying by inches, with not an ounce of medicine, not a hand lifted any where among those in charge of the camp for their relief. On one occasion, where a physician gave notice that he would examine a portion of the sick men, over three thousand poor wretches, scarcely able to crawl, ap-peared before him; some carried on stretchers, and others in blankets, carried by comrades. Many lay before the physician in the last throes of death; and several, who were taken up alive, were corpses before reach-ing the point appointed for the examination, which, after all, amounted only to an inspection. On another occasion a gang of men were em-ployed two hours and a half in carrying out the dead from a section of the camp known as the hospital. On one day in August no less than one hundred and sixty prisoners died, and the average was about ninety deaths daily. From the 1st of March to the 16th of September *sixteen thousand* Federal soldiers, prisoners of war, were carried from that camp to the dead man's trench and the felon's burial! The method of burial was usually as follows: The dead were gathered up by detach-ments of the prisoners, are carried outside of the stockade, where they were laid in a row under a cluster of trees. Thence the bodies were car-ried in wagons, into which they were thrown at random, to a ditch at some distance from the camp, where they were tumbled out, covered with a thin layer of earth, and so left. . . .

But our tormentors did not confine their cruelty to depriving us of proper food and medical attendance. They had another devil's device for maiming and killing, namely, "THE DEAD LINE." This line consisted of a row of stakes driven into the ground—with boards fastened on the top—at a distance of about fifteen feet from the stockade on the inner side. This line was closely watched by a guard, and any prisoner who ap-proached it—and many often unconsciously did, and as, in the crowd, was often unavoidable—was instantly shot dead. Frequently the guard fired indiscriminately into a crowd; on one occasion I saw one man killed and another wounded, both of whom were innocent and standing some distance from the line. There was a standing order that any sentinel who killed a Union soldier for approaching the Dead Line should receive a furlough for two months; and for wounding one, a furlough of one month. This order not only offered a premium for murder, but encouraged the guard in other outrages, against which we had no defense whatever.

Perhaps you wonder what we did in the long days and nights of our imprisonment? What *could* we do? Crowd thirty thousand sick, starving, dying men into a space of thirty acres, and what opportunity is there for any thing but suffering? In all our camp there were but two streets— "Broadway" and "Market" we called them—neither over ten feet wide; and it was impossible, even had we been disposed, to indulge in games and amusements of any athletic nature in avenues like these, along which, lying in the sun or under the starlight, dead men could be seen, pale and ghastly, at any hour of the day or night. What did we do? We talked of home, of wives, mothers, and sisters, upon whose faces we did not expect, many of us, ever to look again; talked drearily of battles past and woes to come. What are they thinking and doing at home? Do they miss us, and long for our coming? Are they still among the living? There were the questions we debated with ourselves and with one another. But chiefly we talked of our daily fare; dwelling with childish pleasure upon those rare meals which more nearly satisfied our clamoring appetites. The nearer we came to starvation the more we talked of choice and dainty dishes; planning for ourselves feasts of all the toothsome things in the day when relief should come; counting up on our fingers the rare substantials and desserts with which our palates should be regaled in that coming time.

On October 27 Confederate authorities decided to transfer all but six thousand of the prisoners from Andersonville to Millen. Wrote Trelease:

How hope stirred within us at the good news! How all clamored to go! How the pallid faces of the dying grew paler still when, begging to be removed, they were told they must remain! Remain to idle—to die away from home and friends, with no soft hand to smooth the rough way into the rest that is starless! No more hope for them! How other faces grew bright at the prospect of deliverance! How scores of weak, suffering ones dragged themselves into line, and, with painful steps and slow, passed out to join the company of the chosen! More than one poor fellow, whose sufferings had won my pity, and whose patience had made me feel for him as a brother, I left behind me that fair autumn day; but their faces haunt me still in the quiet nights, and their sobbing good-byes sound yet in my ears.

At Millen we remained four weeks, and were then conveyed to Savannah for exchange. I shall never forget the feeling that overwhelmed me when, for the first time in months, I saw the old flag again—the dear old flag under which I had so often fought—for which I was ready to die in honorable battle. How we cried when we found ourselves under its folds on the deck of a loyal ship! How we sat down in groups and talked softly one with another of home and friends, and wondered whether, now that the boon we had all longed for was within reach, we should really reach and enjoy it!

Well, we hoisted anchor and sailed out upon the sea and came at last to Annapolis, a sick, maimed, emaciated company. There kind hands cared for us, kind welcomes cheered us, and we knew that we were home at last—home, with the arms of a great nation around us, sheltering and sustaining us with the great love of a noble, loyal heart.

When I left the camp at Millen my apparel consisted only of a blouse, pants and shoes. Many had not even the blouse; some were without shoes; all were ragged, lean, and wretched. But Father Abraham has reclothed us since then—those of us who are left—with the loyal blue, and, God willing, we will wear it again in the battle's front, as, under the old flag, we, with the Cause, keep marching on![5]

Another who endured the horror of Andersonville was Charles Hopkins of the First New Jersey, a native of Hope, in Warren County. Taken during the Battle of the Wilderness in May 1864, Hopkins survived ten months of captivity, where he lost over 100 pounds, returning home to Boonton and a two-year convalescence. In August 1864, Hopkins joined fifteen other prisoners in a daring escape attempt.

The tunnel that I was a party to digging, when I had strength, was nearing completion. . . . August furnished the foggy night acceptable to our party and between twelve midnight and two in the morning fifteen men crawled through the long stuffy hole—like rats—to the end and opening. Now the greatest caution must be observed and it required the stoutest hearts to face it. All could not go at once. Each man must move like a snake and as silent—none to follow until the preceding man was at fairly safe distance in matter of time. They were to have five in each party as near as possible for mutual comfort and protection.

Crawl, crawl through weeds and briars, until the brook was reached, when the crawl was a horror—through mud and filth to the railroad, under that to the site of an old sawmill up the flume, or the remains of it, slimy and dank, to the intake and lastly into the water, covered with frogspawn, briars and rushes—simply a nasty, shallow mudhole backed by a swamp reeking with the seepings through dead vegetation of generations. Wading, crawling, and striving in all ways to place as much distance between us and the Hell behind us, before the daylight gave our trail to the Rebs, and to find some safe place where the tired, starved, almost bloodless frames could rest. Blood was oozing from countless wounds from briars crawled through, and the dead pine and gum branches that met us at every move in the dark. Among our five were two that needed help and received it from the rest of us in every way possible—not caring alone for ourselves. Though pressed by them to make good our own escape, they felt the time had come for them to give way and starve in the swamp. Their plea fell upon deaf ears. Chilly, smothered with mud, weeds, dead pine needles, that had been rotting for years, feeling our way breaking a path or trail for the weaker ones, stepping into holes deeper than the general surface, plunging neck-deep into the slimy mess, even head first into some of them, praying for daylight—at least a little, that we could see our surroundings! Daylight came and found us yet in a swamp—not knowing whether we were nearer or farther from the [prison]. We had been unable to guide by the stars, as one shone, as the fog did not lift during our leavetaking. The sun moved it after daylight. Exhausted from lack of food, pressing labor of escape, the condition of body, the rags upon us, wet, clammy and cold, we had used some water in our mode of transportation, [but] we were not clean. The month of August, in a southern clime, and yet we shivered, though not from fear. We found a little piece of rising ground, carefully surveyed it, painfully dragged ourselves to the high point and lay down to rest—or die—either, was welcome. We had placed as we thought, at least five or six miles between a cruel death and liberty. . . .

Our little party rested and slept as circumstances would permit—the sleep of exhaustion. Two of our party should not have made the attempt. One, we felt sure, could not last long in this struggle; but he was determined not to go back alive. The other was so much of a cripple that he was helped when one could hardly help oneself. . . . A third one was not strong by any means. The night struggle had told very much on his nerves, as he feared recapture and its possible results. Each tried to cheer the other by some funny story, but the eyes never lied, though the lips spoke encouragement. Another of our party was a member of Company "B" of my Regiment. He had lost an eye but the other never failed him, with a nose that was acute in sense of smell, ordinarily of a jovial and devil-may-care disposition—but now, quite subdued . . . !

Our comrade of Company "B" was a little excited, sniffing and looking about. He said, "I smell onions." None of us saw anything about us that would indicate a habitable spot other than our own small island in this great swamp. Our Company "B" insisted that his nose was no liar, and wanted to forage. Being the acknowledged leader of this party of five, I objected on the grounds that where onions grew, enemies might also be found. All were in desperate want of something to eat and the eyes of all pleaded as no voice could. Objection was useless—he pleaded as well as the others that it might be a negro hut and they were our friends. Company "B" started cautiously, following his nose with high hope that he would find something to eat and no enemies. We waited, perhaps twenty minutes, with the little breath in us abated in the act of listening. Soon we heard a dog's bark and instinctively we knew that we were caught. . . . Soon came our comrade, arms full of what are called "leek," a species of the onion family, and he was unconcerned as though no danger was at hand, his whole mind was on his burden, though but a single article of diet they were very nutritious. He most sacredly divided them, each man his actual share. The dog quieted down and we felt more secure.

After a short delay to munch the vegetable we started with the hope of getting farther on in the swamp to avoid being hunted out by bloodhounds. We knew if we had been discovered that the alarm would soon be given and the manhunt would soon follow. Though no one had been seen at or near where the onions were taken, yet the bark of the dog meant to the owner that something unusual had caused him to bark. We had made only a hundred yards perhaps when we were stopped by the sudden breakdown of one of the party. He urged us on—to leave him and save ourselves, but we could not and our progress was slow now, and very laborious on all. Suddenly we heard the bay of hounds some distance away. They had found our trail! We did not know which party they were following, and hoped not ours—which was something selfish, but natural. The sound grew nearer and nearer and hope died within us. We realized it was our trail they were on. Either by the sense of smell to the hounds or intuition as to the direction we had taken, at all events we were being closely hunted. We lifted our comrade to his feet and again started with the desperation that small hope of escape engendered— while the savage baying of the hounds seemed to nerve up all of us. We reached a strip of swamp and entered but a short distance when the weak comrade sank helplessly down and died, while we waited, hoping to be missed by the hounds.

After making sure their companion was dead, Hopkins and his party continued on, hurrying through the brush, stopping now and again "to listen intently for that dreadful bay of the hounds, so near that it seemed our death warrant."

The sound stopped and we were encouraged and for several hours felt safe—night would help us, we parleyed in stifled voices, as to direction. I had made observation before day, and felt that we were going northwest and must soon strike a road leading from Oglethorpe; others argued that I was wrong. Three of us parted with the most obstinate one, he going south and would not be convinced of the fact that we three were moving northwest. Along toward sundown, hearing no sounds of hounds, we thought that we were safe and halted to reconnoiter our position before resting for the night march intended. A few moments later came an awful surprise—the baying of hounds and on our track! We moved to a rising ground and not a moment too soon. We took to some small trees in the opening—two of us were fortunate in having strength enough to swing up clear of the ground and the teeth of the savage brutes at our feet, but the sight that met our gaze when we had recovered from the fright of being hamstrung by the dogs, was one that time could never efface from memory. . . . The other poor emaciated comrade, who had exhausted all his strength to keep up with us thus far toward home and liberty, had no power left to lift himself out of reach of those hellish brutes. They tore him, limb, muscle and flesh—such as there was—so that he prayed his captors to shoot him. He could not stand or move himself from his position, and they did a merciful act, unintentionally—shot him to death; and another "unknown" rested while some fond mother, or other loved one would wait in vain for him or record of his death. Buckalew and I were ordered to come down from our roost. We came down of course, and looked about for our fourth man, whom we had not heard from since he left us. . . .

We moved on but a few yards, when we reached a road, and were bound each to a horse. . . . Why were we made fast to the horses? I thought of everything from hanging to being dragged to death—and this seemed the most suggestive from the preparation. Buckalew and I conversed with each other without notice from our captors—this seemed ominous to us, we concluded to ask the privilege of being shot like a soldier. We discussed the matter as if we were not to be the victims. Why we were waiting was soon answered when a party came up the road, and with them was our comrade who had gone south but did quite as well as we had. He was broken down with his tiresome march, exposure, fright and disappointment. We were soon to know why we were bound to the horses! I, to the one of the left, Buckalew to the right, the returned comrade in the middle, who was fast giving way, being bound by the wrist at right and left to the rope attached to the saddle, and to each other in the same way. The horses moved on quite briskly and the pace was almost too much for Buckalew and me, as the pull on our wrists by the lagging body of our comrade, which made it very painful, the pulling of the muscles, tension on our frames, this became torture to us, what must it have been to the comrade between us? A halt came, which was merciful.

The middle comrade sank to the ground and begged to be shot, as the pace and pain of pulling at arms length was torture to him and was killing his comrades. Our wrists and hands were swollen by the pinch of the rope, to a bursting point, it seemed. Our bodies wrenched by the sidewise pull at the helpless victim in the middle was giving us. Argument availed not, though all three of us were suffering so that our eyes almost popped out of our heads. We move on; our broken comrade fainted and sank to the ground but the horsemen only laughed and ordered him to his feet. He was unable to do so but we dragged him to his knees, they spurred on their horses and he [was] dragged at length over the sandy road and the little so called bridges, composed of two or three poles so the water could percolate through, the poles were rough and knotty. Not a sound from the fallen hero, and we two straining every nerve to keep up and drag his weight. . . . Again we halted, after dragging his limp body nearly a mile—it seemed a thousand—the skin was ground from knees to toe-tips of our dying comrade. He could scarcely speak to be heard, but the bloodshot eyes he turned to his tormentors and gasped, "Shoot me! Do please shoot me!" He was untied from us and we two were lashed together with a good-bye to our comrade so soon to find release. . . .

At dusk the prisoners reached a plantation house.

We were not dead, nor yet, not quite alive, but the human hearted woman gave us milk and bread with some "powk," i.e. some part of a swine. We lived rapidly then, in the course of two hours. We had eaten twice, and slept once. Sweet potatoes were baked in the ashes of the old-fashioned open hearth fireplace. After we had finished our second nap we were given a chance to wash and change our "rainment," so very scant and dirty, and brief at both that we blushed when in the presence of the lady, but the blush may not have been noticed through the accumulations of the past thirty-six hours. After the wash, which was delightful, having had real soap to use, and a good rubbing given us by a colored friend, some "nigger" clothes, they termed them, were handed us so that we might be presentable to the "lady folks. . . ."

Left to ourselves we found in a short time that there was danger in eating. The potatoes were eaten without salt, salt being very scarce. It was very dry eating. We drank much water, as the water was good; the result being a "fullness" quite a stranger to us for several months; so much fullness that it caused pain, which food would have given us, and for the rest of the night we both gulped and retched in misery and severe pains. After awhile we became worn out and actually slept, and morning came all too soon for us. Our relief from pain, with sleep to follow, was due to the kindness of a colored lady, who concocted a dose of hot water and wood ashes mixed, not so palatable but gave comfort in an hour. She knew her business on home remedies. When we awoke, the first topic of conversation was "What will be done with us when we reach camp . . . ?" We were ordered out after our host had given us a square meal of the "inevitable" salt pork and corn pone, but which was delicious to us. At the door was a wagon and team, to our surprise. . . . We rode all the way "home" in the wagon with some sweet potatoes and a few onions, beside them there were two small sacks of potatoes. We wondered why they were separate from the general lot and it worried us, we could not study it out, but when camp was reached we learned to our surprise that they were the "compliments" of the hostess of the night. God bless her, while we enjoyed her hospitality, though we did suffer from excess of sweets . . . ! We bid our coachman good-bye, sending our heart-felt thanks to our hostess for her kindness. . . .

Waiting under guard, we thought "what, oh, what, will be done to us this time, as I would surely be recognized!" This soliloquy ended abruptly. "Eyer, you Yanks, who you-uns as been run away, git up in line! We will take you-uns to see Captain Wirz! . . ." My comrade says, "I will follow your lead, wherever it may be." I replied, "I have only one life to sacrifice and do not want yours to account for." He says, "Never mind, I will go with you." We slowly picked up the little sack of potatoes—I don't know why—I suppose it was mechanical—it seemed just then that I should never want for more of anything in this world, for I was convinced that I was on the last lap of life; if Wirz was to pass on my punishment. Just at this time there were some new prisoners at the South gate in line to march in, and had just commenced to move, we were close both to gate and the moving line, there was some confusion among the guards, and I saw at a glance our only hope. I softly spoke to my comrade, "Step in line and I will follow a file or two back. . . ." I flanked in a few files back and passed to the other side; moved up to his file; and beckoned him to come with me. We passed well up to the front before the gate closed and the inner gate opened, both of us now free to move as fast as we could. We pushed along until inside the dead line, aided by those new men to whom I quietly told in a hurried manner why we were so anxious to get in front before discovered, and two of them did crowd us up front in a jiffy. Once past the dead line we were safe to move anywhere and hurried to our old "home." We had not been missed by the guards until we had made good our escape "inward" this time. Reaching our old place we found it preempted by others, but we were given a hearty welcome by those who knew us before we had taken our French leave.[6]

Hopkins was later awarded the Medal of Honor for distinguished gallantry under fire at the Battle of Gaines Mills.

At last, in early December 1864, several thousand "exhausted, starved, emaciated, dying" Union prisoners were exchanged, reaching Annapolis, Maryland, by ship from Savannah. A New Jersey doctor stationed at the Annapolis Naval Hospital poured out his rage in a letter to Newton's *Sussex Register*:

Nothing during the War has been so calculated to excite the sympathy and arouse the indignation of the loyal people, as the narrative of our exchanged prisoners now being received from Rebel dens of incarceration in South Carolina and Georgia. There is no form of cruelty or neglect that these brave men do not seem to have suffered. Even their prostration by sickness and bleeding wounds does not appear to have had an effect upon the barbarous men who acted as their keepers. Huddled together in open stockades, without shelter, without proper or sufficient food, without clothes enough to even avoid the humiliation of indecent exposure. Sick without medical attendance. Wounded, without surgical care; compassed with filth, stifled by the deadly stench of mortifying wounds and accumulated offal and excrement, history records no such diabolical treatment of human beings in all its most horrible pages. Much of this treatment was sheer brutal neglect; some of it was inhuman vindictiveness. The wan and discolored faces and skeleton forms of the men . . . tell the shameful and doleful story. . . . No appeal, either from the prisoners or their medical attendants, brought relief, or so far as we can hear, any attempt at relief. In all the surrounding region, the richest and best supplied of all the South, the terrible sufferings of our men must have been known, and yet no private succor or expressed sympathy: the pity of the South seems to have been swallowed up in vindictive hate of the loyal people of the North. The general sentiment seems to have been, it is only a Yankee, let him die a dog's death.

Can any adequate excuse be found for such devilish barbarism? If we grant that food is scarce in that section and medical supplies difficult to obtain, where is the apology for huddling the men into such crowded quarters, for smothering them with filth, for leaving wounds undressed until the victim died of gangrene amid terrible suffering; for the failure to provide splints to set fractured limbs, for compelling our men, deathly sick, to sleep on the ground, exposed to all kinds of weather, not even furnishing them with straw. . . .

And what a sacrifice indeed it was. Eleven thousand men died of this cruelty and neglect, the greater part of whom were literally tortured to death and who should have been alive to-day. And these are the tender mercies of the men who are forever declaiming against the barbarism and cruelty of the Union authorities. We return them their prisoners in robust health, they have been well cared for. They return us diseased skeletons—pitiable wrecks, whom extreme suffering has deprived of intellect. Was there ever such a record made by a people pretending to civilization?[7]

A second lieutenant in the First New Jersey when he was captured during the Battle of the Wilderness, May 1864, Joseph Ferguson was held in several Southern prisons until he was paroled in February 1865. Ferguson reached Union lines on March 1, near Goldsborough, North Carolina.

Colonel Mulford and his staff were the first Union officers of whom we caught a glimpse, and no sooner were they observed than they received three of the heartiest cheers ever given by one thousand United States officers. Colonel Hatch, the Rebel Commissioner of Exchange, and Colonel Mulford, the Federal Commissioner, counted us as we passed through the ranks of our soldiers, at an open order, faced inward, with their arms at a present. As each one reached the outer file, he started on a double-quick, shouting, whopping, hallowing, alternately crying and laughing, and running like a wild man. Some jumped as high as they could; others ran down the road for a quarter of a mile, throwing away everything they possessed; many rolled on the ground, cheering, shouting and hugging each other, shaking hands and crying like children. . . .

Those who had bags of corn-meal, untied the mouths of their sacks and threw the course stuff over their companions. Pots, skillets, griddles, bundles of rags, worthless articles, loads of trash and lousy clothing were now thrown away. . . .

We walked about a mile and a quarter from the place of exchange along a road picketed by our troops, singing and feeling gay, and thinking, as we looked upon the bright uniforms and manly forms of our boys, that we were among men and not ragamuffins and butchers. Suddenly turning a bend in the road, "Old Glory," the Stars and Stripes, for the first time, greeted our eyes. A deafening cheer went up from the head of the column, which was caught up and repeated by every voice along its entire length. Again and again every man cheered, until he was entirely exhausted and hoarse. All felt that it was the greatest day of their lives. The Sixth Connecticut Volunteer Infantry were in camp on the north side of the Cape Fear River, and on a small hill . . . they had erected a beautiful arbor of evergreens, and from its center hung their colors, whilst an arch, surrounded a placard, on which was painted the touching words: "WELCOME BROTHERS!" The splendid band of the regiment played "Hail to the Chief," as we marched past it with uncovered heads and hearts filled with gratitude. The troops were drawn up in line. . . . We passed through them receiving congratulations and sympathizing words. Each regiment had its flag, for which, as the officers passed, they gave three cheers. The old prisoners stepped out of the ranks, and, as their eyes filled with tears, hugged and kissed the flag of their country.[8]

SEVEN

"Boys, Your Work Is Done"

1865

Peace was in the air as the year 1865 began. Lincoln had been reelected with a mandate to stay the course until the unconditional restoration of the Union. General Sherman had just captured Savannah, Georgia; George H. Thomas's Army of the Cumberland, fresh from its victory at Nashville, was in hot pursuit of Rebel forces retreating through Tennessee; and the Army of the Potomac, under the determined Grant, was tightening its noose around Petersburg, the gateway to Richmond. At long last, the Shenandoah Valley, pointed like a dagger at Washington, was firmly in Union hands. The Confederacy had shrunk to the Carolinas and Virginia, defended by an army poorly clothed, starving, and wracked by desertions. "Our army is demoralized and the people panic stricken . . . ," wrote one South Carolinian. "The power to do has left us . . . to fight longer seems to be madness."

President Davis's refusal to acknowledge the inevitable meant that the fighting would continue for a while yet. Men died in the trenches before Petersburg, Fort Fisher in North Carolina was captured after a combined land and sea attack, and along Sherman's march from Savannah through the Carolinas, the South burned. When, finally, on April 2 the Petersburg-Richmond line collapsed, the Confederacy's fate was sealed. Events rushed swiftly to a climax: Davis's government fled Richmond in panic later that afternoon, Union troops entered the city the next day, and on April 9, at Appomattox Court House, Lee surrendered his valiant Army of Northern Virginia to Grant. On Good Friday, as the North rejoiced in its victory, a deranged secessionist fired a bullet into Lincoln's head, plunging the nation into grief and mourning.

As the war reached its climax, New Jersey troops saw action on nearly all fronts. While most were with the Army of the Potomac before Petersburg, others fought in Tennessee, or with General Sheridan in the Shenandoah Valley. Still other regiments, part of Sherman's 98,000-man force that had captured Atlanta and Savannah, prepared for the march north through the Carolinas.

Sherman's advance from Savannah, Georgia, to Raleigh, North Carolina, was longer and vastly more destructive than his famous march to the sea. Captain David Pierson of Company E, Thirty-fifth New Jersey, wrote to his hometown newspaper, the *Daily Advertiser*, from camp near Goldsboro, North Carolina:

The late campaign in South Carolina was by far the hardest and most wearing through which we have passed, owing to the season of the year, the rains and the nature of the country. The streams and rivers were high and the low lands and swamps covered with water. These, until we had penetrated far into the interior, formed natural barriers to our progress and materially aided the enemy in resisting our advance. They planted their batteries so as to command the causeways, and our forces were compelled to take the swamps on either side—places impassable to any except Sherman's swamp angels, as the rebels have lately styled us. . . .

We left Pocataligo January 30th, and first encountered the enemy on the 2nd of February at the Big Salkehatchie swamp, where there are no less than sixteen bridges in the causeway. The hostile guns were trained upon this road so as to rake with murderous fire any who might be so rash as to advance by this way. We were almost in such a position before we knew it; but shell from the other side, which came tumbling down the road, duly apprised us of our situation. We were marching by the flank, but immediately formed in line of battle in the swamp. Here we stood in mud and water up to the hips. After having constructed wide foot-paths of boards and logs on which to move back and forth with ammunition and stretchers, we carried the position by the middle of the afternoon of the following day. By the morning of the 7th of February, we reached Midway, a station on the Augusta railroad . . . ; here we destroyed a long line of track, burning and twisting it most effectually. On the 9th we came to the Edisto River. Here the rebels had burned the bridge and put their artillery in position on the opposite bank. While a portion of our forces engaged the enemy's attention in front, pontoons were thrown across below, and in the evening we crossed the river and waded the swamp on the opposite side. This was about the severest performance of the kind we have been called to go through. The swamp was three and four feet in depth and 150 yards wide. The day was the coldest of the season, and ice was forming when we emerged on the hither side. You may imagine the shudder with which the men received the order to take off their cartridge-boxes and string them on their knapsacks, the meaning of which they well understood. One of my men was seized with cramps in the midst of the water and had to be carried out. . . .

Having possessed ourselves of the rebel works on the Edisto, taking the fort and compelling them to retire, and having crossed the train over, the army moved forward and again encountered resistance at Orangeburg on the 11th. The place was taken on the following day and in the evening we entered the town. Here again we destroyed the railroad and continued to destroy it for miles as we moved up toward Columbia. The 16th of February brought us to the Congaree River and the high bluff which commands a most magnificent view of the city of Columbia from the west. . . . Columbia was a beautiful city, with fine institutions and public buildings. . . . Much of the town was unfortunately laid in ashes, having been set on fire by the cotton which was burned in the streets by the rebels, and, some say, also by certain of our prisoners, who escaped from the enemy, in retaliation for the barbarous treatment received at their hands. We left Columbia on the morning of the 20th . . . and marched in the direction of Cheraw. We entered this town on the 20th of March, and remained about three days. Here we obtained a large supply of flour, meal and rice, with which we loaded our trains. Some 25 or 30 guns were captured. . . . I was stationed in a building used by the rebels as an arsenal, but which, besides powder, shot and shell, was stored with expensive furniture, china, Bohemian glass decanters, cut-glass goblets, &c. These things were kept here, for safe-keeping by the people of Charleston! It was, of course, necessary that my boys should thoroughly investigate this stuff, and it was accordingly all hauled over. There was little there which their ready wits did not find some use for during our stay. They lolled about in the elegant cushioned chairs, and lay upon the Brussels carpets, put away their coffee in the flannel powder-bags . . . , eat their bacon off of the beautiful china plates, and had a fine time generally.[1]

In Virginia, meanwhile, the Army of the Potomac was dug in south of Petersburg, a key rail center twenty miles from Richmond. Through this city passed the Confederacy's lifelines: four railways that linked its capital city with the Deep South. The siege of Petersburg had begun in June of 1864 and lasted until the closing days of the war. Gradually, inexorably, Lee's weary forces were ground down until, on April 2, 1865, the Rebels were forced from their trenches.

Brigadier General Robert McAllister, formerly colonel of the Eleventh New Jersey, served as brigade commander of the II Corps during the closing months of the war. In early February Grant ordered McAllister's men, including the Seventh, Eighth, and Eleventh New Jersey regiments, on a flanking movement to the left, hoping to cut even more of Lee's lines of communication with the South. As the troops moved to the left, the Rebels attacked, bringing on the engagement known as Hatcher's Run. Three times the Southern troops "charged with headlong fury" upon McAllister's position, three times they were repulsed. "General McAllister," wrote one who was there, "was the hero of the battle."[2] Five days after the victory, McAllister wrote at length to his wife:

On the morning of [February] 5th . . . , we broke camp and were soon on the march towards the left. All were anxious to know where and what was the move on the board. . . .

After going a very short distance the 1st Brigade . . . took the lead of the whole and moved forward towards the ford. Here this Brigade encountered the enemy. Their resistance was but slight to what we expected, and this Brigade was soon across and in possession of the enemy's works at the ford. The 2nd Division moved to the ford but did not cross the stream. It wheeled to the right and moved forward in line of battle with their left on [Hatcher's] Run. At the same time, I was ordered to wheel my Brigade to the right and take up a position in line of battle at the Tucker House . . . and throw forward a skirmish line well to the front. I was to keep a sharp lookout for the enemy, and also to have my skirmishers connect with those of Genl. Smyth's 2nd Division.

All this was soon accomplished and my line of battle established across the road leading past this house. . . . Our men were now resting. All was now quiet with us, with only a few shots down in front of the ford. At 12 noon Genl. Humphreys and staff came and took a survey of our position. He ordered me to put up breastworks at once. On giving the order to my men, they jumped at it with a will. Rails and timber were carried with dispatch and dirt was thrown up with an unparaleled rapidity. I never saw work go on more satisfactory. My men had now been formed in line of battle (two ranks). But finding that the works for our safety ought to be extended down to a swamp, I had them placed in single rank. A bystander could see our lines growing further and further to the right every time he passed his eyes in that direction. . . .

It was 4:30 p.m. when I heard the firing in my front by the pickets. These pickets were not mine, for I had moved from the rear of my pickets. The pickets in my new front belonged to the 2nd Division. The firing was coming very rapidly towards my front. Our pickets were not firing as they should have don, but were running back with the Rebs after them.

I ordered: "Double quick, and on the right by file into line!" I moved with a rapidity not usual and formed my line along the works that I built . . . all under the fire of the advancing lines of the enemy. All my regiments were now behind breastworks except the 8th New Jersey, commanded by Maj. [Henry] Hartford. The first few companies of it had also filed in. But the works run out, and the [rest of the] men had to be placed in line of battle without works and under a most gauling fire. They faltered for a moment; myself, Adjt. Finklemeier, and aides rushed in and urged them to stand fast and extend their line to the left.

A little to the left of my now extended line were two regiments of the 2nd Division (Genl. Smyth's), which had been placed there to support the pickets. I depended on these two regiments to stand fast and help to fill up the long gap between myself and Smyth. But to my utter astonishment they give way on the approach of the enemy and left me to fight the battle alone.

I at once saw that here the battle must be fought with energy or all would be lost and a terable disaster to our army would follow. The distance now between my Brigade and Genl. Smyth's 1st Brigade on my left across the swamp was at least 300 yards. Through this the enemy might sweep with their heavy columns. I rode along the line towards the center, encouraging the men to "stand firm and the day will be ours." I talked to them as I rode along. I passed the first two regiments on the left, the 8th New Jersey and the 120th New York. I reached the 7th New Jersey (Col. Price) and ordered him to give an oblique fire so as to enfilade the enemy's lines. My works turned here and gave me a splendid chance. . . .

The Rebels recoiled under our deadly fire and the firing ceased in a measure. This gave our boys courage. In a few minutes more the well known Rebel Yell rolled out on the evening breeze and on rushed their massed columns. My line now opened a most destructive fire, so much so that it is said to be unequeled since the Wilderness battles. Again the enemy were repulsed. The fire slacking some, I rode again along the lines, encouraging the men to stand firm and the day would be ours. They all struck up the song, "Rally Round the Flag, Boys." The Rebels replied: "We will rally round your flag, boys!"

The heavy firing had now ceased for the time being, but the pause was of short duration. . . . Once more we heard that unwelcome yell resounding, which told us plainly that they were again charging our lines. But our boys were ready for them. As the darkness of night had closed in upon us, the discharge of musketry and burning, flashing powder illuminated the battle scene. This, together with the roaring of small arms and the loud thundering of artillery, made the scene one of more than ordinary grandure. We thus rolled back the Rebel columns for the last time, and the victory was ours. Cheer after cheer resounded along our lines.[3]

Casualties at Hatcher's Run were fifty-three, most from the Eighth New Jersey.

The men of both armies knew the end was near. Corporal Walter Drake of Company E wrote to the *Newark Daily Advertiser* on February 27 from the Tenth Regiment's camp near Petersburg:

Deserters from their lines all concur in the statement of the speedy evacuation of Petersburg and Richmond; that their cause is fast falling, and that nearly the whole army is disgusted with the Jeff. Davis government and its leaders. They say that if they arm their negroes, the whites will not fight; they will desert first. They have not a brigade in their army they can trust on picket; they have to place three videttes, one to watch us, the one in the rear to watch him, and still another to watch them both. Occasionally the three men [desert to us] together.[4]

On March 26 John Hoffman, now a Second Lieutenant in the Tenth Regiment, had a glimpse of the commander in chief as he toured the lines before Petersburg:

We returned to camp about noon and before we could get our dinner the bugle sounded "fall in" and firing commenced on the left at the same time. So down to the left we went and found that our troops had attacked the rebels in our front. . . . We stacked arms and waited until we should be needed. While we were waiting, "Uncle Abe," Gen. Grant, Gen. Meade, and their staffs together with several carriages containing Mrs. Lincoln and others passed. "Uncle Abe" was on horseback dressed in plain citizens clothing, a beaver hat on his head. There was nothing to indicate that he was anything more than a common citizen and would have passed for a common man if he had been alone and unknown. He is a much better looking man than I had been led to suppose by his pictures. He has a sad, careworn look and has a kind good countenance that leaves a good impression.[5]

Another member of the Tenth Regiment, James Gallagher of Company K, witnessed the surrender of Petersburg.

The morning of April 2d, 1865, I was on the skirmish line in front of Petersburg. As soon as daylight broke I observed a flag being waved from the Confederate breastworks. While watching the flag, Major Fay, of the Fortieth New Jersey, came out to the line and said to me, "Boy, what color is that flag?" I replied that it was white. He then gave the command to fall in, but before giving the order he used his field-glasses to make sure. The line advanced to what they told us was the Halifax road. When we arrived we found a gentleman standing on the breastworks with a white pillowcase tied on a pole. He stated he wanted to surrender Petersburg to save it from being destroyed, as the Confederate troops had all retreated through the night. He stated he was Mayor of Petersburg. The Major then sent word to commanding general not to open fire as the Mayor had surrendered the town. The Mayor and Major Fay then got into a carriage and pushed the white flag out of the back window. A colored man was on the box. He started and we all fell in behind and proceeded on the Halifax road until we came to some woods where the road ran on both sides. It looked to me like a picnic ground. We stayed there a short time, when we were ordered to fall in; then our chase commenced after Lee.[6]

New Jersey's Twelfth Regiment, raised in the southern part of the state in response to Lincoln's call for 300,000 three-year men, left behind an outstanding combat record. William P. Haines of Company F was among the troops in pursuit of the retreating Rebels:

Our regiment broke through near the Crow House, at 8 a.m., April 2d, and soon the whole rebel lines were in our possession, except a few enclosed forts, near Petersburg, which held out till after noon. General Lee, with his whole army, retreated during the night. Next morning, April 3d, Richmond and Petersburg were occupied by our troops, and that long and weary siege was ended. With hardly a halt, we pushed the fleeing Johnnies up the south bank of the Appomattox River to Farmville, where they crossed over the high bridge, which they partly burned; but the low wagon bridge was saved, and we were again at their heels, with no thought of pity, pushing and shoving them back, capturing their artillery and wagons. Their men, weak and faint from lack of food and rest, fall out by the roadside, unable to hold out any longer. We took them prisoners by twos, tens and hundreds. We found two of their brass pieces in the woods, covered with leaves, their horses too weak to haul them any further. We found their guns everywhere: by road, tree and fence. Men too weak to carry them further. Yet that plucky remnant kept up a bold front, the rear often turning and facing us with all their old-time valor; checking our columns and driving back our skirmishers, until outflanked, they fall back to the next hill, and turn again like some wild beast at bay. Pity or mercy we had none; we knew we had them on the run. We kept them going until April 8th, when Sheridan, with his cavalry and the Twenty-fourth Corps, by a long detour to the left, got in front of their retreating columns and planted his troops squarely across the path of the fleeing rebels. On Sunday, April 9th, with this impregnable line in front, and the Fifth, Sixth and Second Corps pushing and shoving their rear, they began to realize that they were whipped. The white flag was shown on their lines, though not in our immediate front. Our brigade continued skirmishing until 9 o'clock, when the order was given to halt and cease firing. We soon knew that they were negotiating with Grant for a surrender; but our position, far to the right and in the woods, kept us from seeing what was going on. Our first certain knowledge of a surrender was gained at 11 o'clock from the headquarters' band, who began playing "Home, Sweet Home," and the long agony was over. Immediately all discipline was relaxed. Our lines were broken up, and confusion reigned supreme; with hats, coats and shoes flying through the air, we whooped and yelled like wild men, till, perfectly exhausted, we dropped down; while tears of joy flowed down those sunburned cheeks, before too tough for tears. This wild demonstration was shared by all, both rebels and Yankees, and kept up for hours. A wild, delirious mob, drunk with joy! Many of the rebels, but rebels no longer, now comrades, came over among us looking for something to eat; and they got it. Everything we had was theirs. No boasting or taunting about being whipped; they were too good soldiers for that. Such plucky, brave fighters had won our respect, and we gladly shared with them our hardtack and coffee, as we swapped reminiscences of the times when we were foemen, now friends. In the evening the Johnnies went back to their own lines, and we established our pickets, just as usual; but no spiteful shots or wild alarms disturbed our happy dreams. Sweet peace had come to stay.[7]

Salem County's George A. Bowen, commander of Company C, Twelfth New Jersey, was barely twenty-one years old as he led his men in pursuit of General Lee. Though the Confederates were on the run, there was still some fighting and dying to do.

We started to march this morning [April 7th] very early, going south, still in column of regiments. . . . We went this way for several miles, coming to a road running east and west, were turned into this road in column, and double quicked to the west, soon arriving at High Bridge, a very high railroad bridge across the Appomattox. This stream runs through low meadows between bluffs on each side; these meadows are probably half a mile wide. Across the stream there was also a wagon bridge; this, as well as the railroad bridge, had been set on fire. We rushed down to the bridge and fortunately were in time to put the fire out before it had done very much damage; this was done by throwing dirt on it.

We crossed and again formed our lines. The Confederates were on the bluff, entrenched. . . . They had some artillery stationed along the railroad to command the bridge; to this we paid no attention, formed our lines, and advanced across the meadow, and would have taken them in the rear if they had not fallen back. Some of our men climbed to the top of High Bridge with axes and cut the burning part of it off. I saw one of these men hit; he fell to the ground with hands and legs sprawled out, and was dead when he hit.

Here Gen. Smyth called for volunteers from this regiment to form a skirmish line. I was one to offer myself; nearly all wanted to go, but I was sent as officer in command of the skirmishers. We advanced across the meadow and into a piece of woods, the enemy falling back as we advanced, and came out to a clearing around a house. They would halt, give us a few shots, and fall back . . . but [we] pressed right forward, shooting as we went. When we got to the house, some of the boys went in and soon came out, each carrying a ham on his bayonet; these were taken from a large cauldron in which the folks had been boiling them for the Confederates. . . . They had left in such a hurry they had not [had] time to take the stuff with them. . . .

Continuing the pursuit, we soon arrived near a road running north and south, leading into Farmville. Here the enemy made a decided stand, planting artillery and giving us sharp fire. Here we re-formed our line of battle and advanced to the foot of a slight elevation. While here Gen. Smyth came out, rode along the crest of the hill accompanied by his staff. While examining their position, I heard a musket ball strike a man, as we could always tell when a man was hit by the difference in the sound from what it was when striking the earth or a tree. I looked to see if anyone fell; then his staff dismounted and caught Gen. Smyth. He had been struck in the jaw, the ball going up and lodging in his head. He lived until the next day. He was the last general officer to be killed during the war. . . . He was succeeded by Gen. Barlow, who came riding along the same ridge where Smyth had been killed. He looked the ground over and said, "When you charge, go easy, don't run."

Someone near me said, "And get cut all to the devil!"

Barlow turned in his saddle, saying, "If anyone does not want to go, don't go; stay where you are." When we did charge, there was not a man that stayed behind. But [the enemy] had gone before we started toward them. . . .

Started at daylight this morning [April 8th] again in pursuit of the enemy. As we started, we passed over the scene of yesterday's battle. Here we found many of our dead lying naked, the enemy having stripped them of their clothing. Marched all day in column of regiments . . . ready at all times to get into line of battle instantly. Did not see the enemy or hear a shot fired that day. We kept it up until midnight without a moment's rest, even to eat, finally halting beside a stream, with orders to march again at daylight.

We were aroused before daylight [on the 9th] and told to get breakfast and be ready to move at once. But we did not start till probably 8 o'clock, then forded the stream. As soon as we got across our lines were dressed, files closed. We kept to the road, marching in column. About 11 o'clock Gen. Meade . . . came up; we were moved to the roadside to allow him to pass. . . . As soon as he passed we again started. In a few minutes one of my men came up to me, saying "Lee is going to surrender." I thought it might be so and certainly hoped it was true; yet it was too good to be true, so I called this man some very hard names, telling him what the consequences would be if he got out of his place again. Soon another man came and told us that Lee was about to surrender. . . .

After going a short distance, we were moved into a field, closed in by a mass of regiments, and told to get dinner. This was the first time since the 2nd when time was given us to eat, let alone to cook anything. The boys gathered a lot of fence-rails to cook with.

During the getting and eating of the dinner there was no noise as is usual in a camp. Everyone was quiet; there appeared to be an air of expectancy abroad. After a while a man came in from the road, saying that a "staff officer had said that Lee had surrendered." He had scarcely passed the word along before Gen. Meade, riding a white horse, came along between our Regiment and the next, and as he got about opposite me he said, "Boys, your work is done; Lee has surrendered and you can go home."

Then arose such a mighty shout as I never heard before. The bands played; the boys made the most absurd manifestations of joy. One of our servants who had packed his horse ready to move at once, climbed on top of horse and load, took the reins in one hand, and rode that horse at top speed up and down the line, waving his hand and shouting. Others placed their caps on their bayonets, caught their guns by the breech and, standing on tip-toes, waved and cheered.

Personally, I sat down on a pile of rails, saying nothing, trying to comprehend the fact and all it included. "The war is over." I had lived to see the Union's arms triumph. The Union was saved. . . . "The war is over," I could not begin to realize what it meant to me. I was afraid it was a dream, that if I stirred I would awaken. Thus I sat without stirring, not being entirely conscious of all that transpired around me.[8]

Charles E. Knox, a member of New Jersey's Christian Commission, which ministered to the spiritual needs of the soldiers, was one of the first to enter the fallen Confederate capital.

It was with the most intense and profound satisfaction that . . . I . . . marched to-day with the first brigade of the Union army into the city of Richmond. Jubilant glee and solemn exultation alternated and mingled . . . in all hearts through the North, as we paced with quick step the short six miles and a half of this triumphant procession. . . .

The news of success at Petersburg yesterday, was followed last night by the news that the already weak line of the enemy had been further weakened. The troops were put under marching orders. Pickets early this morning reported the opposite line deserted. A tremendous explosion between four and five o'clock, since proving to be the blowing up of the Howlett House Battery, was succeeded between six and seven o'clock by another hardly less terrific, which is said to have been the blowing up of the Richmond magazine. . . .

As we sunk into the valleys of the billowy land between Fort Buchanan and Richmond, the city lay concealed. Only the masses of smoke which rose in heavy plumes above the horizon, showed us its site. As the spires of the churches and the State House came into sight, the burning laboratories with their continuous battery of exploding shells, the rising and enfolding balloons of sun-lit smoke from a third great explosion, and the rebellious city shaded in darkness beneath, made a picture at once awful and beautiful. The emotions of sublimity and joyfulness at the thought of the consummation of the hour, lay pictured against the earth and sky, as in lighter form the same feelings were expressed again and again in the jubilant welcome of happy freedmen and suffering poor. . . .

Many things are to be told. . . . The sober enthusiasm of the troops, the masses of ivory in the faces of ebony, the distracted citizens, more distracted by their own leaders, who in firing their tobacco houses and military stores, fired the city, than by the appearance of our army; the famished poor, the last issues of the Richmond *Dispatch,* the capital and its secession churches, the countless papers, Confederate documents, scattered on the streets—the sublime and the ludicrous in the Guard before Jeff.'s mansion of American citizen soldiers of African descent, the street story that Davis tottered as he came out of church, and that Breckinridge walked down the street but twenty minutes before our advance arrived; the bitter silence of secessionists disappointed of their hope; all these and as many more make a long story. Quiet and peace now reign over an orderly city at the early hour of ten o'clock, save only as the light of the dying fires reveals from my window . . . the national soldiers following the "Star Spangled Banner" from the band.[9]

New Jersey rejoiced when the news of Lee's surrender reached the state, reported the *Newark Daily Advertiser.*

Little indeed were the great mass of our religious people conscious yesterday, while celebrating Palm Sunday . . . that during the very moment of their solemn devotions, the victorious chieftain of our armies, and the defender of our liberties, was receiving the surrender of the humbled commander of the rebel hordes; that he was then crowning the national armies with the well-earned fruits of their long suffering heroism, and strewing our pathway with the palms of future peace. . . .

Though this glorious consummation of our long endurance, inestimable sacrifices, and recent triumphs, has been for some days expected, our people awoke to the announcement this morning with demonstrations of joy which defied the power of language to express. . . . Ordinary occupations became tame, indeed; flags were thrown to the breeze from every prominence; hands were grasped in an extacy which completely stifled speech; the clangor of bells resounded everywhere, and the brazen throats of cannon thundered the glad tidings over the hills and far away. Even all this does not satisfy the tumultuous emotions that throb in every breast. . . . Never, indeed, has our generation experienced such patriotic enthusiasm, and never was such cause for its exaltation. . . .

The rainy and disagreeable weather has proved by no means sufficient to damper the enthusiasm of the people. Flags are displayed from the windows and on house-tops; and far up in the misty air from pole and steeple the stars and stripes stream to the breeze. A new and handsome flag, 22 by 30 feet, waves for the first time from the flagstaff of the City Hall. Guns have been fired during the day at different points. Neptune Hose boys planted their guns once more among the graves of the old Burying Ground and testified by its repeated utterances their sympathies with the feeling of the hour. A salute of 200 guns was also fired at the Hospital. The employees of the Morris & Essex railroad at their shops in this city gave vent to their patriotic enthusiasm by the display of flags, the firing of guns and cheering. Many places of business also displayed the stars and stripes. This afternoon a salute of 300 guns will be fired under the auspices of the Union men, and at 5 o'clock the church and factory bells will be rung.[10]

Paterson, wrote the *Daily Press,* greeted the news no less enthusiastically.

This morning, upon the announcement by The Press Bulletin of the surrender of Lee and his army, the city went at once crazy with joy. Business was entirely suspended, the bells were set a ringing their most jubilant peals, the Fire Department turned out for a joyous run, the public schools were dismissed, cheers made the streets vocal, and a forest of flags made the rainy sky radiant and beautiful. Everybody feels that, at last, THE END has come. A procession some thousand strong, of workmen from the shops paraded the streets with ringing cheers.[11]

In New Brunswick another spontaneous parade wound its way through the streets.

The news of the Surrender of Gen. Lee created the most intense excitement in our City to-day. The news spread like wildfire, and the whole population was informed of the joyful event in a few minutes after its arrival. The church, factory, hotel and school bells were rung, guns fired, gongs beaten, steam whistles blown, drums and fifes put into operation—in fact everything that could make noise set at work. The tin shops threw several hundred fish-horns into the excited crowds, and processions of several hundred men and boys paraded through the City making a most terrible din, and calling all into the streets, notwithstanding a severe rain-storm was prevailing. Several thousand persons were thus gathered into the streets, and with their horn-blowing, bell-ringing, gong-pounding, drum-beating, cheers and singing of patriotic songs, created a scene never before seen in this City. Staid, sober and dignified citizens, who would not otherwise have permitted themselves to get excited, were going bareheaded through the rain with tin horns in their mouths blowing as if their very lives were at stake. The stores and places of business were closed up, the college and seminary classes and schools dismissed, factory and work shop operatives discharged for the day, and everybody given up to celebrating the glorious event.[12]

Even the animals joined in the nearly universal celebration of joy, according to Bridgeton's *West Jersey Pioneer.*

Monday evening brought to us the glad tidings that "Babylon" had fallen before the majestic "Grant." The news was too good for any true lover of his country to pass unheeded by, and a grand jubilee was the natural result. Every true American wore a smiling face, and was ready to grasp his neighbor by the hand, and all the patriotic emotions of the soul were indeed felt. . . . How our souls thrilled with delight when we saw the blazing torches and soul stirring music by our excellent band marching along the streets, greeted at every corner with the wildest enthusiasm. Bright illuminations decking the patriots' windows, tokens of love waved by the ladies (God bless them, they are the hope of the country), songs bursting forth to give one to understand that all is not yet buried in chaos. No— the American is still the grand "watchword," and the reply is that onward the nation still marches, achieving victory over victory. . . .

We are told that the dumb brutes caught the inspiration of the glorious news, manifesting it by rearing their heads and prancing with unusual glee. The canary bird owned by E. F. Brewster, to which he has given the name of "Abraham Lincoln," with the Stars and Stripes floating over him, broke forth in some of its sweetest strains in the evening, among the grand public demonstrations, and continued singing for a long time, which he was never before known to do at night. If animals can rejoice why cannot every man?[13]

James S. Knox, a corporal in the Twenty-first Regiment, was in Washington's Ford's Theatre on Good Friday night hoping to catch a glimpse of President Lincoln. A few days later he told his father what he saw instead.

It is with sad feelings that I take up my pen to address you. Last Friday night at 10 o'clock, I witnessed the saddest tragedy ever enacted in this country. Notwithstanding my promise to you not to visit the theatre, I could not resist the temptation to see General Grant and the President, and when the curtain at Ford's rose on the play of Our American Cousin my roommate and I were seated on the second row of orchestra seats, just beneath the President's box. The President entered the theatre at 8½ o'clock, amid deafening cheers and the rising of all. Everything was cheerful, and never was our Magistrate more enthusiastically welcomed, or more happy. Many pleasant allusions were made to him in the play, to which the audience gave deafening responses, while Mr. Lincoln laughed heartily and bowed frequently to the gratified people. Just after the 3rd Act, and before the scenes were shifted a muffled pistol shot was heard, and a man sprang wildly from the national box, partially tearing down the flag, then shouting "'sic semper tyrannis', the South is avenged" with brandished dagger rushed across the stage and disappeared. The whole theatre was paralyzed.

But two men sprang for the stage, a Mr. Stewart and myself. Both of us were familiar with the play, and suspected the fearful tragedy. We rushed after the murderer, and Mr. Stewart being familiar with the passages reached the rear door in time to see him spring on his horse and ride off. I became lost amid the scenery and was obliged to return. My roommate had followed me and secured the murderer's hat. The shrill cry of murder from Mrs. Lincoln first roused the terrified audience, and in an instant the uproar was terrible. The silence of death was broken by shouts of "kill him," "hang him," and strong men wept and cursed, and tore the seats in the impotence of their anger, while Mrs. Lincoln, on her knees uttered shriek after shriek at the feet of the dying President. Finally the theatre was cleared and the President removed. Still greater was the excitement in the City. Rumors of the murder of Sec'y Seward and his son reached us as we gained the street. Mounted patrols dashed everywhere, bells tolled the alarm, and excited crowds rushed about the avenues. Despair was on every countenance, and black horror brooded over the city. Until long after midnight I was detained at Police Hd-Qrs. giving my evidence, and when I sought my room, in a distant part of the city, dark clouds had gathered in the heavens, and soldiers sternly paced their patrol. May I never see another such night. I could not sleep, I could not think. . . . Yesterday morning the President died. At 8.30 o'clock, the kindest, noblest, truest heart ceased to beat, and Abraham Lincoln was dead. . . . Andrew Johnson has been sworn. His speech was simple: "The duties are now mine, the results are God's." I trust he may perform his task faithfully, but oh, for the confidence and the hope that we had in Lincoln. Like a ship without a rudder is the Nation tossed. Outwardly are we quiet, but in each heart, what terror, misgiving, and despair.[14]

The assassination of Abraham Lincoln stunned the nation as no event in its history ever had. Lincoln's sudden death plunged New Jersey into grief, overwhelming the people "with sorrow and indignation and surprise." Patriotic bunting was exchanged for the purple and black of mourning, flags were lowered to half mast, and men and women walked the streets disconsolate with black bands on their arms and eyes red from tears. The reaction in Hightstown was intense, said the *Hightstown Gazette*:

A nation mourns the loss of its Chief Magistrate. A great, noble man has fallen by the hands of a bloody assassin. In the height of his glory and the fullness of his fame he was stricken down. His work is finished, and impartial history will place his name alongside of the purest and noblest martyrs of the Revolution.

Not alone as a public grief was the lamentable fate of the President received on Saturday morning. Gloom and sorrow was depicted in every countenance. Strong men were seen to weep, and everywhere, without preconcerted action, business was suspended. The joy that only the day before beamed in every countenance was changed to the deepest sadness. Every family circle felt that it had lost a cherished member. On Sunday our churches were thronged . . . and everywhere the emblems of mourning were to be seen. Never before has been witnessed in the United States such a day of gloom so overwhelming in its intensity.[15]

News of "the assassination of President Lincoln . . . created the most profound sensation" in Newark.

The flags that but yesterday floated in honor of our great triumph, are to-day at half-mast in token of the general sorrow over a calamity without parallel in our history. By direction of the Mayor, the public offices have been closed and draped in mourning. Many places of business are also closed, and the city everywhere presents an aspect of mourning, the streets being filled with groups of citizens discussing in subdued tones the event which has so suddenly dashed the joy and overshadowed the hopes of the people. The Hospital is hung with crape, and the carriage of Neptune Hose Company has been tastefully decorated in mourning. It is recommended, as a further evidence of the prevalent grief, that all the bells of the city be tolled between the hours of five and six o'clock this afternoon. Services in expression of the feeling of the hour will be held in many of the churches tomorrow.[16]

In Bridgeton, reported the *New Jersey Pioneer,* the people were despondent:

On Saturday last extensive preparations were made in this city for a general illumination, torch-light procession and other demonstrations of joy, on account of the capture of Petersburg and Richmond, the surrender of Gen. Lee and his army, and the prospect of a speedy termination of hostilities, but alas, joy was suddenly turned into mourning on the reception of the sad news by telegraph, which was confirmed in a short time by the arrival of the morning newspapers. The excitement was intense, and the news depot was thronged, and many stout-hearted men wept bitter tears of grief. Almost every one showed some signs of grief. The escape of the assassins caused additional sadness, and many swore vengeance on rebels and traitors, both home and abroad. The various bells of the city were tolled in the afternoon. The news depot was again crowded on the arrival of the evening papers, and it was difficult to procure a whole copy. . . . On Sunday the churches were draped in mourning.[17]

At first the people of Morristown refused to believe the telegraphic reports:

The news of the Assassination of President Lincoln produced in the Town, as everywhere throughout the land, the most profound sensation. When the news was first received on Saturday morning, it was generally disbelieved, but as it became certain that it was too true, every countenance looked sad, and every heart felt stricken. Flags were put at half mast, and the symbols of mourning soon appeared upon many of our places of business. The churches were appropriately draped, and in all of them feeling allusions were made on Sunday to this great national calamity.[18]

On the field one New Jersey soldier said that the assassination "fills every soldier's heart with the most bitter hatred against a Rebel." The *Jersey City Daily Times*, a fervent supporter of Lincoln and the war effort, grimly called for retribution:

A terrible blow has fallen upon the nation— a crushing blow in the hour of our supremest joy. . . . President Lincoln has been horribly, brutally murdered. That human life, on which more than upon any other, the hopes of a nation hung, on which perhaps rested the most momentous interests, and for whose continuance the prayers of all the good ascended, is violently, inhumanly taken away. The pistol and the dagger of the assassin have completed the culminating atrocity of the slaveholders' rebellion. The cup is full, and its bitter waters are wrung out this morning for a nation to drink. This murderous deed of the fell spirit of slavery, secession, and treason, is one of unparalleled and ineffable horror. . . . Good men have thought, that God in his justice was trying this nation by the severe and bitter ordeal of the bloody and remorseless war, and they have rejoiced, that at last the scourge was lifted, the plague stayed, and in the dawn of blessed peace that has just flashed its rays across a gladdened continent, there was evidence that our punishment had been enough. But now comes this crowning woe, this unlooked for stroke, that has fallen like a chilling ice bolt on millions of loyal hearts. We thought that there would be no more mourning houses, no more orphaned families, no more precious blood flowing as to the sacrifice to the Moloch of slavery, the demon of treason. And now the nation's head is fallen, the most precious blood of the country has been shed, and that cold, lifeless form, weltering in its gore, [is] lying there in Washington, in the habiliments of the grave. . . .

Abraham Lincoln, the beloved President, the pure patriot, the sagacious statesman, the champion of human liberty, the captain of the great host of the noble defenders of the Union, in the hour of his greatest triumph, at the meridian of his earthly glory, has fallen a victim to the rage and hate of traitors and assassins. . . . It is not possible, in this first moment of overwhelming and mingled grief and wrath, to predict what the people will demand as an atonement for this gigantic crime. The immediate instruments in this villany will, doubtless, be seized and pay the penalty of their guilt as far as the forfeit of their wretched lives can pay it. But the spirit that incited, the cause that prompted these murders must not, cannot be overlooked or forgotten. . . . There must be a total end made now of all these enemies of the republic, and adequate expiration of this concentrated criminality of treason.[19]

Not everyone in New Jersey mourned Lincoln's death. A farmer in Cape May draped his hog pen in black, a few brazen citizens of Princeton rejoiced openly, and a man in Bridgeton boasted that he would illuminate his home in celebration. William H. Hornblower, a Paterson minister, spoke for the vast majority, however, as he eulogized Lincoln the Sunday after his death. The nation, he said from the pulpit, had been "baptized in the blood of their President."[20]

On April 21 a nine-car funeral train carrying the coffins of Abraham Lincoln and his little son, Willie, left Washington for its 1,600-mile roundabout journey to Springfield, Illinois. Along the route hundreds of thousands paid their final respects to the man many called the savior of the nation. The train passed through New Jersey on April 24.

The special train which on the morning of Friday last left Washington with the remains of the murdered President, reached Philadelphia on

Saturday afternoon at about 5 o'clock. . . . At the depot a large and elegant funeral car was in waiting, to which the coffin was transferred and at six o'clock the long procession which had been formed for the purpose, conducted the body through the principal streets to Independence Hall, where it remained open to the gaze of the public until midnight of yesterday. . . .

At midnight the means of access were closed and after two o'clock this morning, the body was again placed in the hearse and conducted to the Depot by a body of soldiers and the Republican Club and members of the Fire Department bearing torches. . . .

The special train to convey the funeral party to Jersey City was composed of nine cars—a restaurant specially fitted up for the purpose immediately in the rear of the locomotive, six passenger cars, the funeral car containing the coffins of the President and of his son Willie Lincoln, and another car containing the chief dignitaries. The train was drawn by engine No. 72, which, as well as the pilot engine No. 24, was appropriately draped with flags and the insignia of mourning. The pilot engine received instructions to precede the train by 10 minutes. . . .

The magnificent funeral car with its drapings of black and silver . . . was built especially for the use of the President and Cabinet, but has never been put to any other service than the fulfillment of its present and funereal office. A beautiful wreath of flowers rested on the head of the coffin, the offering of the ladies of Philadelphia, and a cross of camellias from the ladies of the Sanitary Commission, was placed upon its foot. On little Willie's, also, were a wreath and cross of camellias.

Promptly at but a few minutes after four o'clock this morning, just as the eastern horizon began to purple with the first rays of dawn, the funeral train, with every car muffled in mourning, moved out from the [Philadelphia] depot and passed slowly northward between the lines of sorrowing beholders. . . .

At thirty-five minutes past five, a.m., the train entered New Jersey, passing slowly through the crowded streets of South Trenton, where thousands of spectators had assembled to witness the melancholy spectacle. At the main depot were drawn up on the platform, the Old Detachment New Jersey Volunteers, and several companies of the Veteran Reserve Corps. Lischer's band was also in attendance, and as the car bearing the honored remains came slowly up, the military presented arms, the dirge-like music of the band sounded forth, the bells of the city tolled and the minute guns boomed from a neighboring eminence. . . . There were probably some five thousand people in the neighborhood of this depot alone. . . .

The course of the new road was taken from Trenton to Dean's Pond, the Princeton depot being passed with slakened speed at 6:40 a.m. The platforms were covered with subdued and awe-struck beholders, including a number of students from the College. At Dean's Pond large numbers had gathered from the neighboring farms, and stood with heads uncovered, while the cars passed by.

New Brunswick was entered at 7:35. . . . In the outskirts of the city, along the line of the railroad, the waiting multitude extended in long procession. Individuals of every age and class were seen standing side by side with their hats in their hands and with the same expression of grief upon their countenances; many, indeed, were unable to repress their emotions, and many eyes were moistened with the tears of bitter sorrow. In the neighborhood of the Depot the crowds were great. All available eminences were occupied, the tops of cars and sheds being sought after as well as the windows of surrounding houses. Business had been temporarily suspended. Bells were tolled and minute guns fired at regular intervals. . . .

At Rahway and Elizabeth the assemblages were also very large. Minute guns were fired in both places, and the bells were tolled. On a road this side of the latter city, a group of school children turned out and displayed appropriate banners. Not only, however, in the larger towns along the route were such unmistakable evidences of the universal grief of the people at the untimely death of him whom they had learned to look upon as a father, but at the smallest stations were seen, as the train moved by, little groups of sincere though humble mourners; and the poor laborer ceased from his work in the field, and stood with uncovered head and tearful countenance while the sad procession passed.

Shortly after 7 o'clock this morning crowds of people began to gather upon [Newark's] Railroad avenue between Market and Chestnut streets, and soon not only covered the entire street but all the adjoining housetops, sheds and windows. A feeling of deep sorrow appeared to pervade the entire mass, while the fluttering of the black trimming from the neighboring buildings, the mourning badges upon the coat or mantle, and the other tokens of grief gave an unusually sombre cast to the scene. . . . As the trains with the remains passed slowly along the avenue, heads were uncovered and bowed with reverence, many persons shedding tears. The cars remained at the depot only a few minutes and then proceeded to Jersey City, passing large numbers of citizens who had gathered at the various street crossings. . . .

The depot at Jersey City was appropriately decorated with the habiliments of mourning, and the clock at the west end was stopped at 7:22—

the hour of the President's death—being encircled by the motto, "A Nation's Heart is Struck." At the west end the American flag was festooned, draped in mourning, and over it was suspended the motto, "Be still and know that I am God". . . . At 3 minutes after 10 o'clock the funeral train entered the depot. . . .

[The remains were taken from the train] and borne on the shoulders of ten members of the Veterans Reserve Corps. Immediately following the body marched Governor Parker . . . followed by the city authorities and Councils of Jersey City, Hoboken, Hudson City and Bergen. The procession marched . . . into Exchange Place, where the body was placed in a hearse drawn by six iron-gray horses, each covered with a heavy black pall. The mournful procession then passed upon the ferry boat "Jersey City," which had been handsomely trimmed in mourning, and upon which the New York Common Council was in waiting. . . . Upon the arrival of the boat on the New York side, the Hoboken German singing societies chanted a mournful dirge while the remains were being conveyed to the shore.

All business places were closed in Jersey City between the hours of 9 and 10 o'clock, and upon the arrival of the train in the city limits the church bells were tolled and minute guns fired. Around the depot and in Exchange Place an immense throng had congregated, but the utmost quiet and good order prevailed, and with one accord, the spectators remained uncovered during the passage of the procession.[21]

The war did not officially end until May 10, when President Andrew Johnson proclaimed that all resistance had ceased. By then 6,400 men from New Jersey had died in the service of their country. Thousands of others had been wounded, many maimed for life. Writing from the headquarters of the Thirty-third Regiment in Raleigh, North Carolina, a Jerseyman who came through the conflict alive expressed the feelings of most:

The War is ended, the Government is saved, and the traitorous South is taught a lesson of obedience to law that cost her dearly. . . . What a glorious achievement! In the midst of the sickening sorrow and gloom overwhelming us because of the tragic end of Mr. Lincoln's administration and life, we have great cause for rejoicing and much to elevate our hopes for the future of our nation. . . . Everything is assuming a shape for as rapid a march towards the national metropolis, as the circumstances of our situation will permit. We hope to celebrate the grand old 4th of July with our friends at home. . . . Not the least glad at this intelligence . . . is the soldier of the Republic. Home, sweet home, is the burden of his thought by day, and the subject of his dreams at night. He thinks and talks of it incessantly. Nearly three years separation from it by the necessities of his calling and the perils of his country, have only whetted his appetite to a keener appreciation of its worth, and produced a stronger desire to share its blessings. Parents, brothers, sisters, wives, sweat-hearts, are now yearned after with a passion, before concealed, and only now made known, because its cherished object is nearer and more probably attainable than ever before.[22]

On May 23 and 24 the victorious armies of the eastern and western fronts marched triumphantly down Washington's Pennsylvania Avenue, cheered by President Johnson, General Grant, and two hundred thousand ecstatic spectators. Thomas Marbaker of the Eleventh Regiment was there:

At seven A. M. we left camp and marched across the long bridge and up through the city to the east of the capitol, where we remained until nine o'clock, when the signal for the column to move was given. The line of march led up Pennsylvania avenue. The sidewalks were thronged with citizens, whose enthusiasm knew no bounds. All along the line of march the heartiest cheers greeted us, while from nearly every window flags and handkerchiefs were waving; flowers were scattered in profusion, so that nearly every soldier carried a bouquet in the muzzle of his musket. On the steps of public buildings were grouped the children of the public schools, who sang patriotic songs as we marched by. Theirs were the first childish voices that many of us had heard for nearly three years, and the sweet tones of their voices echoing above the strains of martial music seemed to us a guarantee of peace and home. As we passed the reviewing stand occupied by President Johnson, Generals Grant, Meade and others, someone proposed three cheers for the officers and men of the Eleventh New Jersey, and they were given with a will.[23]

A reporter for the *Newark Daily Advertiser* who watched the parade proudly described those "gallant veterans from New Jersey, whose thinned ranks, bronzed faces, and tattered battle flags attested to the hardships they had endured in the nation's service." New Jerseyans in the reviewing stands, he added, "looked upon their representatives with mingled pride and sorrow—pride at the achievements of the ever-brave 'Jersey Blues,' sorrow at the absence of many daring leaders, who now filled honored graves."[24]

On June 2, General McAllister issued his final order to the men of his brigade:

As we are about to separate, allow me once more to congratulate you on your past and brilliant career, which now becomes a matter of history. The war is over, the contest is ended. The glorious old flag of our country—consecrated by the blood of our fallen heroes—under the folds of which you have so often, so long, and so gallantly fought and bled—and to defend which your comrades have died—now floats in triumph over our land. The war brought us to the field. Peace returns us to our homes. Our work is done, and we go to enjoy the fruits of our victories with our friends in the several States represented in this command. . . .

In parting with you, I feel more than I can express or than language can convey. We shared each other's dangers, toils, and fatigues—on the march, in battle, in the charge, whether attended with victory or defeat. Ties of more than an ordinary kind bind us together. Goodbye, Comrades in Arms. God bless you, and the widows and orphans of those of our number who have fallen by our side. And if we never meet again on earth, may we meet in a brighter and better world.[25]

Notes

ONE. *"A Carnival of Patriotism"*

1. Quoted in William Gillette, *Jersey Blue: Civil War Politics in New Jersey 1854–1865* (New Brunswick: Rutgers University Press, 1995), 125.

2. *New York Times,* February 22, 1861; *Newark Sentinel of Freedom,* February 26, 1861; and *Philadelphia Inquirer,* February 22, 1861.

3. *Trenton State Gazette and Republican,* March 1, 1861.

4. *Somerset Messenger,* February 21, 1861.

5. *Newark Daily Journal,* April 4, 1861.

6. *Newark Daily Advertiser,* April 6, 1861.

7. *Princeton Standard,* April 12, 1861.

8. *Trenton State Gazette and Republican,* February 8, 1861.

9. *Princeton Standard,* February 8, 1861.

10. *Newark Daily Advertiser,* April 15, 1861.

11. *Somerset Messenger,* May 9, 1861.

12. *New-Jersey Journal,* April 23, 1861.

13. *Newark Daily Advertiser,* April 13, 1861.

14. *New-Jersey Journal,* April 23, 1861.

15. *Bordentown Register,* April 19, 1861.

16. *New Jersey Herald and Sussex County Democrat,* April 27, 1861.

17. Ibid., quoting the *Princeton Standard,* April 27, 1861.

18. *Newark Daily Advertiser,* April 15, 1861.

19. *Trenton State Gazette and Republican,* April 22, 1861.

20. Hermann J. Platt, ed., *Charles Perrin Smith, New Jersey Political Reminiscences, 1828–1882* (New Brunswick: Rutgers University Press, 1965), 110–111.

21. John Y. Foster, *New Jersey and the Rebellion* (Newark: State of New Jersey, 1868), 26.

22. *Ocean Emblem,* April 24, 1861.

23. *New Jersey Pioneer,* May 11, 1861.

24. *Bordentown Register,* April 26, 1861.

25. Ibid.

26. *Newark Daily Mercury,* April 30, 1861.

27. *Bordentown Register,* May 10, 1861.

28. Quoted in John T. Cunningham, *New Jersey, America's Main Road* (Garden City, N.Y.: Doubleday & Co., 1966), 179.

29. *New Jersey Mirror and Burlington County Advertiser,* May 16, 1861.

30. Foster, *New Jersey and the Rebellion,* 42.

31. *Monmouth Democrat,* May 16, 1861.

32. *Trenton State Gazette and Republican,* May 24, 1861.

33. *New Jersey Mirror and Burlington County Advertiser,* June 6, 1861.

34. Camille Baquet, *History of the First Brigade, New Jersey Volunteers* (Trenton: State of New Jersey, 1910), 411–412.

35. *New-Brunswick Fredonian,* May 30, 1861.

36. *American Standard,* May 6, 1861.

37. Frank H. Stewart, ed., *Gloucester County in the Civil War* (Woodbury, N.J., 1941), letter dated July 2, 1861.

38. *Newark Daily Mercury,* July 25, 1861.

39. Ibid.

40. James I. Robertson, Jr., ed., *The Civil War Letters of General Robert McAllister* (New Brunswick: Rutgers University Press, 1965), 50–53.

41. *New Jersey Mirror and Burlington County Advertiser,* August 6, 1861.

42. *Trenton State Gazette and Republican,* July 26, 1861.

43. *Newark Daily Journal,* July 2, 1861.

44. *Trenton State Gazette and Republican,* July 26, 1861.

45. Ibid.

46. *Newark Daily Mercury,* August 14, 1861.

47. *New-Brunswick Fredonian,* August 28, 1861.

48. *Newark Daily Advertiser,* September 6, 1861.

49. *The Jerseyman,* September 7, 1861.

50. *Morristown Banner,* quoted in the *New-Brunswick Daily Fredonian,* August 31, 1861.

51. *Monmouth Democrat,* September 12, 1861.

52. Ibid.

53. *Trenton Gazette,* quoted in the *Newark Daily Advertiser,* September 12, 1861.

54. *Newark Daily Mercury,* September 10, 1861.

55. United States, *The War of the Rebellion: A Compilation of the Official Records of the Union and Confederate Armies* (Washington, D.C., 1880–1901), Series 2, Vol. 2, pt. 2, 801–802, quoting Record Book, State Department, "Arrests for Disloyalty."

56. *The Jerseyman,* October 5, 1861.

57. *Paterson Daily Guardian,* October 1, 1861.

58. Ibid., October 8, 1861.

59. *Monmouth Democrat,* August 26, 1861, quoting the *Newark Daily Mercury.*

60. *Paterson Daily Guardian,* October 8, 1861.
61. *Monmouth Democrat,* December 26, 1861.
62. Ibid.
63. *Paterson Daily Guardian,* October 8, 1861.

TWO. *"Rally, Boys! Rally!"*

1. Robertson, ed., *McAllister Letters,* 106.
2. Quoted in W. Woodford Clayton, *History of Union and Middlesex Counties, New Jersey* (Philadelphia: Everts & Peck, 1882), 147.
3. *Daily State Gazette and Republican,* March 3, 1862.
4. Foster, *New Jersey and the Rebellion,* 210.
5. *Daily State Gazette and Republican,* March 29, 1862.
6. *Paterson Daily Guardian,* May 16, 1862.
7. *Falls City Register,* May 21, 1862.
8. *Paterson Daily Register,* July 12, 1862.
9. *Newark Daily Mercury,* July 10, 1862.
10. *Paterson Daily Register,* July 12, 1862.
11. Ira Seymour Dodd, *The Song of the Rappahannock* (New York: Dodd, Mead and Co., 1898), 44.
12. Joseph E. Crowell, *The Young Volunteer* (Paterson, N.J., 1906), 10.
13. *Morristown True Democratic Banner,* July 24, 1862.
14. *Easton and Phillipsburg Standard,* August 8, 1862.
15. *Sentinel of Freedom,* August 5, 1862.
16. *Newark Daily Mercury,* August 11, 1862.
17. *American Standard,* August 19, 1862.
18. *Monmouth Democrat,* September 4, 1862.
19. Ibid.
20. *Millstone Mirror,* August 28, 1862.
21. *Newark Daily Advertiser,* August 28, 1862.
22. *Orange Journal,* September 6, 1862.
23. *Trenton State Gazette,* September 5, 1862.
24. *Monmouth Democrat,* September 4, 1862.
25. *New York Times,* September 22, 1862.
26. Crowell, *The Young Volunteer,* 128–143.
27. Ibid., 147–149.
28. *Bergen Democrat,* October 3, 1862.
29. *Trenton Weekly True American,* November 14, 1862.
30. *Paterson Daily Guardian,* December 25, 1862.
31. *Hunterdon Gazette,* December 24, 1862.
32. *Newark Daily Mercury,* December 27, 1862.
33. Ibid., December 17, 1862.
34. *Newark Daily Journal,* December 17, 1862.

THREE. *"We Will Give Them Hell Yet"*

1. *Hunterdon Democrat,* February 11, 1863.

2. *Newark Daily Mercury,* January 26, 1863.

3. Crowell, *The Young Volunteer,* 315–317.

4. *Hunterdon Republican,* February 6, 1863.

5. Foster, *New Jersey and the Rebellion,* 544.

6. *Hunterdon Democrat,* February 11, 1863.

7. *Paterson Daily Guardian,* February 2, 1863.

8. Letter, Jacob Young to his father, January 4, 1863, author's collection.

9. *American Standard,* March 2, 1863.

10. *Bergen Democrat,* February 20, 1863.

11. Quoted in Gillette, *Jersey Blue,* 208.

12. Quoted in Bruce Catton, *Glory Road* (Garden City, N.Y.: Doubleday & Co., 1954), 145.

13. *Newark Daily Mercury,* March 7, 1863.

14. Ibid., March 12, 1863.

15. *Newark Daily Advertiser,* April 20, 1863.

16. *New-Brunswick Fredonian,* May 15, 1863.

17. *Newark Daily Journal,* May 14, 1863.

18. *Somerset Messenger,* May 14, 1863.

19. *Orange Journal,* May 16, 1863.

20. Quoted in Edmund Drake Halsey, *History of Morris County, New Jersey* (New York: W. W. Munsell & Co., 1882), 93–94.

21. Samuel Toombs, *Reminiscences of the War . . .* (Orange, N.J., 1878), 68–69.

22. *Jersey City Daily Advocate,* September 15, 1863.

23. Henry R. Pyne, *The History of the First New Jersey Cavalry . . .* (Trenton, N.J.: J. A. Beecher, 1871), 117–119.

24. Samuel Toombs, *New Jersey Troops in the Gettysburg Campaign . . .* (Orange, N.J., 1888), 56–58.

25. Pyne, *History of the First New Jersey Cavalry,* 120–123.

26. *Jersey City Daily Advocate,* September 15, 1863.

27. *Trenton Daily True American,* June 20, 1863.

28. Gillette, *Jersey Blue,* 238.

29. *Newark Daily Mercury,* quoted in the *Plainfield Union,* June 16, 1863.

30. Michael Hanifen, *History of Battery B, First New Jersey Artillery* (Ottowa, Ill.: Republican-Times printers, c. 1905), 66–83.

31. William P. Haines, *History of the Men of Co. F . . .* (Camden, N.J.: C. S. Magrath, 1897), 39–43.

32. *Paterson Daily Guardian,* July 6, 1863.

33. *New-Brunswick Fredonian,* July 7, 1863.

34. *Newark Daily Mercury,* July 10, 1863.

35. *American Standard,* July 8, 1863.

36. Toombs, *Gettysburg Campaign,* 316–317.

37. Henrietta Stratton Jaquette, ed., *Letters of a Civil War Nurse, 1863–1865* (Lincoln: University of Nebraska Press, 1998), 4–6.

FOUR. *"It Was a Godforsaken Place"*

1. *Somerset Messenger,* February 11, 1863; *Bergen Democrat,* October 3, 1862; *Newark Daily Journal,* June 1, 1864.

2. *Somerset Unionist,* November 19, 1863.

3. Foster, *New Jersey and the Rebellion,* 772.

4. *Newark Daily Advertiser,* November 11, 1865.

5. *Trenton True American,* November 7, 1862.

6. *Bergen Democrat,* May 9, 1862.

7. Charles Merriam Knapp, *New Jersey Politics during the Period of the Civil War and Reconstruction* (Geneva, N.Y.: W. F. Humphrey, 1924), 83.

8. *Newark Daily Advertiser,* July 30, 1862.

9. *Newark Daily Journal,* February 16, 1863.

10. *Newark Daily Mercury,* February 16, 1863.

11. *Hunterdon Republican,* February 6, 1863.

12. *Newark Daily Mercury,* March 21, 1863.

13. *Sentinel of Freedom,* March 24, 1863.

14. *Newark Daily Mercury,* April 3, 1863.

15. Cunningham, *New Jersey's Main Road,* 183.

16. *Newark Daily Advertiser,* April 15, 1863.

17. Quoted in Earl Schenck Miers, ed., *New Jersey and the Civil War* (Princeton: D. Van Nostrand Co., 1964), 108.

18. *Somerset Unionist,* July 9, 1863.

19. *Newark Daily Mercury,* March 17, 1863.

20. *Newark Daily Journal,* July 14, 1863; *Sentinel of Freedom,* July 21, 1863.

21. *Morristown True Democratic Banner,* June 2, 1864.

22. *Newark Daily Advertiser,* August 15, 1864.

23. *The Jerseyman,* June 18, 1864.

24. *Newark Daily Journal,* July 18, 1864.

25. *Trenton State Gazette and Republican,* July 21, 1864.

26. *Paterson Daily Press,* February 25, 1865.

27. *Morristown True Democratic Banner,* June 11, 1863.

28. *Jersey City American Standard,* March 7, 1863.

29. *Paterson Daily Press,* November 18, 1864.

30. Quoted in Gillette, *Jersey Blue,* 288–289.

31. *Paterson Daily Press,* November 18, 1864.

32. Ibid., November 4, 1863.

33. *Trenton Daily State Gazette,* November 7, 1864.

34. Ibid., November 1, 1864.

35. Ibid., October 10, 1864.

36. *Paterson Daily Register,* October 18, 1864.

37. *Trenton Daily State Gazette,* October 27, 1864.

38. *Morristown True Democratic Banner,* November 9, 1864.

39. *Flemington Republican,* November 25, 1864.

40. *Trenton Daily State Gazette,* November 22, 1864.

FIVE. *"Go in, Jersies, We Will Follow You!"*

1. *Newark Daily Journal,* March 4, 1864.

2. *Paterson Daily Press,* June 4, 1864.

3. *Newark Daily Advertiser,* August 15, 1864.

4. Ibid., January 3, 1865.

5. Alanson A. Haines, *History of the Fifteenth Regiment, New Jersey Volunteers* (New York: Jenkins & Thomas, 1883), 145–149.

6. Ron E. Davis, ed., *The Civil War Diary and Letters of John Bacon Hoffman of Shiloh, New Jersey* (Plainfield, N.J.: Seventh Day Baptist Publishing House, 1979), 6–7.

7. Foster, *New Jersey and the Rebellion,* 397–400.

8. Ibid., 115.

9. Quoted in William B. Styple, ed., *Death Before Dishonor: The Andersonville Diary of Eugene Forbes* (Kearny, N.J.: Belle Grove Pub. Co., 1995), 191–193.

10. Thomas D. Marbaker, *History of the Eleventh New Jersey Volunteers . . .* (Trenton, N.J.: MacCrellish & Quigley, 1898), 173–174.

11. Ibid., 175.

12. Foster, *New Jersey and the Rebellion,* 400.

13. Letters of William S. Van Fleet, Parsippany (New Jersey) Historical & Preservation Society, Inc.

14. Foster, *New Jersey and the Rebellion,* 363.

15. William P. Haines, *History of the Men of Co. F., with Description of the Marches and Battles of the 12th New Jersey Vols.* (Camden, N.J.: 1897), 66–69.

16. Baquet, *History of the First Brigade,* 349–350.

17. *Newark Daily Advertiser,* May 17, 1864.

18. *The Jerseyman,* May 28, 1864.

19. Foster, *New Jersey and the Rebellion,* 671.

20. *Newark Daily Advertiser,* July 16, 1864.

21. *Monmouth Democrat,* July 21, 1864

22. *Jersey City Daily Times,* October 6, 1864.

23. *Ocean Emblem,* November 3, 1864.

24. Robertson, ed., *McAllister Letters,* 526–530.

25. Marbaker, *History of the Eleventh New Jersey Volunteers,* 251–261.

SIX. *"Exhausted, Starved, Emaciated, Dying"*

1. John Bray, "My Escape from Richmond," *Harper's Monthly*, April 1864, 662–665.

2. Baquet, *History of the First Brigade*, 350.

3. Haines, *History of the Men of Co. F.*, 166–170.

4. Foster, *New Jersey and the Rebellion*, 870–872.

5. Edgar H. Trelease, "Letter from a Soldier," *Harper's Weekly*, January 11, 1865, 93–94.

6. Charles Hopkins, "Hell and the Survivor," *American Heritage* 33, no. 6 (October/November 1982), 89–92.

7. *Sussex Register*, December 16, 1864.

8. Joseph Ferguson, *Life Struggles in Rebel Prisons . . .* (Philadelphia, 1865), 202–204.

SEVEN. *"Boys, Your Work Is Done"*

1. *Newark Daily Advertiser*, April 11, 1865.

2. Quoted in Robertson, ed., *McAllister Letters*, 575.

3. Robertson, ed., *McAllister Letters*, 580–584.

4. *Newark Daily Advertiser*, March 3, 1865.

5. Davis, ed., *Hoffman Diary and Letters*, 20.

6. Baquet, *History of the First Brigade*, 410.

7. Haines, *History of the Men of Co. F.*, 88–89.

8. Diary of George A Bowen, April 6–9, 1865, Salem County (New Jersey) Historical Society.

9. *Newark Daily Advertiser*, April 12, 1865.

10. Ibid., April 10, 1865.

11. *Paterson Daily Press*, April 10, 1865.

12. *New-Brunswick Fredonian*, April 13, 1865.

13. *West Jersey Pioneer*, April 8, 1865.

14. James Suydam Knox, "The Assassination of President Lincoln," *Princeton Alumni Weekly* 17 (1916/17), 407–409.

15. *Hightstown Gazette*, April 20, 1865.

16. *Newark Daily Advertiser*, April 15, 1865.

17. *New Jersey Pioneer*, April 22, 1865.

18. *The Jerseyman*, April 22, 1865.

19. *Jersey City Daily Times*, April 15, 1865.

20. Quoted in Gillette, *Jersey Blue*, 308.

21. *Newark Daily Advertiser*, April 24, 1865.

22. *Sussex Register*, May 12, 1865.

23. Marbaker, *History of the Eleventh New Jersey Volunteers*, 308.

24. *Newark Daily Advertiser*, May 25, 1865.

25. Robertson, ed., *McAllister Letters*, 619.

Selected References

Bilby, Joseph G. and William C. Goble. *"Remember You Are Jerseymen!" A Military History of New Jersey's Troops in the Civil War.* Hightstown, N.J.: Longstreet House, 1998.

Cunningham, John T. *New Jersey: America's Main Road.* Garden City, N.Y.: Doubleday & Co., 1966.

Faust, Patricia L., ed. *Historical Times Illustrated Encyclopedia of the Civil War.* New York: Harper & Row, 1986.

Foster, John Y. *New Jersey and the Rebellion.* Newark: State of New Jersey, 1868.

Gillette, William. *Jersey Blue: Civil War Politics in New Jersey, 1854–1865.* New Brunswick: Rutgers University Press, 1995.

Jackson, William L. *New Jerseyans in the Civil War: For Union and Liberty.* New Brunswick: Rutgers University Press, 2000.

Knapp, Charles Merriam. *New Jersey Politics during the Period of the Civil War and Reconstruction.* Geneva, N.Y.: W. F. Humphrey, 1924.

McPherson, James M. *Battle Cry of Freedom: The Civil War Era.* New York: Oxford University Press, 1988.

Miers, Earl Schenck, ed. *New Jersey and the Civil War.* Princeton: D. Van Nostrand Company, 1964.

Mitros, David. *Gone to Wear the Victor's Crown. Morris County, New Jersey and the Civil War: A Documentary Account.* Morristown, N.J.: Morris County Heritage Commission, 1998.

Siegel, Alan A. *For the Glory of the Union: Myth, Reality, and the Media in Civil War New Jersey.* Rutherford, N.J.: Fairleigh Dickinson University Press, 1984.

Sinclair, Donald A. *A Bibliography: The Civil War and New Jersey.* New Brunswick: Friends of the Rutgers University Library, 1968.

Stryker, William S. *Record of Officers and Men of New Jersey in the Civil War, 1861–1865.* Trenton, N.J., 1876.

Wright, William C., and Paul A. Stellhorn. *Directory of New Jersey Newspapers, 1765–1970.* Trenton: New Jersey Historical Commission, 1977.

Wright, William C. *The Secession Movement in the Middle Atlantic States.* Rutherford, N.J.: Fairleigh Dickinson University Press, 1973.

Index

About the Author

A graduate of Rutgers College, Columbia University, and Rutgers School of Law, Alan A. Siegel is a practicing attorney in Chatham with an abiding interest in state and local history. *Beneath the Starry Flag* is his eighth book and second for Rutgers University Press. *Smile*, his illustrated history of Olympic Park, has been in print continuously since it was first published nineteen years ago. Mr. Siegel's works have twice won the New Jersey League of Historical Societies' Certificate of Excellence.